Arrest the Music!

TEJUMOLA OLANIYAN

# Arrest the Music!
# Fela and His Rebel Art
# and Politics

INDIANA UNIVERSITY PRESS
*Bloomington and Indianapolis*

This book is a publication of

Indiana University Press
601 North Morton Street
Bloomington, IN 47404-3797 USA

http://iupress.indiana.edu

*Telephone orders*   800-842-6796
*Fax orders*   812-855-7931
*Orders by e-mail*   iuporder@indiana.edu

**Library of Congress Cataloging-in-Publication Data**

Olaniyan, Tejumola.
Arrest the music! : Fela and his rebel art and politics / Tejumola Olaniyan.
p. cm. — (African expressive cultures)
Includes bibliographical references (p. ), discography (p. ), and index.
ISBN 0-253-34461-1 (cloth : alk. paper) — ISBN 0-253-21718-0 (pbk. : alk. paper)
1. Fela, 1938- 2. Musicians—Nigeria—Biography. 3. Afrobeat—Nigeria—History and criticism. I. Title.
II. Series.
ML420.F333O43 2004
781.63′092—dc22
2004002138

1  2  3  4  5   09  08  07  06  05  04

To Fela

The gold, the lead,

all undecidable

in between around and beyond.

Esu accepts.


And


To us, all of us, his fans worldwide.

# Contents

# Acknowledgments

The last time I presented part of what became this book at a conference, a few members of the audience referred in their responses to parts I had presented "two or three years ago." It is humbling indeed to have a project so dedicatedly monitored by peers. I am grateful to all those members of the African Literature Association and the African Studies Association, both in the United States of America, who have followed the project these past years and offered incisive comments. I have been teaching Fela over the years and have benefited from the critical enthusiasm of my students. For assistance and/or encouragement in a variety of direct and indirect ways, I am grateful to Adeleke Adeeko, Nkiru Nzegwu, Olakunle George, Olufemi Taiwo, Oyeronke Oyewumi, Biodun Jeyifo, Isidore Okpewho, Abiola Irele, Kofi Agawu, dele jegede, Mobolaji Aluko, Akin Adesokan, and Ogaga Ifowodo. My deep appreciation to the Nzegwu family: Nkiru, Uzoamaka, and Azuka; I wrote parts of the book while a guest of theirs in upstate New York.

In Nigeria, I was welcomed and aided by individuals and families too numerous to mention; I am thankful to them all, especially the families of Kolawole Babatunde, Kunle Ajibade, Babatunde Adeyemo, and Niyi Bankole; and to Yemi and Shade Ogunbiyi, Femi Osofisan, Lemi Ghariokwu, Demola Balogun, Femi Osunla, Ayotunde Lawal, Mahmood Ali-Balogun, Edwin (Jahman) Aiyudu, and Edmund Enaibe. Publishers of *The News* generously gave me the use of their office space as and when needed; I am grateful to the entire staff and management, especially Ajibade, Idowu Obasa, Babafemi Ojudu, and Bayo Onanuga. Special thanks to the Anikulapo-Kuti family. Yeni Anikulapo-Kuti promptly answered my request, and Dr. Beko Ransome-Kuti's proper direction saved me much time. I am grateful to them, the Estate of Fela Anikulapo-Kuti, and the law firm of Olajide Oyewole and Co.

I am above all most indebted to Mojisola Olaniyan for her usual resilient support in all ways and to Bolajoko and Olabimpe Olaniyan, who insisted they must be fully acknowledged, "and not just in tiny print." Their gargantuan contribution? They reduced their pestering of dad, at least until the last plea or threat wore off; plus they endlessly arranged and rearranged scores of compact discs, cassettes, and LPs, now upstairs, then downstairs, depending on where I chose to write at the moment, and meticulously typed out every discographic detail. I also acknowledge the Union of Nigerians in Madison (UNIMA) and the Association of Africans in Madison (AAM); their activities provided a psychologically boosting context for the composition of the book.

My gratitude to Dee Mortensen, my editor at Indiana University Press, for her steadfast and active interest in the project. An earlier version of Chapter 8 appeared in *Research in African Literatures* in 2001. I am grateful to the editor and publisher for the permission to republish.

# Arrest the Music!

# 1 Introduction
## "Living In The Interregnum": Fela Anikulapo-Kuti and the Postcolonial Incredible

The scene has stuck in my mind for over two decades now, but I can no longer remember whether I actually saw it or imagined it. Veteran watchers of Fela Anikulapo-Kuti (1938–1997)—simply "Fela" to his fans—dismissed my "positivist" worries and instead wagered their reputations on its plausibility. Here then, the (in)famous spectacle: a half-literate officer of the Nigerian army and lorry-loads of fully armed soldiers swooped down on the venue of a performance by Fela, their AK-47s fully drawn. Amid the commotion by the startled audience, the officer bellowed out to his soldiers, "Arrest the music!" A few soldiers approached the stage tentatively and stopped at the footlights, apparently not sure how to execute the strange command. Their glance back at the officer was met with an even more thunderous "Arrest the music, I say!" this time with the officer's own pistol drawn. The soldiers scrambled to cart away Fela's musical instruments. I did not wait to see or could not remember what happened next.

I have often wondered why the officer's particular phrase refused to leave me, more so when the whole scenario may really be no more than the product of an imagination gone overactive for a moment. Fela had infinitely more and *real* violent visitations from the security agents of successive Nigerian governments over the course of the three decades of his musical career. One such on February 18, 1977, resulted in the invasion and sacking of his residence by nearly 1,000 soldiers. Residents—including Fela—and guests were brutally beaten and bayoneted and scores ended up with broken heads, legs, backs, shoulders, arms, and ribs; women were sexually assaulted; Fela's ailing mother, Nigeria's foremost anticolonial nationalist and feminist, was tossed from a second-floor window; and the house itself was razed—all in broad daylight, with thousands of citizens in the mostly lower-class neighborhood watching in disbelief. The government's commission of inquiry into the cruelty by its agents acquitted it of responsibility because, it said, "unknown soldiers" committed the acts. Not even the subsequent global popularity of the phrase "unknown soldier," thanks to Fela's musical account of the episode in the album *Unknown Soldier,* was able to remove the poignancy of "Arrest the music!" in my consciousness.

"Arrest the music," I now discover, can actually be a suggestive conceptual key to approaching the music of Fela and the contexts of its production, circulation, and consumption. It reveals, for example, the peculiar character of the relations between art, specifically oppositional music, and a postcolonial African state. It is also an inadvertent homage to that part of Fela's image as a musician that is most familiar to the world: the "political." Above all, the unvarnished crudity, unhidden ill-bred megalomania, killjoy morbidity, and sheer incredibility of the unusual command speak volumes about the political order—and those who manage and profit from it—on behalf of which it is uttered. Indeed, if there is one overarching conceptual thread running through Fela's music, it is that the postcolonial Nigerian, and African, condition is an incredible one. The "incredible" inscribes that which cannot be believed; that which is too improbable, astonishing, and extraordinary to be believed. The incredible is not simply a breach but an outlandish infraction of "normality" and its limits. If "belief," as faith, confidence, trust, and conviction, underwrites the certainty and tangibility of institutions and practices of social exchange, the incredible dissolves all such props of stability, normality, and intelligibility (and therefore of authority) and engenders social and symbolic crisis. Evident in Fela's body of work is a gargantuan will to articulate, to *name*, the incredibility and thereby inscribe its vulnerability. To the extent that Fela's expressed objective is the overthrow or at least the amelioration of the reign of the incredible, he obviously conceives its dominance at the moment as a transition, an "interregnum." His exertions, in all their recalcitrant multidirectional sprawl, are best seen as meaningful confrontations with a presupposed interregnum that increasingly threatens to become the norm, a norm with a rapidly consolidating hierarchy of privileges feeding on and dependent on the crisis for reproduction. This crisis-as-norm is what I call the "postcolonial incredible," signally marked by "a great variety of morbid symptoms."[1]

If Fela, even in death, remains Africa's most controversial popular musician, it is primarily because of his complex response to the postcolonial incredible. That response appears to most people to be utterly peculiar and paradoxical. On the one hand is his irreproachable feat of a comprehensive venomous critique of both institutions and individuals he sees as causes and perpetuators of the reigning incredible social anomie. On the other hand is his far more reproachable cultivation of an antisocial counterculture of drugs and sex and a flamboyant cult of charisma that both fed on and were part and parcel of the anomie that Fela condemned. The one, in the extensive garish tableau of the postcolonial incredible it dramatizes with all its attendant social and psychological costs, brooks no notion of the incredible present that is not a transition.[2] The other, in its indulgent countercultural pleasures irrespective of the social cost, already implicitly votes for its enabling order. The one is transcendentalist in aspiration—a powerful exploration of the wherewithal to surmount the incredible and its rule—while the other wallows in a sustaining relationship with it.

Sustenance *and* transcendence do appear to be discrepant; they are, however, actually complementary in Fela's creative universe, and it is useless to speculate on whether they need be so. That would not be discoursing on the figure we have but the one we would like to have (ah, if only we could choose our artists the way we elect politicians!). I have instead followed in this book the more challenging option that fundamentally affirms our subject in space and time and have not shied from wherever my inquiries may lead. Approaching Fela this way, I suggest, produces an effect similar to Bertolt Brecht's "complex pleasures," an aggregate of gratification "more intricate, richer in communication, more contradictory and more productive of results."[3]

By the time Fela died on August 2, 1997, he had successfully cultivated and made hegemonic in global consciousness an image of himself as a quintessentially "political musician." From his many statements in interviews, lectures, lyrics, and other social activism activities, we can deduce that by "political musician" he means a musician who devotes his or her musical resources to evoking, interrogating, and pronouncing judgments on the partisan political arrangements and attendant social relations of his or her context. In this regard, Fela was right: he was a political musician, and I am sure that many of his fans and scholars were drawn to him in large part for that reason. But Fela was not always a political musician; his musical career is infinitely richer and more dramatic than this, once we refuse the reification of the "momentous present" that Fela himself now and then encouraged. To robustly historicize Fela's career is to see distinctive patterns or clusters of patterns over time and the relationships and differences among them. There are, it must be acknowledged, grave risks in doing periodization, for periods of cultural history are very often blurred and uneven at the edges. The real task is to find the mean between watertight compartments and vast, indistinct seamlessness. Conscious of this challenge, we can approach the engaging multidimensionality of Fela's career by recognizing distinct yet related phases of his career at levels of both style and ideology. Style and ideology are mutually embedded, but that does not mean they are collapsible, for it is possible for a particular style to support a variety of ideological positions. Such is the case with Fela. At the level of style, two distinct phases can be recognized: the avant-pop (after avant-garde) and afrobeat. At the level of ideology, however, three distinct stages are recognizable: the apolitical hustler, the moral reformer, and the dissident political activist. I have synthesized these phases of style and ideology into three: the apolitical avant-pop hustler, the afrobeat social reformer, and the afrobeat political activist. I consider each of these phases in detail in Chapters 2, 3, and 4, respectively, showing their distinctive sonic and extrasonic features and the different social and historical circumstances that produced and gave them depth.

Fela was and remains one of a few popular musicians anywhere to have won any sustained serious attention from the scholarly community. Since the 1980s, the critical attention to Fela has been fairly enduring. Scholars have written books, dissertations, chapters, and articles on him across continents, not to mention extensive magazine and newspaper reviews and profiles. I have benefited from many of these, especially Carlos Moore's quasi-biography *Fela, Fela: This Bitch of a Life* (1982); the more recent robust biography by Michael E. Veal,

*Fela: The Life and Times of an African Musical Icon* (2000); and the hagiography by Mabinuori K. Idowu, *Fela: Why Black Man Carry Shit* (1986). These books provide me with useful details of a primary nature, and they are so acknowledged in my citations, especially in my contextual, more genealogically oriented chapters 2, 3, and 4. However, the books—and the two writings mentioned below—follow very little of the conceptual and analytical directions I pursued in this book. If we were to conclude from this selective mention that the biographical is the ruling mode of Fela scholarship, we would be right. Fela invented a musical genre, and he also, it seems, determined in large part the genre in which scholars would write about him. The spectacular, dramatic nature of his life and career —the chameleonic, roller-coaster stylistic and ideological changes, the politically charged lyrics and antiestablishment politics, the many encounters with the law, the twenty-seven wives, the open marijuana-use culture, and the general flamboyantly nonconformist lifestyle—appears tailor made for nothing but the biographical. Nonbiographical scholarly analyses have been harder to come by. Iyorchia Ayu's long chapter "Creativity and Protest in Popular Culture" in his *Essays in Popular Struggle* (1986) is an early Marxist analysis within the context of Nigeria and the "Third World," while an early example of the recent swell of scholarly interest since the musician's death is Sola Olorunyomi's book *Afrobeat! Fela and the Imagined Continent* (2003). Although the latter is not strictly a biography, it is nevertheless classified partly as such by the publisher; old expectations, apparently, die hard.

I come to Fela as both a passionate fan—beginning from high school when I would save up my lunch money to buy his records—and a dispassionate scholar. In fact, over the last several years since I began teaching Fela in my courses, I have discovered that the more enthusiastic I am about his music, the more unrelenting I become in scrutinizing it, fundamentally accepting its self-presentations and representations but at the same time insistently identifying and exploring its gaps, cracks, and silences. The reason scholars are attracted to Fela's musical practice—a reason they have yet to fully identify or acknowledge—is in part its vast intellectual density, made even more complex by the practice's swashbuckling yet entirely unpretentious incongruities. Far more than in currently available scholarship, I analyze this dimension of intellectual density of Fela's musical practice at length. It is rare that the work of a popular musician intervenes so cogently in current dominant problematics in the social sciences and humanities: the nature of the postcolonial state and the character of its bureaucracy; the relationships between art, especially oppositional art, and the state; sex, gender, class, and oppositional politics; cities and citizenship; democracy and (dis)empowerment; music, pedagogy, and cultural identity; history, memory, and the refashioning of new subjectivities; the complex interaction of racial and cultural identities; authenticity and hybridity; popular culture and the (im)possibility of radical politics; the sociology and psychology of a counterculture; language, cultural imperialism, and postcolonial modernity; and nationalism, afrocentrism, and cosmopolitanism. I critically explore different strands of these issues in Fela's musical practice in Chapters 5–9.

A note is in order on my treatment of Fela's music. On the one hand, I am not seduced at all by Fela's sensational politics to focus my analyses solely on his lyrics. My research tells me that Fela is to a large extent a musician's musician; that is, a musician interested more in the ensemble of nonverbal sounds that make music than in the lyrics laced around and between them. In another place and time, he might have played solely what musicologists call "absolute music," that is, instrumental music that is free of any overt connection or association with words. In many instances, reading the ideology from the sonic style actually proves much more rewarding than reading from the obvious lyrical content. On the other hand, I am ambivalent about going the way of notations. This is not because I think they are irrelevant—I have in fact wondered to no end why notation is not a much more common practice among professional musicologists working on African popular music.[4] My ambivalence is informed by my disciplinary take-off point and by the fact that for the vast majority of my readers—surely they will not be professional musicologists—notation would be no more than a distraction. My only other viable solution then is detailed description (this would still be so even if I were to prepare an accompanying compact disc of cited examples) of the music, its sound and stylistic components. This is what I have done, but with full acknowledgment of the humbling universal fact that music, a veritable form in solution, will never be totally captured by language.

In the eyes of the world, Fela was the charismatic face of afrobeat, a kind of music and an attitude he invented in response to a context he articulated in his own unique way. In Chapter 6, I go behind the shop front to the shop floor to register the labor of many others, without which there would have been no afrobeat the way we know it. In Chapter 10, I celebrate the widespread influence of Fela and the current explosion of afrobeat bands across continents. Focusing on younger musicians he has influenced such as his son, Femi, and Lagbaja, I explore the manner and politics of current directions of appropriation of afrobeat.

Scholars have often noted that music, because of its distinctive power to activate emotional intensities, inscribes experience with greater potency than any other art. If there is one most pervasive experience that afrobeat has invested with such intensity, it is the experience of the postcolonial African state. But this is also an acknowledgment of how greatly the state decisively imprints its mark on the music. Without those features of the postcolonial African state that we know so well (see Chapters 4–5), Fela and afrobeat would have been vastly different from what they were. To listen to Fela's music then is to listen to a kind of cultural, specifically musical, "biography" of the postcolonial African state: an account of the state's crisis-ridden life so far as seen by an oppositional music—whose potency as oppositional music depends on the continued tumultuous life of the state! Everyone knows that this "political engagement"—not so much as an act or series of acts bounded in space and time but as a discourse to be broadcast widely over time and space as an example—was very dear to Fela's sense of himself as a musician, and it is in conceding the point that I end here with this deeply affecting homage to the master composed by one of his musical heirs, Lagbaja, in the tribute album *Abami* (2000):

| | |
|---|---|
| When he start to dey yab | When he starts to banter |
| Dictator go dey shake | Dictators shudder in alarm |
| Oppressor go dey fear | Oppressors quake in fear |
| When he put mouth for song | When he begins to sing |
| Philosophy go dey flow | Philosophy issues forth |
| When he put horn for mouth | When he blows his horn |
| Melody go dey blow[5] | Melody flows in a stream |

# 2    The "Apolitical" Avant-Pop Hustler

## Contexts

I have borrowed the military metaphor of the avant-garde—advance guard—to describe the first phase of Fela's musical evolution as avant-pop—advance pop. By this I mean a form of popular music that is self-consciously experimental, new, and distinct from existing forms in its sociocultural context. Such music transgresses the boundaries of established styles, the meanings those styles reference, and the social norms they support or imply. The avant-pop is the form of Fela's musical practice from when he started in Britain in the late 1950s through his return in the early 1960s until the end of the decade. His band was at various times during that period known as Fela Ransome-Kuti and the Highlife Rakers, the Fela Ransome-Kuti Quintet, but mostly as—once briefly discarded and then reassumed—Fela Ransome-Kuti and the Koola Lobitos. The particular genre of his music during this time was the hybrid called highlife jazz. This was a composite that synthesized an older form, highlife, and a newer one, jazz, that was then beginning to make an inroad among the elite in West African capitals.

Highlife emerged in the coastal cities of Anglophone West Africa such as Accra and Lagos in the early decades of the twentieth century. In its stylistic varieties such as the brass band, the guitar band, or the most widespread and popular, the ballroom dance band, highlife is a fusion of local dance melodies and rhythms and imported European brass, string, and woodwind instruments.[1] The sonic properties were strange—there were no indigenous orchestras with such a wide assemblage of horns—but the familiar tunes and songs amply compensated for this. It is best to conceive of highlife as the product of a mutually disciplining relationship between foreign instruments and indigenous melodies. It quickly became so popular that by the end of the 1930s, there were already dozens of bands in Ghana, Sierra Leone, and Nigeria playing local tunes as well as European concert music in soft, abbreviated versions and favorite ballroom types such as foxtrots, two-steps, and waltzes. These European forms diminished in significance in the late 1940s as highlife came in contact with Afro-Cuban dance-music varieties such as mambo, rumba, and cha-cha. From a creative blending of these and other indigenous materials, Ghanaian E. T. Mensah,[2] generally regarded as the "grandfather" of highlife, fashioned the modern form of dance-band highlife; through Mensah's performance tours, that particular modern form spread to and became the vogue in other places, most notably Nigeria. Newly established local branches of European recording companies significantly contributed to the spread and popularity of highlife. By the close of the 1940s, these companies had produced thousands of 78 rpm shellac discs of highlife for the West African market.[3]

The name "highlife" literally and unashamedly indexes the class character of the music it refers to as for the elite, meaning, in context, the *westernized* elite. Highlife's means of production—the instruments as well as the elaborate and lengthy period of training needed to master them—excluded all but the privileged, lucky, or well connected. The mode and protocols of its consumption—the classy night club with, of course, an equally classy entrance fee and strict codes about dressing and being in couples—left no one in doubt as to the status of the clientele.[4] At the peak of its popularity in Nigeria in the 1950s to mid-1960s, highlife boasted such distinguished bandleaders as Bobby Benson, Victor Olaiya, Eddie Okonta, Zeal Onyia, Stephen Osita Osadebey, Cardinal Rex Lawson, Roy Chicago, and Celestine Ukwu. Those were the giddy years of Nigeria's struggle for independence from colonial rule (which was finally won in 1960) and the first few years of victory celebration before the civil war (1967–1970) hastened the already spreading gangrene of the failure of the postcolonial state and consequent general public disillusionment. The music embodied the heroic struggle and optimism of the years before the fall. The mastery and incorporation of instruments from diverse climes testified to the creativity and cultural resilience of the colonized as well as the expansiveness of the mindset of the anticolonial struggle. After all, the struggle was conducted mostly in English, and the model of government the nationalists struggled to establish after they overthrew European colonial rule was borrowed from Europe. Their great expectation was that the new system would work well to realize all the preindependence dreams on the part of the colonized of egalitarian social relations and "rapid modernization." The hope was gargantuan. Lofty stump speeches during the day were affirmed later at night by the hypnotic rhythms of highlife, as politicians boogied down with musicians and both looked forward to a new dawn. As a decidedly nonethnic music, highlife is perhaps Nigeria's first truly national music, and it helped to widely broadcast, in sensuous form, intimations of loyalties beyond the ethnic group. Bands traveled widely and sang in various languages. Unlike existing popular musics such as *juju, apala,* or *sakara,*[5] highlife's verbal and aural imagery were profoundly secular and cosmopolitan, tied to the pressures of the modern urban context—the meeting place where ethnic identities and interests are renegotiated and reshaped—that gave birth to it. There is little doubt about it: highlife was the quintessential soundtrack to Nigerian independence, the upbeat music of an arriviste bourgeoisie with a modernist ideology that by its refined cultured outlook and hard work would peel off the colonial shame and transform Nigeria into a modern, developed, and respectable nation.

This was the reigning music when Fela left for Trinity College in Britain in 1958. He had spent the last few years—the last years of his high school education—immersed in the exciting Lagos highlife scene, where he had his first professional experience playing the music. That was during his brief stint as a back-up vocalist with the second-tier Cool Cats (the first band was already full!)

band of the legendary Victor Olaiya.[6] There is no reason to doubt that highlife is the music Fela would have played all his life had he not gone abroad. Even his main goal at Trinity, which was to learn to be a trumpeter, appeared aimed at the Nigerian highlife scene, where the most famous names and bandleaders were trumpeters.

Fela studied formally during the day, but he was more eagerly absorbing the exhilarating confluence of musical cultures the nightclubs of metropolitan London offered him, thanks to people like him, students and immigrants from far-flung parts of the British colonies and former colonies. "In England I was exposed to all these things," Fela said of jazz performance cultures specifically, but no doubt also of others such as mambo, calypso, and ska.[7] Along with his longtime friend J. K. Braimah, who had also come to London but to study law, Fela formed a band, the Highlife Rakers, composed of Nigerian and West Indian musicians. They would later change the name of the group to Koola Lobitos.[8]

By far the biggest musical influence on Fela at this time was jazz. It is not that jazz influence was entirely absent from Fela's musical experience up to this point; highlife bears the unmistakable influence of dance-oriented and more commercial entertainment jazz styles such as swing and big band. Bobby Benson and his Jam Session Orchestra, perhaps more than any other highlife band in Lagos in the late 1950s and 1960s, is a classic example. "Modern" jazz as such—bop, cool, "free jazz," and other abstract styles, which were radical in their social orientation and opposition to commercialism—were studiously ignored by the bandleaders because the disarticulated harmony and irregular beats of the styles made them undanceable, suitable only for contemplative listening. It was natural then that when Fela began to immerse himself in jazz outside the filter of highlife, it was to the commercial forms that he turned, not the more socially conscious modern forms.

I say "natural" to emphasize the fact that it is only in the context of Fela's later radical politics that Michael Veal's "ironic" in the quote below more graphically hits home:

> Fela's take on jazz was initially rather conservative. While the dominant trends during his college years were hard bop and cool (which were gradually being supplanted by modal and avant-garde styles), his initial exposure was to the older, more commercial styles. It might strike some as ironic that the future "Black President" of African music would cite two Sicilian-American musicians as formative influences: "I had this single I was listening to all the time, Frank Sinatra's 'Mr. Success.' . . . But the first guy who really got me was Louis Prima. Then I went to hear Louis Armstrong at ballroom club in London and he knocked me out."[9]

Of course, as Veal himself has shown in greater detail elsewhere, Fela's overall appropriation of jazz is much more complicated. He absorbed more contemporary styles such as bebop made famous earlier in the 1940s by Dizzy Gillespie, Thelonious Monk, and Charlie Parker and the modal style of the early 1960s popularized by Miles Davis and John Coltrane.

Benson Idonije, who met Fela in 1963 and became his early manager, once tried to methodically unpack the layers of jazz influences on Fela between the late 1950s and the mid-1960s. On trumpet, Fela admired Miles Davis because of his "wonderful tone, phraseology, and economy of notes." On piano, he learned from Wynton Kelly and Red Garland, but Herbie Hancock was his "favorite because of his funk-oriented compositions such as 'Watermelon Man,' and his ability to introduce some lightheartedness to his piano playing with evocative phrases." On saxophone, which would later become central to afrobeat, Fela

> listened a lot to Charlie Parker[,] who influenced every other modernist on the instrument. But of particular interest to him at the time was the tenor saxophone sound of Harold Land who usually teamed up with Teddy Edwards. He listened to Hank Mobley[,] whose phrases were at the time unusual and unpredictable, playing with Art Blakey and the Jazz Messengers, and later the Miles Davis Sextet. He also admired John Coltrane but he rather preferred his modal interpretations with the Miles Davis Sextet of the late fifties to the Sheets of Sound he unleashed on his fans in the mid sixties.[10]

Fela was right in his claim that this "lot of jazz . . . had cultural information that enriched my mind,"[11] but he had to absorb the influences very strategically. The Nigerian social scene he had left and to which he would soon return was dominated more by music for social dancing than by music for meditative attention. So in spite of how inspirational these jazz forms and figures may have been to him, there was no way he could have emulated them without committing professional suicide.

Fela returned to a much-changed Nigeria in 1963. For one thing, the country had won its independence from British colonial rule in October 1960. A raucous political scene notwithstanding, the attitude that defined the elite and new professional class to which Fela belonged was an optimistic and "can-do" one. Highlife, the preeminent music of that class, boomed high-decibel vindication and triumphalism at every party occasion. Finally, the hawk was vanquished and now the rooster could have, and did have, all the stage to perform, to create the new dawn it had crowed about all along. But during momentary ebbs of euphoria, any discerning eye could see that there were already serious fissures in the new political dispensation. This was not a new political culture after all, but a revamped older one in which goals other than the pursuit and entrenchment of the proclaimed democracy and egalitarian social relations determined political action if not also, in a vulgarly obvious manner, policy.[12] But highlife could care less—"the music must go on," to borrow the cliché. That is, until a few years later when historical events—the civil war, especially—decreed the contrary, showing that even handy clichés do now and them come up against the ugly withering truth of their own contingency.

Fela could not discount his London jazz experience and return to highlife; jazz was such a creative revelation to him that it could not be discarded so easily. But Fela also could not abandon the entrenched highlife in favor of jazz if he wanted to play for an audience larger than a handful. To resolve the conundrum, he came up with the creative mixture he called highlife jazz. There was an audience for highlife and a tiny cultic one for jazz, but there was none at all for a music called highlife jazz. In truth, highlife jazz was more jazz than the advertised hybrid. Through jazz, Fela had become enamored of the culture of quiet virtuosic performance, improvisatory metric freedom, and lyricism of pure instrumental sound. By comparison, highlife was rougher, louder, more rigid in format, too fixated on meeting popular expectations, and above all, seemingly less dignifying for the university-trained musician—and more so for a "been-to," "oversea" or London-educated musician. In relation to highlife, jazz had a more elitist and exclusivist class character. It was the music of a coterie among educated Lagosians who were well read in, and identified with, the history, art, and politics of jazz in America and, of course, were not at all averse to the distinctions in image, in social capital, that jazz consumption in 1960s Lagos conferred on them. Plus, with his university degree, Fela could have played "art music," consciously Africanized versions of essentially western classical music, which was even higher up on the scale of elitism and exclusivity.[13] While his musical skills prepared him to follow any of these three directions—highlife, jazz, and art music—his original grounding in the popular dance-band highlife and later self-absorption in jazz complicated any easy decision. Highlife jazz was the creative compromise, and Fela's true stylistic preference in the hybrid is much evident in the naming of his band on return: the Fela Ransome-Kuti Quintet, in the typical manner of jazz groups abroad. Ideally, Fela wanted to tame, refine, in short, "classicize" highlife with more jazz; he wanted to change a very popular taste without sacrificing popular and commercial success.

Fela took a job with the Nigerian Broadcasting Corporation as producer, but he was sacked not long after for, among other things, coming late work, not recording new programs, and, above all, using his position to promote his own hybrid fusion, highlife jazz, rather than the standard form the station wanted. He changed the name of his band back to Koola Lobitos, a sort of tactical step down from the "Quintet" high horse to the popular realm. Yes, band names do signify, but the music must at least sound right enough to command popular attention. But as both the Quintet and the Koola Lobitos, success, in terms of mass acceptance, eluded Fela. Even his mother admonished him to "start playing music your people know, not jazz."[14]

## Avant-Pop Avatar

One cannot be certain which particular music Fela's mother meant in her admonition. She probably meant highlife, since given the family's westernized middle-class background, as well as Fela's own university training, she could not have been referring to such other existing urban popular forms as *sakara, apala,* or *juju* that are not associated with the highly educated class at the level of production, are of stronger local and ethnic provenance, and are much less cosmopolitan in outlook. Fela stuck to the apparently new and strange mixture called highlife jazz. But it was only the nonverbal sonic element—that is, the sound produced by the mostly nonindigenous instruments—which was strange. In a cultural context where the instruments of the indigenous musics are heavily percussive, Fela's highlife jazz used mostly brass and woodwind instruments. Of course, some of these kinds of instruments are also used in highlife, but the percussive element of highlife never strayed from being dominant, and the horn arrangements are many times shallower and far less extensive than in Fela's highlife jazz.

To some extent, then, highlife jazz could not but sound strange to the majority of its would-be audience; that is, the consumers of highlife. But the verbal sonic elements such as the lyrics were often very familiar and were composed mostly in Yoruba, the language of the majority in the musician's immediate cultural context, even if the titles were in English or pidgin. Also, the subjects of the songs were most often, as in straight highlife music, based on common popular themes such as love, sensuality, fidelity, friendship, and the myriad pressures of city life. So while the musical sound was somewhat outlandish, the lyrics and the subjects they addressed were far less so; they were only mildly eccentric. It is for this creative mixing of the strange and the familiar that I label Fela's musical practice at this stage avant-pop. Precisely because he situated himself at the interface of the well known and the little known, he was able to push against the frontiers of Nigerian popular musical taste and culture, even if he was commercially unsuccessful at the time. Some of Fela's more well-known recordings of this phase, dating mainly from the 1960s, include "Ololufe," "Mio fe," "Obinrin," "Fine Fine Baby," "Araba's Delight," "Bonfo," "Onidodo," "Wa Dele," "Laise, Lairo," "Omuti ti de," "Highlife Time," "Wakawaka," "Everyday I Got My Blues," "Mo ti Gborokan," "Fere," and "Home Cooking." A few were released as singles, while most were collected in the LPs *Fela Ransome-Kuti with the Koola Lobitos* (1969) and *Live at the Afro-Spot* (also 1969). Some of these recordings are now easily available on the compact disc *Koola Lobitos 64–68/The '69 Los Angeles Sessions*, released by MCA in 2001 as part of its massive project of reissuing Fela's works in their original forms.

To Fela's potential audience of highlife consumers, there were three major alienating features of highlife jazz. First, and this is no surprise, was the fact that there is too much jazz and too little highlife in the hybrid. Fela's jazz instrumental arrangements were too crowded with high-pitched saxophones and trumpets that were foregrounded in repeated vigorous solos. Where in highlife, the horns served a carefully modulated function leading, following, underscoring, breaking away from but never straying too far from the vocals, in highlife jazz, the horns assumed an identity all their own and took off on different tangents. They became too obvious, and since the taste for the kind of sound they produced was as-yet rudimentary, their obviousness was a distraction. Highlife consumers were not used to the horns declaring their independent identity with their aggressive blaring pitch and solos that sometimes lasted longer than the vocals. No less than two-thirds of the nearly four minutes each of such well-known tracks as "Bonfo" or "Fere" were devoted to the instruments, whether as solos or as group acts. Rather than serving as brief interludes of wordless musical intensity between the vocals as in highlife, the horns in highlife jazz presented themselves as the main act. A typical track from the Koola Lobitos sounds like no more than just a pretext to stage a show for the horns. In a sense, this had to be so, for how else could Fela demonstrate the result of the highly professional compositional approach that he and his band members had adopted? Idonije writes that "[r]ehearsals for one song usually took three sittings, each of which often lasted five hours on the average. Sometimes members such as bassist Okeji had to practice their own scored parts in their times at home. Little wonder they were rich in musical embellishments from the beginning to the end."[15]

Second, an inevitable outcome of Fela's thick horn arrangements—a result of those "embellishments from the beginning to the end"—was the element of unpredictability in rhythm and harmony. Highlife jazz could be danced to, but its much more complex and varying harmony ran against the grain of popular dance taste. The Koola Lobitos was a small group of four horns and a rhythm section, but it nevertheless managed to follow the five-part harmony technique in arrangements. Fela was using a small band to achieve a big band effect. His procedure, Idonije explains, "split the horns into fragments that created structural progressions as [a] sequence for the songs. But in a style reminiscent of the Count Basie and Duke Ellington orchestras, Fela was able to establish question-and-answer sessions as the horns created riffs. Solos were shared between himself on trumpet and Isaac Olasugba on the alto saxophone."[16] This small band was compositionally very busy compared to highlife. Tony Allen, Fela's master drummer, adds his own observation: "In five minutes, we'd use about five different arrangements. . . . It was far too complicated for the audience. They couldn't understand what was happening; except, possibly the musically inclined[,] who knew that the music was different from all the local things they'd been listening to. It was a bit like showing off."[17] Fela was unsatisfied with the simplicity of highlife; he was certain it could be enriched and made more sophisticated, but he could not seem to get the formula right. Joni Haastrup, a competing musician, gleefully remembers Fela's doomed "jazz-highlife-fusion," for "the people couldn't relate to it because he had all these horns and all these arrangements, and it was all too much for the people to comprehend. . . . He was playing to empty houses while we were packing [them]."[18] Understandably, Idonije provides a different reading: "In spite of the legendary fame with Afrobeat, Fela's timeless melodies are usually associated with the Koola Lobitos days of the sixties."[19] The level of Fela's mass appeal at the time contradicts this upbeat retrospection.

Third, part of the mass appeal of highlife was not just the music but also, and perhaps this is more important, the songs, the lyrics. In the context of a predominantly oral culture where verbal dexterity is unquestionably treasured, the songs and the vocalization of those songs articulate all the other musical elements and anchor meaning. There is just no delicate way to put it: Fela of the Koola Lobitos may not have been the most dreadful singer around, but he was not even among the average singers. This was not a question of skill but of emphasis. Because of the deep influence of jazz, Fela approached the songs as unnecessary bother. One can decipher that attitude in the casualness or conceited harriedness of his vocals, as if he considered them no more than mere asides. It is not that the lyrics are trivial, incoherent, or meaningless, but that they are schematic and badly sung: often jarring, unsteady in rhythm, and only clumsily melodious when at all. Even the ever-affirmative Idonije had to concede that in the music of Koola Lobitos, "obviously, the singing was not the main consideration. It was the arrangement and the ability of the . . . hornmen to improvise."[20]

We can see a composite of these features in attenuated form in several Fela's Koola Lobitos recordings. The annunciatory "Highlife Time" is divided into three sections. In the first, the horns enter for a few seconds to briefly but energetically mark out the tune, followed immediately by Fela's vocals, singing the song's only verse:

> It's highlife time
> A morning time
> And jump for joy
> At this swinging club
> It's a brand new place
> That plays the latest craze
> It's got the beat
> It's got the hit!

The horns follow him closely, underlining his short phrases, while Fela repeats and makes slight improvisations on the lyrics. This tapers off into the second section, devoted exclusively to instrumentals. A nearly one-minute trumpet solo initiates the section, riffing briefly on the main tune and then improvising extensively. The trumpet is then joined by the other horns for the chorus. This last call-and-response act transitions into another solo performance, following the formula of the first: the soloist riffs briefly on the main tune, branches off improvisationally, and then returns to interact with the group. The third section essentially repeats the arrangement of the first, with Fela's vocals and the horns mutually interrelating. It is unmistakable that the goal of the track is to showcase Fela's jazz pedigree, though the title only mentions highlife. This is evident not only in the showy arrangements in the first and third sections but also in the chunky middle section (a good half of the track's entire five-and-a-half minutes), where the horns are given complete free reign. While the first and third sections are obviously well arranged, largely because they are composed mostly of short repeated phrases and because of the disciplining effect of the lyrics, the middle section falls into unwieldiness now and then; sometimes the percussionists seem unsure of what direction to follow while the soloists play. Beneath all the blaring horns are the drums, muted but nevertheless pulsating deeply in the background, exercising a coordinating centripetal effect on the horns. This up-tempo track would have been much poorer without the heroic efforts of the percussion section.

"Omuti tide" ("The Drunkard Is Here") is a similar up-tempo track about

the just reward for lack of diligence at work: a drunkard is dismissed for dere-
liction. As in "Highlife Time," the horns enter first to graphically outline the
tune, followed by Fela singing the song's only verse:

| | |
|---|---|
| Omuti ti de o | The drunkard is here |
| Ewa w'aye omuti | Come and see the life of a drunkard |
| O f'ise s'ile | The drunkard abandoned assigned duties |
| O wa beer lo | In search of beer |
| Ise wa bo o | The drunkard is sacked |
| On ronu o | Now see the drunkard gloomy |
| Eje ka sora ka ma kabamo | Let's be diligent and avoid later regrets |

The pattern of the relationship between the vocals and the instruments in
"Highlife Time" is repeated here, except that that we have two sections instead
of three. Fela's vocals follow immediately after the delineation of the tune by
the horns. For some reason, the subsequent tempo of the horns is a notch faster
than that of the opening introductory phrase that was repeated twice. While
Fela repeats and improvises on the basic lyrics and even scats twice, the horns
bellow their accents forcefully. This goes on for about half of the nearly four-
minute track and then transitions into the second section, which is devoted to
horn solos, although the drums become louder and more prominent. Overall,
the rhythm is stiff and irregular, and the song is far less polished than "Highlife
Time." On the other hand, the leisurely tempo of "Ololufe Mi" ("My Lover")
seems, strangely, to subdue the usual overenthusiasm of the horns and attenuates the inequity of exposure between them and the drums. The result is that
brief breathing spaces open up between the horn arrangements during which
the drums shine. This remains so even during the unusually long instrumental
segment—a whopping four of the nearly five-and-a-half-minute track. The effect of the subdued horns is a much richer sound in which the varieties can be
heard and appreciated. The horns still dominate, but they do not overpower
the drums. Of course, the melody is far from lilting and Fela's voice is uninspir-
ing, but from time to time, one can rock lightly to the beat, especially when
the resolute horn solos do not distract attention. One could say that the flow
of the horns here is more intuitive; they actually tarry long enough to repeat
short phrases into a predictable pattern and thereby create an accessible har-
monic arrangement. I suppose this is what Idonije means when he writes that
Fela backgrounds his jazz in this track: "He based its melodic structure on the
12-bar blues, a format whose progression was emphasised by the bass movement."[21] Again, the lyrics are slight, a short stanza upon which Fela improvises
repeatedly:

| | |
|---|---|
| Ololufe mi, tie ni mo fe | My lover, it is you I want |
| Alayanfe me, mio se tiwon mo | My darling, I am no longer with them |
| Ololufe mi, tie ni mo fe | My love, it is you I want |
| Wa fenu ko mi lenu | Come and kiss me |
| Wa fara ro mi lara o | Come and cuddle me |
| Alayanfe mi, iwo ni mo ri | My darling, only you I see |

It is clear that the lyrics here are no more than convenient routines to cue instrumental arrangements.

"Bonfo" (literally, "if flying," but idiomatically used to mean high up, whether one is discussing a miniskirt or trousers) is an up-tempo lusty serenade for a woman with tantalizingly long legs accented by her miniskirt.

| | |
|---|---|
| Arabinrin, ese re ga | Lady, your legs are classy |
| Arabinrin, se bonfo ni | Lady, yours is an inviting miniskirt |
| Ye o, ma ba e lo o | Yes, I'll go with you |
| Se America ni | Even if it is to America |
| Ye o, ma ba e lo | Sure, I'll follow you |
| Se Jamaica ni . . . | Or to Jamaica . . . |
| Se Ghana ni | Or to Ghana |
| Se Nigeria ni | Or to Nigeria |

An instrumental section opens the track, setting the tone and pace for nearly one minute. This ushers in Fela's vocals, as usual repeating and varying the basic lyrics of the song and scatting ever so briefly now and then. Fela sings for no more than a minute, then the signature lengthy instrumental show commences with the usual horn solos. This goes on for a good one-and-a-half minutes before Fela's vocals return for a half-minute lyrical wrap-up that basically repeats the second section. Although "Bonfo" has four recognizable sections, unlike the tripartite division of "Highlife Time" or the binary partition of "Omuti tide" and "Ololufe Mi," the structural content and relationships are basically the same: instrumentals, including extended horn solos, and lightweight monochromatic songs woven around them, always with the longer duration allotted to the horns. The track is cluttered, with the lead horn and keyboard wobbling perceptibly a few times, though there are moments in which the trumpet solo delivers a muscular performance.

Arguably the most popular Koola Lobitos recording is the three-minute up-tempo "Onidodo" ("Fried Plantain Seller"). Again, the lyrical narrative is very scant: the fried plantain seller has not had many sales all day and so is ready for a fight at the slightest provocation.

| | |
|---|---|
| Onidodo, oni moin moin | The fried plantain and beancake seller |
| Nigba ti o ta, o gbe 'gba kale o | Didn't sell all day and so rested the cart |
| Ewa wo'ja ni Lafiaji | My, you should have seen the brawl in Lafiaji! |

This track is much more accomplished technically. The wind instruments are scaled back just a bit so that the percussion instruments can clearly delineate the rhythm, an arrangement that contextually makes great cultural sense. It is no surprise that this is the only Koola Lobitos song that still remains a party favorite today. It follows Fela's by-now-standard three-part division of brief instrumental introduction mixed with vocals, then extended instrumentals with at least one horn solo and a repeat of the first section for the finale. Idonije lists "Onidodo" as one of the few songs that Fela and the Koola Lobitos borrowed and then rendered differently; in this recording, then, Fela has obviously been tamed by at least one previous popular version: "Onidodo had been kicking around for years before Fela picked it up and redressed it. It was made popular by veteran musician, Chris Ajilo, whose combo gave it an appealing version in the fifties as a song from the folkloric circuit."[22]

We can compare the foregoing samples with conventional highlife tunes to underscore Fela's similarities with and departures from the established norm. One of the most popular songs of Victor Olaiya, Fela's one-time mentor, is "Omo Pupa" (literally, a light-complexioned child or person, but idiomatically, a light-complexioned woman). It is a mid-tempo appeal by a London-bound man to his light-complexioned woman to love him and come and join him soon in London—he will send the fare and be waiting.

| | |
|---|---|
| Omo pupa o, omo pupa lemi nfe | Light-complexioned woman, I love you |
| Omo pupa o, jowo ko feran mi o | Light-complexioned woman, please love me |
| Ti m'ba de London | When I get to London |
| Ma wa f'owo oko ranse | I will send you the passage fare |
| Omo pupa o, jowo ko b'oko de o | Light-complexioned woman, please come |

One can clearly discern here Fela's transformation of the conventional three-part division: instrumentation and vocals, an extended middle instrumental section, and finally instrumentation and vocals. Apart from the articulation of instruments and vocals that skews attention in favor of the former, the structural location of the horns in the middle section further privileges them. In "Omo Pupa," in contrast, a 58-second instrumental opens the track, laying out the melody with a lilting, soothing regularity. There is no horn solo; a brief guitar solo substitutes. The middle section—which lasts for over a minute—is devoted mainly to vocals and instruments. The final section, which lasts about forty seconds, is mainly instrumentals; although the horns are prominent, they perform as part of an ensemble. The horn solo is given thirty seconds, while the last ten seconds recap the vocals. The horn solo that Fela so often foregrounded is put in the background here. This arrangement approximates popular expectations—created in the first place by the sedimented practice of the leading musicians—that the opening instrumentation would "invite" the audience to the dance floor, the middle vocals would engross them in the main business of the song, and the last short instrumental section, gradually fading in volume in the last moments, would gently steer the sweating dancers back to their seats. The articulation of the instruments and the vocals is much more harmonious, and the percussion section includes the *dundun* talking drum, an instrument whose sound would resonate powerfully with any Yoruba audience.[23]

Later in his career, Fela would sometimes play songs of yesteryear, mostly highlife, at his nightclub, Africa Shrine, on less formal nights. He hardly ever returned to any of his Koola Lobitos highlife jazz songs, but the one you were most likely to catch him singing is the straight highlife classic "Sawale" by Cardinal Jim Rex Lawson. The song is an enchanting mid-tempo brew of very measured but sprightly drums laced with low-key but unrelenting maracas; a gripping, throaty introductory trumpet solo; Lawson's own mellifluous singing; and a sparkling saxophone solo positioned in such a close, knowing relationship with the vocals that the latter actually serve as an accenting chorus to its improvisations, subtly suggesting and exacting rhythmic regularity from it. Fela never played this sort of highlife, but it is also clear that he never stopped loving this form he so desperately wanted to change.

Fela struggled heroically all through the Koola Lobitos years. He was not commercially successful, though this was not necessarily because he was just another amateur musician trying to find a niche. The main problem was that he was trying single-handedly to reorient Nigerian popular musical taste. This was great hubris, and the endeavor took place well before we came to recognize and accept that quality as distinctive of his identity as a political musician. His highlife jazz was too jazzy, he turned his back on accepted melodic arrangements, and apparently he thought his high-decibel jazz instrumentation would block out his inept singing in the ears of his audience. He was wrong on all counts. In mid-1960s, he thought Ghanaians, who gave birth to highlife, would be more receptive to his innovations, but that dream was exploded by the new invasion from abroad, soul music, and its West African embodiment, Geraldo Pino of Sierra Leone. But Fela was imaginative, committed, and professional enough to invent a musical form ahead of its time and stand by it against all odds. His determination alone shows that although he was sure of where he was going, he could not master the confounding twists and turns and thickets on the road at the time. Today, neither the history of the evolution of African highlife nor that of the global appropriation of jazz would be complete without an account of Fela's impressive avant-garde labors.

## The "Apolitical" Hustler

Years ago, I delivered a conference paper that became the nucleus of this chapter. The title was "The Avant-Pop Hustler: The 'Apolitical' Fela Anikulapo-Kuti." Many of those who attended the panel confessed at the end that they came because of the title of my presentation. They just could not believe, they said, that Fela was ever " 'apolitical,' " "with or without quotation marks." Fela, I realized, was a known entity, and the attitude out there was a skeptical, "now convince me *what else* there is to know" one. This attitude is not baseless, for this earliest phase of Fela's professional development is generally little known, musically or ideologically. That part of his career was not treated in any detail in the two books on Fela that were available for a long time, Carlos Moore's *Fela, Fela: This Bitch of a Life,* and Kayode Mabinuori's *Fela: Why Black Man Carry Shit.* Not a single title of the recordings of Koola Lobitos is mentioned in these books. And it does not seem that Iyorchia Ayu in his long essay "Creativity and Protest in Political Culture: The Political Protest in Popular Music of Fela Anikulapo-Kuti" is even aware of that earlier professional life of Fela. The first (and still only) close attention—albeit primarily biographical—to that phase is Michael Veal's *Fela: The Life and Times of an African Musical Icon,* published only in 2000. Thus the predominant image of Fela securely imprinted in global public consciousness in the last thirty years is the radical, controversial, daringly antiestablishment Fela; that image is complicated enough for anyone to make sense of without additional surprises. For many of my listeners at the panel, I was retouching their image of Fela with such surprises.

Ideologically, at the early phase of his musical evolution Fela exhibited nothing of the concerns for Africa or blackness or the quest for a radical trans-African musical aesthetics that he later engaged in. He was at this point what one might call, very charitably, "apolitical." Of course, we know that there is no such thing as being "apolitical," just different kinds of politics. Fela was at this stage not political in the sense he implicitly embodied later on in his career; that is, as someone who is actively engaged in a carefully calculated social action ultimately aimed at refashioning existing norms and social relations in society. At the early stage of his career, he was more concerned about aesthetic innovation within the context of the "classy" musical genre from abroad, jazz, and he was quite satisfied pouring old wines of flagrant sexism and conservatism into new bottles of musical form.

In a very significant sense, it is quite a surprise that Fela did not become sensitized to political issues long before he did. His grandparents and parents were distinguished social and political activists. His grandfather, the Reverend J. J. Ransome-Kuti (1855–1930), was a leading Christian, church builder, and pioneer of Christian music in Yorubaland. He was a thorn in the flesh of the colonial administration and defied church authorities even while aggressively campaigning for conversion. As part of his burgeoning cultural nationalism, he had several Christian songs pressed for EMI in the 1920s. J. J.'s son and Fela's father, the Reverend Israel Oludotun Ransome-Kuti (1900–1955), also distinguished himself as a clergyperson, church musician, educator, nationalist, and labor activist. He helped establish the Nigerian Union of Teachers in 1931 and the Nigerian Union of Students in 1940. He was an associate of well-known nationalist political leaders such as Obafemi Awolowo and Nnamdi Azikiwe. Israel Oludotun's wife and Fela's mother, Funmilayo Ransome-Kuti (1900–1978), was a leading feminist activist and builder of women's institutions. She was at one time the president of the more than 20,000-member Abeokuta Women's Union. Under her leadership, the union fought successfully for the abdication of the king of Abeokuta for his alliance with the colonizers in administering unjust and specifically gender-discriminatory colonial tax laws. She traveled widely— to Peking, Moscow, Vienna, Budapest, for example—to participate in conferences on women's issues. She was also the country's foremost female nationalist, rubbing shoulders on equal footing with the likes of Nnamdi Azikiwe and Obafemi Awolowo, and was a close friend of Kwame Nkrumah, the nationalist leader who led Ghana to independence and became the country's first president in 1957, one year before Fela left for Trinity in Britain. A vocal leader of the anticolonial nationalist party, the National Council of Nigeria and the Cameroons (NCNC), Funmilayo Ransome-Kuti was one of only seven top leaders chosen by the party in 1947 to visit the United Kingdom to protest against the new Richards constitution imposed on the country. Subtle or unsubtle persecution was not strange to her: she was once denied a visa by the U.S. government, and her passport was seized between 1956 and 1961 by the Tafawa Balewa government. Both of these events took place because of her alleged communist links. She broke with the NCNC in 1959 to form her own political party, the Funmilayo Commoners' Party. In 1960, the Soviet Union awarded her the prestigious Lenin Peace Prize for her work for the advancement of women. This is a high pedigree of political involvement indeed, and Fela was a witness to many of his parents' activities, especially those of his mother, but I suppose the old adage is still apt: you can lead a horse to water, but you can't make it drink.[24] Decades later, Fela would recall that he was very interested in his mother's political activities and in fact liked them a lot, but only because "when she was running around doing politics she didn't have time to flog me. The more she got into politics the less time she had to beat me. So I, too, began liking politics."[25]

Even Fela's experience of racism in Britain appeared not to strike him much beyond the surface. He was interested in music, and that was his obsessive focus. He recalled hearing of race riots in Britain and seeing newspaper headlines screaming "Notting Hill, August 1958. Stick-Wielding Police Contain Negro Rioters." But, he explained, "I wasn't ready for that!"[26] Not that Fela was an unusually meek and gentle young man who did not want to get involved in the hustle and bustle of politics. On the contrary, he had been naughty and antiestablishment since his elementary school days. He was what you would call, in Nigerian parlance, a "rascal," an irredeemable young mischief-maker who was always getting into trouble with authorities, familial or otherwise. His colleagues at Trinity did not fail to notice that in him, and one of them remembered that "[h]e was loud and jovial, and he seemed to regard the whole collegiate environment as comical. The feeling was mutual."[27] But this antiestablishment streak never metamorphosed into any socially directed politics. This remained the case even when he was extremely close to such social action. Wole Soyinka, Fela's cousin, who would later win the Nobel Prize in Literature in 1986, was also in Britain at the time, starting his career as a creative writer. Soyinka recalled engaging Fela to supply the music for a reading of his protest poems and noted the apprentice musician's moving performance:

> Fela Anikulapo-Kuti was a principal musician—together with Ambrose Campbell, another Nigerian musician—when I had that Sunday night poetry-cum-drama stand at the Royal Court Theatre in December 1959. I recall he supplied the musical background for the reading of my two "Immigrant" poems, and also for the poem I have already referred to, my versified outburst against the explosion of the French atomic bomb in the Sahara. I have never forgotten his trumpet improvisation on all of those themes.[28]

It is not unkind at all to suggest that Fela was probably too absorbed in his trumpet to care much for the larger significance of the occasion. It is not surprising then that he never recalled this event in his later accounts of his London years.

Shortly after Fela began college at Trinity, his mother arranged a vacation trip for him to East Berlin. It is not clear why she chose that city, but it was no secret that she was well known in many countries of the communist bloc, where she was highly appreciated for her democratic, antiimperialist activities. The obvious goal did not appear to be to politicize Fela; if that was the subtle goal, that failed too. After initial misgivings about visiting a communist country, thanks to what he called "brainwashing" by western propaganda, Fela settled down to enjoy the trip. "I had the most beautiful time of my life in those ten days I spent there," he said, and added: "All the racist thing [sic] I experienced as a student in England wasn't there. . . . So I took a different view on that whole shit about communism."[29] That "different view," like the earlier one, remained largely personal and private, not employed as basis for civic social action or interaction or even solidarity. The closest Fela came to the latter, psychologically, was when he noticed the regard accorded to Kwame Nkrumah whenever he visited London: "He was so respected. Anytime he came to London, they put him in the front page of the newspapers. . . . I was so proud of Nkrumah, all African students were proud of him." One of his own judgments on his ideological outlook during his Trinity years is that "I was a 'jaiye-jaiye' [happy-go-lucky] man. I was just enjoying myself. Politics was not in my brain. I spent all my time playing music."[30]

The decade of the 1960s was the most revolutionary in twentieth-century Africa; countries were throwing off the colonial yoke, a task that many only a few years before had thought would take another generation to accomplish. It started as a trickle in 1957 with Ghana and had become a flood by 1960. Over twenty countries had become independent by the time Fela returned to Nigeria in 1963, and most others had raised their own flags by the end of that decade. But in many instances, people had barely savored the sweet taste of freedom before it turned sour in their mouths. Congo-Kinshasa celebrated its freedom in June 1960, and by September it had exploded in crisis. By 1965, there had been military coups and countercoups in several countries, including nearby Dahomey and Togo. Nigeria—and other countries, of course—joined the inglorious ranks a year later. Nkrumah, the leader who made Fela proud in Britain and had been a guest at the Kutis' residence and met Fela, was overthrown in a military coup on February 24, 1966. The Nigerian civil war, which dealt a crushing blow to highlife, started barely a year later. No, it was not as if all African or Nigerian musicians were commenting upon or protesting these crises in their music and Fela for some reason did not. But that is precisely the point—that he was just another ordinary young musician hustling for, as he himself liked to put it, "bread" while the momentous political events of the day passed him by. In fact, more may be expected of him, given his peculiarly opportune background. "Politics! Man, I was so fucking ignorant about world politics then, I didn't know shit! And I really didn't give a fuck either!"[31] His frankness is admirable and redeems him.

Benson Idonije writes that the music of Koola Lobitos "sounded progressive."[32] He then outlines Fela's borrowings from the artists of the "progressive jazz" era. I suppose then that Idonije means that highlife jazz is "progressive" in the sense in which "progressive jazz" is considered progressive. There is a lot to unpack here. The "progressive jazz" artists rebelled against the crass commercialization of jazz and introduced innovations of various kinds to dam that tide. Unlike the big band era, this form of jazz was emphatically not for dancing; the fast tempo made sure of that. Many of the artists were also known for their antiracist civil rights views and actions. Fela never made any declaration against existing conventional highlife or disagreed with the dominant culture of music for social dancing. All he wanted to do was distinguish himself on the highlife scene by his incorporation of more jazz sounds and protocols. He articulated no express ideology to anchor the changes, so his practice lacked the self-reflexivity that characterized the "progressive jazz" artists.

One can reasonably surmise that his catalyst was a mixture of the genuine power of conviction that jazz exerted over him and a much less clean desire for distinction that usually manifests itself in an extraverted mentality in the educated colonial, especially a "been-to."[33] Highlife already had the streak, in its showy jazz instruments, that in the Nigerian context produced not just music but also social status. "Progressive jazz" abroad may be radical, but in 1960s Lagos, it was extremely elitist. Of course, what is elitist can be progressive too; it is just that cultural tastes, open but bound by space and time as they are, are not that amenable to transregional "progressive" calculation. Jazz was the music of the "ultra-civilized" Lagos elite, and while that was not worth many pounds and shillings in the bank, the production or consumption of a chic classic music—or a rough facsimile of it—from abroad that embodies a critique of the dancing rabble is great psychological capital for invested egos in the erstwhile colony and dependent periphery. Fela's mother, ever the perceptive nationalist, saw through her son's hankering when she admonished him to start playing the music his people know, not jazz. In context, the only sense in which Fela's highlife jazz is progressive is that sense in which most borrowings from abroad are seen automatically as improvements upon the local.

Koola Lobitos's Fela was an aestheticist through and through. His instrumental innovations in highlife jazz were meant to be auto-referential; they were not intended mean anything outside of his music. He was uninterested in the larger social determinants of his musical practice and did not worry about the intricacies of musical "persuasion," or resubjectification of the audience, other than the commercial success that that implies. To this extent, he could be regarded as apolitical, and therefore politically conservative, by omission rather than commission. However, no matter how auto-referential, his music could only be meaningful in relation to the other forms he was trying to distinguish his own from. But even in that direction, our conclusion is the same: in relation to highlife, highlife jazz, in the elitism of the content and form of its instrumentals and the vacuous form and sexist and masculinist content of the lyrics—though highlife was this too—can only be regarded as politically conservative, this time by commission rather than omission.

It was not just in his music that Fela was at this period doing something confounding and untraditional. His notoriety as a "rascal" began to blossom into the image of a social rebel, the jazzy boy of highlife. If not for his skills, he would have been regarded as a drifter and ne'er-do-well. The only structure of authority he could stand was the one proposed and run by him. He had smoked marijuana briefly in London and by 1966 had returned to it. He was already getting noticed as garrulous and opinionated and as a womanizer. On his penchant for high drama, Michael Veal writes that in one incident, "he is said to have blown his trumpet outside the house of the veteran highlife star Cardinal Rex Lawson, to prove himself the better trumpeter."[34] All of these, coupled with his peculiar mode of elocution that seemed straight out of American gangster movies, began to form the building blocks of a counterculture.[35]

# 3   The Afrobeat Moralist

## ". . . . just another musician"

It is now well known that Fela's transformation to a socially conscious exponent of afrobeat began during his famous trip to the United States of America in 1969, though few actually had any idea what he was "transforming" from: an apolitical avant-pop hipster playing highlife jazz. Periods of musical, indeed, artistic, history always blur at the edges; let us note this as a humbling check on our addiction to "exact" dates. Fela had indeed been groping for a new and revitalizing musical form and ideology well before the 1969 trip. Faced with the increasing popularity of imported soul music and its bland imitations in the preceding two years, he had been stricken with the bug of continental and nationalist consciousness. Even at the risk of playing to empty clubs in Nigeria or in Ghana, where he went to try his luck twice between 1967 and 1969, he simply could not capitulate to the new trend.[1] The soul copycat extraordinaire, Geraldo Pino, whom he considered his nemesis,[2] was one model he could have followed. In 1968, he thought long and hard: "Everybody was playing soul music, man, trying to copy Pino. I said to myself: 'This James Brown music. . . . This is what's gonna happen in Nigeria soon-o.' I saw it so clearly. That's why I said to myself, 'I have to be very original and clear myself from shit.' I was still hustling. Hustling to make bread."[3]

For the first time in his professional and ideological development, Fela began groping, conceptually, in the direction suggested by his mother years before, though without his knowing it. He began to think about such large issues as Africa, the world, culture, and identity—matters he had before thought were distant and extramusical. He was now thinking of music as a bearer of African cultural specificity in the global marketplace of cultures. A cultural nationalist was born. Fela concluded to himself with determination: "'I must clear myself from this mess. I must identify with Africa. Then I will have an identity.'"[4] He became dissatisfied with "highlife jazz" as the name of his music, arguing that "[h]ighlife is a loose term which has no reference to any concrete happening in actual life. And besides, my music is much stronger than what people are already used to as highlife music. . . . It is my desire to create a new trend worthy of emulation in the music scene of this country in particular and Africa in general, which will be a pride to the black race."[5] This turned out to be deeply prophetic, though Fela was doing little more than bragging to stir himself into creative seriousness. He began searching for "a real African name that is catchy." He called a press conference and announced a new name for his music, Afro-beat, and established a club called Afro-spot, the prefix "Afro" signifying the emerging consciousness.[6] It was the next year, 1969, that the opportunity to travel to the United States presented itself to him and his band.

I begin with the foregoing not to minimize the radicalizing effect of the ten-month U.S. trip on Fela. It was in the United States that his tentative cultural nationalism of the previous year and a half was forcefully catalyzed and definitively shaped. That process began from his own immediate observations and deductions about American society and its infrastructure well before he was introduced into the politics of civil rights and African-American nationalism. Fela's expectations were great. Undertaking a successful American tour would boost his image and the band's fortunes tremendously on return home. Although it was not yet the era of such successful trips by Nigerian *juju* stars— Fela was a kind of pioneer in this regard—a few African musicians such as Miriam Makeba and Hugh Masekela were already popular in the United States. The accomplished Nigerian percussionist Babatunde Olatunji could be counted too, though he was based in the U.S. and not Nigeria. Fela might finally be able to secure a solid niche for himself in the Nigerian popular music scene after the trip. But the goal of his tour, he announced in the typical sanitized, near-duplicitous, high-flown language of marketing and publicity, was to "promote Africa in the United States and help the cause of the Afro-Americans."[7]

Not even Fela's years in London prepared him for the shock of New York City. One enduring popular image of him is that of an immensely creative musician who is also a rascal and confused professional rebel with a Kilimanjaro-sized ego. I submit that most of this was a performance. At least one contrary aspect of his character has not been as widely acknowledged, but it remained the most critical in his artistic and ideological growth. Fela was a genuinely humble and transparent human being who had a babyish impressionability that could sometimes border on naïveté. Benson Idonije, Fela's early confidant and manager, perceptively notes this trait in interpreting Fela's pursuit of jazz as a case of him being "overwhelm[ed]"[8] by the music's influence. Fela was awed by jazz and he succumbed to it, though creatively, and never looked back. He would have been awed by soul too, but it came to him in a vulgar, second-hand form that lacked the power of conviction. Fela was positively awed by America—and New York in particular—especially its evident technological sophistication and its apparent social and institutional orderliness. His immediate response was to compare New York to the jumble of postcolonial Lagos. And, of course, the latter came out woefully inadequate: "I said to myself: 'Fuck! Look those motherfucking tall buildings! Africans ain't shit! Just savages, man! When did black man ever build things great like that-o?' Oh, I was so impressed by America!"[9] Part of his wonder appears to be about what in the world could account for the gigantic disparity in living standards when both places existed in the same historical time. He was a little more diplomatic in another account: "I started thinking; I saw how everything works there, everything functions. I saw how great America is. I realized that to be a great man you have to have a great country behind you. I had no country, just a bunch of Africans running around in suits trying to be

Englishmen."[10] Like the earlier influence of jazz, Fela completely absorbed this negative affect as a catalyst for his later critique because of the power of conviction it had on him, and it would show up in myriad ways in several songs, of which one of the most famous is "Upside Down" (1976). He kept the critical cudgel handy, even though he would later learn that beneath those enchanting glitters of America were centuries of unspeakable barbarism in which Africans were, and continue to be, the victims. In contrast to his earlier observation that Africans never built anything so great, he later learned that Africans were the originators of civilization itself. "So blind, man!"[11] He later condemned his earlier ignorant and therefore overly credulous self.

The great expectations of the Koola Lobitos shriveled in no time like a raisin in the sun. Their sponsors failed to show up and performance engagements or recording contracts were not waiting for them everywhere, as they had hoped. Between New York and Los Angeles, where they were finally stranded, the group managed to secure appearances only in Washington, D.C., Chicago, and San Francisco, and all the trips were done by road. A few times they came close to a breakthrough, but each time something happened to slam the door shut at the last moment. A showcase performance for leading entertainment and business figures such as Bill Cosby and Frank Sinatra turned into disaster when the band's bassist Felix Jones disappeared. Jones, of Igbo ethnicity, had apparently calculated that such a distinguished audience could include officials of the U.S. government, which was then a staunch supporter of the Nigerian federal side against the seceding Igbos of the declared "Biafra Republic" in the ongoing civil war back home. During each number, in addition to singing vocals, Fela had to switch between playing piano, bass, and trumpet—hardly the kind of performance that would impress a potential sponsor. The band's three-month cultural exchange visa soon ran out, making it illegal for them to still be in the country. Their contract disagreements with the promoters who showed up later filtered to U.S. immigration authorities, and only the services of a lawyer saved them from deportation.[12]

With what might have been the coup de grace of the band's American tour staved off, at least temporarily, Fela and a Ghanaian record promoter he met, Duke Lumumba, began frantic efforts to raise funds through recording. Their alliance resulted in the now-(in)famous recording "Viva Nigeria." The civil war was raging in Nigeria.[13] As in all wars, the propaganda sections of both sides were on overdrive with all sorts of misinformation, half-truths, and, especially, vulgar simplifications. The main theme on the Nigerian federal side was "unity" at all costs to "Keep Nigeria One," even when the crass venality of a medieval-minded middle class that instituted ethnicity as the basis for the distribution of national wealth had led to pogroms of ethnic cleansing primarily against the Igbos in many sections of the country, especially the north. Every other minute on the Nigerian radio, one heard the jingle "To Keep Nigeria One Is a Task That Must Be Done." Even the name of the Nigerian leader prosecuting the war, General Yakubu Gowon, became a jingle, figured by inventive propagandists to mean, by nothing short of divine blessing on the task at hand, "Go On with One

Nigeria." This is the gross federalist propaganda that Fela and Lumumba decided to tap into in a desperate anticipation of recognition and therefore financial assistance from the Nigerian government. Here are the lyrics of "Viva Nigeria," which are liberally sprinkled with recognizable lines from the jingles and the national anthem at the time, in all their leaden glory:

This is Brother Fela Ransome-Kuti
This is one time I would like to say a few things
Men are born, kings are made
Treaties are signed, wars are fought
Every country has its own problems
So has Nigeria, so has Africa
Let us bind our wounds and live together in peace
Nigeria, one nation, indivisible
Long live Nigeria, viva Africa!

The history of mankind
Is full of obvious turning points and significant events
Though tongue and tribe may differ
We are all Nigerians
We are all Africans
War is not the answer
It has never been the answer
And it will never be the answer
Fighting amongst each other
Let's live together in peace
Nigeria, one nation indivisible
Long live Nigeria, viva Africa!

Let's eat together like we used to eat
Let's plan together like we used to plan
Sing together like we used to sing
Dance together like we used to dance
United we stand, divided we fall
You know what I mean
I hope you do
Let us bind our wounds
And live together in peace
Nigeria, one nation, indivisible
Long live Nigeria, viva Africa!

Brothers and sisters in Africa
Never should we learn to wage war against each other
Let Nigeria be a lesson to all
We have more to learn towards building than destroying
Our people can't afford any more suffering
Let's join hands, Africa
We have nothing to lose, but a lot to gain
War is not the answer
War has never been the answer

And it will never be the answer
Fighting amongst each other
One nation indivisible
Long live Nigeria
Viva Africa!

Were it not for the particular character of Fela's later achievement, we would have had to conclude that he missed his calling and that he should have been one of those government jingle-makers; he surely would have made a lot of "bread," and much faster, too.

But "Viva Nigeria" also marks a less striking irony. Fela would perhaps have been more successful had he been playing his music the way he did in this recording. The instrumental track is not new—it is from one of the band's earlier songs, "Waka waka" ("Walkabout"), about the one who walked endless miles in pursuit of a beautiful beloved. The two arrangements, however, are worlds apart. The tempo of "Viva Nigeria" is a click slower, the track is generally less busy, and the sound of the instrumental groups is more distinct. No doubt because of the supposed gravity of the content of the lyrics, the overall tone is more subdued—one of the distracting features of "Waka waka" is an exaggerated, choking rowdiness that is afraid to pause for breath, created by the drums and horns competing to match and outdo Fela as he howls the flimsy lyrics. It was as if Fela was trying to create the impression of a rambunctious stadium-size live show in place of the small live club audience that was incorporated into the recording. In contrast, the usual abrasiveness of the horns is downplayed noticeably in "Viva Nigeria"; they yield to the percussion and to percussive textures. The result is one of only three or four of the more than twenty recordings of Koola Lobitos that can actually coerce perceptible rocking movements from you before you know it. Fela's serious, coolly magisterial voice—the first time it sounded that way on a recording—only adds to a surprisingly rich musical experience. If you are unaware of the historical context of the lyrics, you could take the track for the most honest and enthralling pacifist song on record.

In the context of Fela's later reputation as a radical, progressive, even if anarchic, political musician, "Viva Nigeria" turned out to be his most politically scandalous and compromising composition. He tried at every opportunity to minimize the embarrassment with his usual lucid explanation and disarming unpretentiousness:

The Biafran war was still on. One day Duke came up with an idea: to release a pro-government record just so we could get some bread, man. I wanted to hustle the Nigerian government to back my band. So I wrote a song: "Keep Nigeria One." Now, wait a minute-o. You see, it wasn't my idea. It was Duke Lumumba's idea. It was he who was putting the money down. You see, Duke had this old woman he would take money from. He went to the old woman and she gave him $2,500. So he got this studio to do the recording and said to me, "Fela, I have to make just one record that the Nigerian government will like, just in case the government will want to back the band." So we made this tune. It was just bullshit: "Nigeria, we must not fight ourselves we must be like brothers." I feel so bad about that record now; I was on Biafra's side. But it wasn't my idea. Anyway, nothing came of it.[14]

He insisted that the song actually went against his deeper convictions at the time: that the Igbos were right to secede because of the injustices done to them and that the federal government was wrong. He then consoled himself: "Anyway, at that time . . . I wasn't politically minded at all. I made my comments as a citizen. I was just another musician, playing with Koola Lobitos and singing love songs, songs about rain, about people. . . . What did I know?"[15]

## The American Africa: The Paradox of Self-(Re)Discovery

Picture Fela years earlier before a haughty futurologist with all the paraphernalia of his mumbo-jumbo trade spread out around him, pronouncing casually, with unhurried authority, Fela's inexorable fate: he can run but he cannot hide from the political life he must live. "Bullshit" would have been Fela's reply. After all, uncountable momentous political events had whirled by and around him without leaving a mark, like water on a hippo's hide. Another instance of that was about to happen again in the fall of 1969 in Los Angeles. Fela was invited to perform at a function of the local chapter of the National Association for the Advancement of Colored People (NAACP), the largest civil rights organization in the United States. "[N]ot because I was political," Fela is quick to say. In fact, the occasion was just another musical engagement for him: "I just wanted to play, to make bread."[16] Remember this is the same Fela who announced with fanfare months before in Lagos that he was taking the Koola Lobitos on a tour to "promote Africa in the United States and help the cause of the Afro-Americans." A beautiful African-American woman that his roving lustful eyes caught in the audience was supposed to be just another of Fela's conquests, but even the most commonplace events sometimes engender quite uncommon consequences. Meaning that stargazers, even self-important ones, are sometimes right.

Sandra Smith Isidore and Fela soon became quite close. She was a former member of the militant black nationalist organization, the Black Panther Party.[17] As a political activist, she had been imprisoned for three months in 1967 for attacking a police officer during the Los Angeles riots. Fela was confronted with the idea and reality of determining political goals and fighting for them, even at great personal risk. Sandra's personal sacrifice for a larger political cause left a particularly strong impression on Fela, especially—sexist that he was—given Sandra's gender: "I got jealous. 'How can a woman do that and a man can't do it, a man like me?'"[18] I have underscored Fela's imperviousness to political influence until now, in spite of his great impressionability in other matters. So I will not point out the noteworthy irony here that Fela's mother herself had for decades been an exemplary model of such commitment.

Sandra became Fela's mentor. She introduced him to the history, ideas, literature, and personalities of the black struggle for civil rights. Fela absorbed all these and in the process learned even more about himself. Sandra was the midwife of this personal self-(re)discovery:

> Sandra gave me the education I wanted to know. She was the one who opened my eyes. I swear, man! She's the one who spoke to me about . . . Africa! For the first time I heard things I'd never heard about Africa! Sandra was my adviser. She talked to me about politics, history. She taught me what she knew and what she knew was enough for me to start on.[19]

Roland Barthes, the late distinguished French cultural critic, could have been talking about Fela when he wrote in a short and famous critique of the avant-garde published in 1964 that "to tell the truth, the *avant-garde* is threatened by only one force, which is not the bourgeoisie: political consciousness."[20]

Barthes could have extended his observation to the pimp, the dope addict, and the numbers runner, for those were some of the occupations of Malcolm X before the bug of political consciousness bit him. The specifics are very different, but Fela himself could not have failed to recognize faint echoes of his own unfolding trajectory in Malcolm's carefully documented movement from a self-destructive asocial life to political revelation and social and psychological rebirth. The story of Malcolm's life had a deeply significant influence on Fela:

> But this book, I couldn't put it down: *The Autobiography of Malcolm X*. . . . This man was talking about the history of Africa, talking about the white man. . . . I never read a book like that before in my life. . . . Here was a *true* story, about a man! I said, 'This is a man!' I wanted to be like Malcolm X! . . . I wanted to *be* Malcolm X, you know. I was so unhappy that this man was killed. Everything about Africa started coming back to me.[21]

*The Autobiography* is a gripping, expansive chronicle of the uplifting transformation of Malcolm from a life of petty thievery and hustling to that of a spiritual leader and internationally recognized political spokesperson of the African-American struggle against racism and for equality. Whether as a minister of the racialist and religious organization, the Nation of Islam, or later as the head of his own more secular Organization of Afro-American Unity, his whole public life is articulated in *The Autobiography* as a polemical counterdiscourse to the prevailing Euro-American hegemony characterized by racial apartheid and all the imaginable inequities that attend it. His central idea was that endless pleas or meekness would not free blacks from the stranglehold of a pathologically racist America but that only blacks' own independent determination, cultural self-confidence, and active struggle "by any means necessary" would free them. This idea was the backbone of Black Power, a composite movement of black political radicalism and cultural nationalism that effected an epochal shift in the psychological constitution of African America by detaching the power of truth from the entrenched myth of Euro-American racial superiority.

From *The Autobiography* Fela took away at least three main lessons. The first is a palpable reaffirmation of an old cliché that knowledge is power. To *understand* the world in which one lives—its previous configurations and how it came to be the way it is now, the shifting role of oneself in it in relationship to others, how those positions came to be determined, and how they can be consolidated or reconfigured—was as important to Malcolm as overcoming systemic impoverishment. And his own personal example in a context in which centuries of racism had imposed on blacks a self-subverting inferiority complex made it clear to him that mental rebirth or resubjectification was actually more important than immediate food on the table.[22] His extensive self-education and re-education in the history and cultures of the world, especially Africa, gave his life a new purpose and the insight to pursue it. Henceforth, he would never stop wielding the weapon of the central contradiction in European civilization as he saw it: great technical achievement, on one hand, and great moral depravity, on the other. It was this depravity that catalyzed one of the central themes in the book, that of an oppositional religion to Christianity, Islam, which he used to counter the historic complicity of Christianity with black enslavement and the colonization of Africa. If Christianity was used to support and broadcast the myth of black inferiority, he would use Islam to do the opposite: glorify black ancestry and demonize whites.[23] Fela, as someone conscious of indigenous African religions and at least the originary alienness of *both* Christianity and Islam to Africa, overlooked Malcolm's unjustified valorization of Islam, but he would hold dear Malcolm's veneration of historical knowledge as a veritable resource for the psychic empowerment of Africans.

But of what use is a liberating knowledge that is not openly and boldly broadcast to the oppressed millions who need it? Speaking truth to power, at whatever personal cost, is the second crucial lesson that Fela learned from the example of Malcolm X. Malcolm X remains perhaps the most courageous African-American leader of the twentieth century. This is more so given the context in which he lived. In an era when black leaders were supposed to be "reasonable" and "diplomatic," Malcolm was Frantz Fanon's untamable, unassimilable Negro who "knocks down the system and breaks the treaties."[24] With the kind of acerbic wit that would define Fela's songs later on, Malcolm stood tall and said things the way he saw them. "No, I am not an American," he famously and polemically declared in 1964, "I am one of the twenty-two million black people who are the *victims* of America . . . [v]ictims of 'democracy'—nothing but disguised hypocrisy. . . . I don't see any 'American Dream,' I see an American Nightmare!"[25] In an era of black unfreedom, he plucked freedom for himself and lived it so his people could borrow his example. His effect was incalculable.[26]

Malcolm X toured Egypt, Sudan, Nigeria, and Ghana in 1959. And after his resignation from the Nation of Islam in 1964, he made his well-publicized pilgrimage to Mecca and traveled to several African countries. President Kwame Nkrumah of Ghana honored him royally, and students at the University of Ibadan in Nigeria christened him "Omowale," a diaspora-disciplining Yoruba name meaning "the child comes home." Fela, the apolitical highlife jazz musician in Lagos, had missed all of that, of course. But better late than never:

he now learned from Malcolm's story—his third lesson—what he could have learned earlier from Malcolm in person in Nigeria: the significance, indeed the necessity, of advocating and cultivating pan-African political and cultural relations and unity.

The lessons would later constitute pervasive themes in Fela's music. Malcolm's story and statements were not the only sources of his influence. It is unclear whether Fela was aware of it, but Malcolm also influenced Fela's favorite and inspirational jazz artists at this time, especially Miles Davis and John Coltrane but also Albert Ayler and Archie Shepp.[27] It is also in this context of close connections between black nationalism and black music, in which both the music and the star status of performers were made part of the weapons of struggle, that Fela made his peace with the music of James Brown, which he had tentatively sampled back home but whose overwhelming influence on the public he had consistently lamented.[28]

Enveloped in a sweeping sociopolitical, racial, cultural, and musical education of an oppositional character, Fela rediscovered his blackness and Africanness in a radically new way. I say "rediscover" advisedly, to acknowledge his groping of the previous two years for such an anchor. The conviction struck him forcefully that he had not been playing "truly African" music:

> [O]ne day I sat down at the piano in Sandra's house. I said to Sandra: "Do you know what? I've just been fooling around. I haven't been playing AFRICAN music. So now I want to write African music . . . for the first time. I want to try." Then I started to write and write. In my mind I put a bass here . . . a piano there. . . . Then I started humming, then singing. I said to myself, "How do Africans sing songs? They sing with chants. Now let me chant into this song: la la la laaa."[29]

He thus created a new musical aesthetic which the "afrobeat" name he had invented a year earlier would more properly describe: a fusion of indigenous Yoruba rhythms and declamatory chants, highlife, jazz, and the funky soul of James Brown. His first composition was titled "My Lady Frustration," dedicated to Sandra for the strain he and his band had placed on her and on her family's resources, running up phone bills without recompense because he could not get rewarding engagements in Los Angeles nightclubs. But this composition changed all that; the first time he performed it at the club where he had been working for two months, the owner and barman screamed, "'Fela, where did you get this fucking tune from? Whaaaaaat!' The whole club started jumping and everybody started dancing. I knew then that I had found the thing, man. To me, it was the *African* tune I had written till then."[30]

Based on the seven-minute recorded version, "My Lady Frustration" is not wholly unrecognizable from Fela's highlife jazz. There is the familiar tripartite arrangement: Fela's vocals and the horns interact in a call-and-response manner to set the theme, then two extended solos are backed up in interspersed stretches by the horn section to reiterate the founding theme, and finally, the first section is repeated with improvisatory variations mainly by Fela's vocals. However, the track does show some significant distinguishing features. Although Fela's vocals are prominent, he does not bother to sing at all; he apparently could not find an appropriate topic or return to his usual puerile love songs. He said in recounting his epiphanic moment above that he was inspired by African "chants," but the predominant scatty "Ho! Ho! Ho! Ho!" "Hei! Hei! Hei! Hei!" and the like in the track are hardly "chants," much less uniquely African. However, the different ways he stressed these nonverbal vocals in both duration and pitch to make them musical has a firm anchor in many African languages, especially tonal ones such as Yoruba. Although he was working at the interface of Yoruba and English and with mostly European instruments, Fela appeared to have decided to employ Yoruba speech patterns as the operative mode.[31] He seemed to recognize that since the tonality of most African languages contracts the gap between speech and song, he needed to pay particular attention to how speech and song and the sounds of instruments mutually enable or constrain one another.[32] As he "dialogues" effortlessly—and not just in short safe phrases but in far more exploratory ways—with the horns, his own voice becomes another distinctive instrument in the ensemble. And indeed, in the closing moments, he sings unaccompanied by the instruments. The horn solos are much more unwearied and melodious—of course, the track's overall mid-tempo pace helps, allowing the repetitive main theme to clearly mark the rhythm, but the horns sound purposive though without anxiety. The James Brown trademark exhortations to the instrumental sections, soloists, back-up vocals, or even the audience, are here in the usual abbreviated form ("One more time!") but in a structurally far more meaningful way; something close to the kind of robust interactive presentation we find in Brown's "I Feel All Right" would come much later in Fela's recordings such as "I.T.T."

Other songs collected in the album *The '69 Los Angeles Sessions* include "Viva Nigeria," "Obe," "Ako," "Witchcraft," "Wayo," "Lover," "Funky Horn," "Eko," and "This Is Sad." "My Lady Frustration" is the greatest revelation among them. Some in fact are refurbished from the Koola Lobitos repertoire. Both "Wayo" and "Ako," for instance, had been released before in different versions.

Fela went to the United States with the two intertwined goals of finding financial and musical success to boost his so-far-lackluster career back home. Both eluded him. However, he gained something more fundamental and therefore most important: the lasting potential to meet those two objectives and a lot more. The optimism, by no means bubbly since a potential holds no guarantee, is evident in the new name he gave his band, Nigeria 70, as if announcing to all that the dawning decade belonged to him. In March 1970, the nine-person band, which had remained intact through the rough nine months, set for home. Fela was not known to enjoy extended or abstruse jokes or anecdotes, either as teller or listener, but he was obviously inspired when he recounted for Carlos Moore one he had heard in Los Angeles in 1970; Fela's eloquence alone makes the anecdote worth quoting in full:

As me and my band headed back to Lagos, I remembered a joke told to me only a few days before getting on the plane. I kept laughing to myself, thinking about it. . . . It was this man in Los Angeles who had thrown a party in his house. LSD liquid, acid, was passed around. They all took small small. Then this guy went to the toilet. Suddenly he runs out with a towel around him. "Goddamn, there is a fucking gorilla in the bathroom!" Everyone was so high, man. "A gorilla?" they asked. "In Los Angeles?" The man himself was so fucking confused, he said: "I tell you I saw a fucking gorilla in the bathroom. Shit! I know what I saw. Fuck L.A.!" So they all decided to go and see the gorilla in the bathroom for themselves. They're all so scared, but they go and push open the door ever so s-l-o-w-l-y. Then put in head bit by bit to see the gorilla, "There ain't no fucking gorilla in here, man. Shiiit!" Now the guy who said he'd seen a gorilla came and went inside. There was a mirror on the wall. When the guy looked up, he screamed: "The gorilla! The gorilla!" They all said, "That's you, motherfucker!" I laughed and laughed over that one.[33]

Fela told this joke immediately after emphasizing "My Lady Frustration" as "the first *African* tune" he had written till then and immediately before raising the rhetorical query, "Who was I?" That Fela remembered the joke in the context of his ruminations on his own developing consciousness of cultural identity makes it much more suggestive than just another common "boys' night out" gag. Could it be, for instance, that Fela saw his previous ideologically barren highlife jazz self in the drugged man who misrecognized his own image in the mirror? Does this have anything to do with his mother's earlier counsel to him to play the music his people knew? Looking at a mirror—a moment that is normally a harmless but illusory and vainglorious affirmation of one's "whole" self—becomes for the addled man an ego-shattering experience. The moment of the shattering also marks the commencement of reconstitution, but the brief moment between paradigms during which one can only have a tenuous hold on reality can be extremely discomfiting. Fela imagined himself seeing the man in that vulnerable moment and laughing at him. However, because we cannot laugh at someone in a vulnerable moment without imagining ourselves in the person's shoes, our laughter can only be a hidden anxious quest for our own safety, certainty, relief. Fela reflected, after relating the story: "Who was I? It was in America I saw I was making a mistake. I didn't know myself. I realized that neither me nor my music was going in the right direction."[34] When he recalled his moment in that risky space between realization of mistake and institution of correction—a recollection that happened years later when he was already a successful musician—Fela could only laugh the substantive, relief-laden, mirthless laughter that comes after a close shave, after the lucky escape of successfully crossing the gulf.[35]

## The Birth of Afrobeat

Fela returned home to Nigeria with the crucial ingredients for a new beat and a new outlook. Although he recalled later that he returned "with the intent to change the whole system,"[36] it was clear that he had not the vaguest idea how or where to effectively begin. Mabinuori K. Idowu wrote euphemistically that

Fela's "first appearance at the 'Afro-Spot' was a pointer to the difficult task ahead of him. He greeted the audience with the Black Power Salute, but there was no response from the crowd—because at this time, they did not know what a Black Power Salute stood for."[37] To compound the alienation, he was not sure what to sing about that would interest the audience. Love songs were the staple for a musician of his kind (educated, thoroughly westernized, urban-based), and though he had not been successful with them earlier on, he was now vehemently opposed to them ideologically. Even with the free shows he did to reintroduce himself to the public, his early recordings "bombed," to use the music-industry term. He still had not made it when James Brown toured Nigeria in December 1970, though Brown thought his music significant enough to call him an "African James Brown."[38] He was settling into what looked like an extension of the pre-trip quagmire when a well-meaning brother advised him to invite Geraldo Pino to be a guest at the Afro-Spot, to attract the audience. It was probably the specter of this old nemesis that finally stung Fela into deeper creative exploration.[39] The result was his first successful record, "Jeun Ko Ku" ("Chop and Quench"), released in 1971. It was a wildly popular hit that sold more than 200,000 copies within six weeks of its release, setting Fela on the path to musical stardom. He had finally found the formula for success.

It was clear up until then that in Fela's quest for a dance music that would be culturally popular and also sophisticated, he had found the horns the most difficult to tame. This was partly the result of his own ambivalence about the kind of music he really wanted to play or be associated with. In "Jeun Ko Ku," he at last discovered a direction that suited his talents and temperament and a musical vision that yielded an appropriate modality for aligning and integrating the instrumental groups in his ensemble. Over very sprightly drums and other percussion that set up a graceful, funky rhythm, the horns begin briskly to delineate the popular tune in sparkling, bold strokes. Indeed, part of the sonic stimulation comes from the expert choreography of the horn section in delivering those strokes. Underneath, the drums and other percussion instruments are positively inspired, with the congas, *shekere,* and sticks cheekily stealing into the limelight in between the breathing of the horns. The congas repeatedly taunt by doing what party-hardened Lagosians call "*re ilu,*" meaning to beat the drum in brief light patterns to achieve a tantalizing effect. Horn solos loop and twist and, collectively, return to the tune and even simulate the lyrics. Fela does not use talking drums, instruments of prime significance in Yoruba ensembles, but he tries to make the horns perform at least the simplest of the functions of those drums.[40]

Lyrically, "Jeun Ko Ku" is not a great distance away from earlier inconsequential highlife jazz songs:

| | |
|---|---|
| Jeun ko ku o, o de! | The glutton, here he comes! |
| Waki and die, o de! | The overeater is here! |
| Chop and quench, o de! | Chop and quench has arrived! |
| Waki and quench, o de! | Gorge and die has come! |

| Mo gba'mala 'le o fa'tan o | I put amala down, he ate it all |
|---|---|
| Mo gb'eba sile o je'tan o | I dished up eba, he devoured it all |
| Mo gbe'su sile o je'tan o | I set down yam, he gobbled every crumb |
| Mo gb'obe sile o laa tan o | I served stew, he licked it all |
| Mo gb'eja sile o jee tan o | I presented fish, he finished it all |
| Mo gb'emu sile o ba mi muu tan o | I supplied palmwine, he guzzled it all |
| Mo gb'obinrin le o ba mi je mbe | I brought women, he played with them |

| E ba mi le kuro n'ile mi o o | Help me drive him away from my house |
|---|---|
| Onigbese, e ba mi le lo o | The squanderer, help me chase him away |
| Ole! e ba mi le lo o | Thief! Help me hound him off |

The song is thematically similar to "Omuti" and in its presentation recalls "Onidodo," both from Fela's Koola Lobitos years. It is, however, in a class by itself. Songs—or artistic renderings in general—about the drunkard do not necessarily sell a dozen a penny in Yoruba popular culture, but they are not uncommon. Nearly two decades earlier, the distinguished novelist Amos Tutuola had made world famous the fantasy of one Yoruba gourmet palmwine drinker who went up to heaven to command back to earth his dead favorite tapster. This is in his *The Palmwine Drinkard,* which was subsequently adapted into a popular opera by the veteran Kola Ogunmola and his theater troupe. In plays, songs, proverbs, anecdotes, mothers' pleas, fathers' warnings, spouses' protests, and above all, in government health division campaigns, it could be said that drinking was oversymbolized in the general culture. Gluttony, on the other hand, had not figured so extensively in popular culture, and the effect on the audience of such a totally off-beat theme in a track that had every other thing going for it was electric. Also, "Omuti" is preachy and judgmental in a distant, condescending manner and completely humorless. All it offers is wholesome fatherly advice, and who does not already have a surfeit of that? In contrast, it is clear that the singer in "Jeun Ko Ku," even while reproaching and begging to be freed of the glutton, actually has a soft spot for him. They have no doubt been good friends, seen in the singer's unforced generosity: he does not object to sharing, he just objects to the fact that the glutton greedily finishes every dish set down. The catalyst of the song is the leech's abuse of that generosity. In this scenario, the singer's rejection of the glutton, though it is a moral condemnation, harbors less condescension and more pragmatic self-preservation; the latter was the number-one survival rule among the teeming mass of Lagosians as they eked out their daily existence in a postwar confusion yet to be tempered by the oil boom. And then there is the exaggerated dramatic presentation, complete with rib-cracking and often sexist street humor, and Fela's own decidedly "unsingerly" hollering and highly theatrical voice. It was no surprise that the song was a sensation. The architecture of afrobeat as a distinctive genre of music was complete.

"Jeun Ko Ku" was the first critical milestone in the five years from 1970 to 1975 which I have labeled Fela's second stage of artistic and ideological growth. Immensely productive, he released nearly fifty songs in the period. I have divided these into three main types based on their subject: metro songs, racial/cultural nationalist songs, and appropriated folk songs.

The metro songs are those that implicitly or explicitly take as their theme the sights and sounds of the metropolis. Lagos, Nigeria's capital city until the 1980s and still the premier commercial center, is Fela's immediate inspiration for them, but he might as well been talking about any major West African city. Because the metro songs constitute a good four-fifths of all Fela's musical production at this time, it is important to explore why. The city, of course, exerts its own pressures on artistic creativity, and this is very much a part of the equation. But Fela's metro songs are not about just any aspect of city life. There are, after all, a million things to inspire anyone in the city. The city is the incomparable and ever-busy red-light district of the muses. Fela's metro songs are of a particular kind: they exhibit a decidedly lower-class orientation. They are about the quotidian urban experiences of the teeming lower and under classes as they jostle against one another to negotiate "the system" in search of the elusive dream of a comfortable and dignified existence in a pitiless urban sprawl. Some of the better-known metro songs include "Jeun Ko Ku" (of course), "J'Ehin J'Ehin" ("Chop-Teeth Chop-Teeth"), "Let's Start," "Who're You," "Shakara (Oloje)," "Roforofo Fight," "Igbe," "Go Slow," "Je'Nwi Temi" ("Don't Gag Me"), "Noise for Vendor Mouth," "Ariya," "Swegbe and Pako," "Mattress," "He Miss Road," "Eko Ile," "Monday Morning in Lagos," "It's No Possible," "Trouble Sleep Yanga Wake Am," "Na Poi," and "Open and Close."

Think of the 1950s and 1960s as the age when an ostentatious arriviste pseudo-bourgeoisie looked so awesomely busy as they steered the ship of state. Highlife, with all its sonic pretensions to "modern" good breeding and sophistication, was its music. The civil war (1967–1970) shattered all that, and by 1970, when the country settled in for a long stretch of military rule, that bourgeois class had lost the moral authority it had begun to accumulate since wresting power from the colonizers formally in 1960. The pace of urbanization accelerated after the war as people escaped the destruction and poverty of the countryside to try their luck in the promising neon lights of the city.[41] In October 1973, a barrel of crude oil went for US$3.80. By January 1974, it was selling for US$14.70. The oil boom was on, and most of the benefits would be concentrated in the cities.[42] The new breed of Nigerian leaders was brasher and more venal and made no pretence of morality. On the contrary, it placed all its stocks on brute force. Even if it did try pretence, it was not certain that the people would buy it, for the experience of the breakdown of democratic process and subsequent tragic civil war because of the intellectual and moral bankruptcy of the ruling class had profoundly changed the people too. They were now generally savvier in their relations with "the system": less trusting and more cynical until actual government performance dictated otherwise. They could be cowed by military force, but they would not automatically accord any regime with moral recognition; they did not control power, but the hordes outside the door now constituted perpetual headaches to those sitting on gilded thrones inside. It is in this sense that Nigeria of the 1970s could be described as the age of the (urban) masses. They were overworked, underpaid, and stressed out by the pressures of the new petrol-fueled economy; and in the overcrowded slums of the metropolises, where primordial loyalties and languages could hold on to only a tenuous existence, they created a unique common symbolic language and mode of social relations. This was the humble pool from which afrobeat drew its complex of oral-aural imagery. In that sense, it is the quintessential music of this new Nigerian social form, the urban masses.[43] These were (and still are) the people whose faces and actions never make the news except as lawbreakers; they are never the subject of great works of art except as caricatures. Fela took their daily social life and artistically—musically—monumentalized it in their very own language. They recognized themselves in the music and embraced it wholeheartedly. Thus, afrobeat introduced profoundly new dimensions to the nation's sonic landscape, and it fundamentally transformed it in the process.

Gluttony, boastfulness, Lagos, traffic jams, fights, boisterousness, shit, water, newspaper vendors, sex, the colonial mentality, electricity, skin bleaching, and more. Afrobeat became not just a new kind of music but a new way of looking at the world in which repressed, marginal, or tabooed themes, figures, and desires were freely acknowledged, debated, and even frequently affirmed, in a musically pleasurable manner, with inventive catchy phrases or words—"jeun ko ku," "shakara," "swegbe," "na poi," "je'nwi temi," and so forth—that soon entered into widespread usage. Fela knew he was blazing a trail, and apparently he had thought about what surprises might lie around the corner. In a very prescient track, "Je'Nwi Temi" ("Don't Gag Me"), released in 1973, he expressed his determination to pursue that social interventionist course without fear:

| | |
|---|---|
| Ti mba r'oto ma so, o le panu mi de | If I see the truth I will say, and you can't shut me up |
| Je'nwi temi o, o le panu mi de | Let me say mine, you can't close my mouth |
| Ma la'nu bi apere o, o le panu mi de | I will open my mouth like basket, and you can't shut me up |
| Otito ko ro, o le panu mi de | Truth is bitter, you can't shut me up |
| Bo ti mi mo'le o, o le panu mi de | You can imprison me, but you can't close my mouth |
| Padlock mi o si lowo e, o le panu mi de | You don't have the key to my padlock, so you can't shut me up |
| Agadagodo mi o si lowo e, o le panu mi de | You don't have the key to my padlock, so you can't shut me up |
| Je'nwi temi se O! | Let me say mine |
| *Chorus:* Je'nwi temi. . . . | *Chorus:* Let me say mine. . . . |
| Otito koro o, omo araiye o fe | The truth is bitter, the world hates it |
| Be fe, befe o, mi a wi temi | Like it or not, I will say mine |
| O le panu mi de | You can't close my mouth |
| *Chorus:* O le panu mi de | *Chorus:* You can't close my mouth |

Defiance is evident enough in the lyrics, but it is actually in the context of the sound arrangement that its true extent can be gauged. Fela introduces the mid-tempo track, unusually, with a sort of withholding of sonic access: the bass, radically pared down in range and pitch, and a taut, droning, energetic guitar line combine to sketch a subdued theme upon which Fela sings—more precisely, announces in a brawny voice—the first three lines of the lyrics. It is only after this, a minute into the thirteen-minute track, that the horns and the full drums and percussion enter with a dramatic convivial intensity. It is as if he does not want the core message to get lost in the music, hence the introductory clear drawing of a line in the sand. Fela bellows and shouts scats; he vocally leads and underlines the instruments, then intersperses them with brief theatrical stops in which only the maracas can be heard before the ensemble roars in again. The stop-starts are unfailing emotional hooks on the audience, goading them to discharge and recharge, catch some breath, and more intensely resume the dance. Fela sings more of the lyrics, and the band then repeats the enchanting arrangement. A horn solo serenely takes over and for about two whole minutes it wails, sinuously weaving intricate mellifluous patterns, backed up heavily now and then by all the horns together. Underneath, the drums reverberate cavernously, with tantalizingly choppy undertows furtively ornamenting the basic repetitive pattern in a hide-and-seek manner. And just as serenely, the whole carnival settles down into minimalism, allowing Fela, supported ably by the chorus, to emphatically repeat the lyrics again and even sell his tradition-deprived city-dweller audience a line or two of Yoruba pseudo-incantation. No matter; the musician and his audience probably shared the same level of shallow immersion in that part of the culture. A much longer and prominent keyboard solo answers Fela's vocal "ma'gbo" (listen). It is quite impetuous, restlessly skipping hither and thither in a zigzag pattern, and in a stretch of particular willfulness due to overexcitement, the pacing contracts rapidly and it whips itself into a keening loll, squeezing itself—and no doubt the dancing torsos of diehard fans—to the ground at an enervating speed, to the point of complete dissipation. It actually vanishes, dies! Thankfully, the drums and percussions underneath keep their cool unfailing regularity and receive the dancing bodies tenderly back into the more gentle flow of the sturdy rhythm. In the last two minutes of the track, Fela's vocals, chorus, horns, and drums come together to replay both the musical and lyrical theme with Fela's additional improvisatory scatting. The track does not end with ebb as one would expect, given all its drama, but as is usual with Fela in many tracks, he ratchets the instruments to exit on a high flourish. "Je'Nwi Temi," if I still need to say it, remains a favorite party classic. Not only does Fela sing defiance; he makes defiance a pleasurable object of desire. "Je'Nwi Temi" became a pat response to bullies and aggressive interlocutors.

Two more samples of the metro songs should suffice to demonstrate their texture and ideological orientation. "Eko Ile" ("Lagos, Home") is less musically adventurous, but it is significant as one of the most popular of Fela's many songs about the metro itself, Lagos, his professional home. Others include "Eko," an earlier version of "Eko Ile," "Monday Morning in Lagos," and "Go Slow." "Eko Ile" is a tongue-in-cheek but also genuinely felt homage to this city, popularly known as the home of wisdom. Over a vivacious up-tempo beat, the horns and drums lay out the basic pattern of repeated short brief strokes followed throughout the track. They trace and underline Fela's vocals, the horns more vigorously and at a higher pitch, as he sings:

| | |
|---|---|
| Ko ma sibi ti mo le f'ori le, ko si o, a f'Eko ile | There is nowhere I can head to, nowhere else, but Lagos home |
| Bi mo ba rajo lo London o, ma tun pada s'eko ile | If I travel to London, I will return to Lagos home |
| Bi mo ba rajo lo New York o, ma tun pada s'eko ile | If I travel to New York, I will return to Lagos home |
| Eko o, Eko ile | Lagos, Lagos, home |

This transitions into a long horn solo, which takes two of the song's nearly seven minutes, mimicking the main tempo by riffing short, choppy patterns of different kinds. There is a striking structural irony here that cannot be overlooked. After praising Lagos as a homey, welcoming place, and ceremonially accenting that with a gorgeous horn solo, all that is left to do is to offer concrete examples in order to convince the audience. What follows—and Fela returns and sings all the lyrics this time—is a most unusual exemplification in the circumstance, since all it narrates is the confusion and danger that is Lagos:

| | |
|---|---|
| Bi mo ba wa moto ni London o, ma tun sese wa ko ti wa n'ile | Even if I drove in London, I would have to learn driving anew when I return home |
| Bi o ba wa moto ni New York o, wa tun sese wa ko ti wa nile | Even if you drove in New York, you would have to learn driving anew on return |
| Tori Turn Right l'Eko o, la'ju e, Turn Left l'ori o | Because "Turn Right" in Lagos, open your eyes, is really "Turn Left" |
| Nitori o to ba ri Turn Right l'Eko o, ore mi, Turn Left lo ri o | Because if you see "Turn Right" in Lagos, my friend, it is really "Turn Left" you see |

As if suspecting that you would notice and point out the inconsistency in the presentation, the song cheekily advances the apologia of difference, "Ours is different from yours, you hear":

| | |
|---|---|
| Ti wa tun yato si tiyin o se e ngbo o, eko ile | Ours is different from yours, you hear |
| Chorus: Eko ile [repeats] | |
| Ka ma tun sese so tawon obirin wa o | Let's not even talk about our women in Lagos |
| "Lady" ni won o | They are "Lady" |

Logically ordered London and New York should go and mind their own business. There is just no place like homey Lagos. Fela's voice, thunderous as usual, is by turns serious and playfully mischievous. But it is doubtful that anyone would think this is problematic, for the track, in spite of its wordiness, seems in fact to be organized more around the sizzling thumping rhythm than by anything like logical lyrics. Another, but much shorter, horn solo leading the ensemble ushers the track to an end.

Toward the end of the lyrics above, Fela presents "*awon obinrin wa*" (our women) as part of the difficult obstacles to negotiate in the testy terrain of Lagos. It is clear, then, that the proclaimed homeyness of Lagos, obstacles and all, appeals to men like Fela only and does not apply to women. Women are part of the Lagos man's tricky problems such as the deceptive traffic signs. Fela apparently has a lot more to say about this but has run out of time. "Let's not even talk about our women in Lagos" now, he pleads, in a tone pregnant with meaning.

He created more time elsewhere to sing about women, from Lagos or elsewhere, in the most infamous among the metro songs, "Mattress." The mid-tempo song, fourteen minutes long, has the space and time to robustly exhibit its wares, both instrumentally and lyrically. The song, released in 1975, incorporated some of Fela's early practice of prefacing his songs with very extended instrumental introductions. In this song, a thin keyboard line noodles a plaintive note while drums, unusually heavily, and the horns sketch a tune around it. From then on, drums heave and cymbals clash, consistently maintaining the rhythm in the background while horn solos weave in and out of the horn section and keyboard solos moan and wail, interspersed with the entrances and exits of the horns. Fela's vocals do not begin until eight minutes into the song:

| | |
|---|---|
| Mattress, mattress | Mattress, mattress |
| Call am for me! | Name it for me! |
| *Chorus:* Mattress, mattress | *Chorus:* Mattress, mattress |
| The thing wey we dey sleep on top call am for me | The thing we sleep on top name it for me |
| If e be mat, wey dey cold for ground | If it's a mat on the cold floor |
| If e be plank, wey dey hard for back | If it's a hard plank |
| If e be spring wey dey bounce like ball | If it's the bouncy spring |
| If e be cushion wey dey soft like wool | If it's soft cushion |
| E be mat, e be plank, e be spring, e be cushion | Mat, plank, spring, cushion |
| Anything wey we dey sleep on top call am for me | Anything we sleep on top name it for me |
| So when I say woman na mattress I no lie | So when I say woman is a mattress I am not lying |
| *Chorus:* You no lie, my friend | *Chorus:* You are not lying, my friend |

Note how carefully Fela the singing "I" draws everyone in with a nondiscriminating "the thing wey we dey sleep on top," as if all the voice wants to do is teach *all of us,* male and female without distinction, a lesson about mattresses. There is no doubt that a lesson is there, but as is characteristic of Fela, in generalizing from a universal to a gendered particular, it turns out that the "we" is exclusivist, gendered, and vulgarly masculinist. The music of the song is not particularly notable in the corpus of Fela's metro songs, but it is alluring enough to fuel the sexism of his male audience—especially the most dangerous kind, the urban lower-class sexism that can frequently ignite into violence against the most vulnerable group of women. One cannot fail to note the irony as Fela's female chorus, crisp and professional, repeatedly and shrilly underscores "Mattress, mattress" and "You no lie, my friend" in response to Fela's crude and demeaning analogies. We could literalize Fela's imagery and ask, What if he were not too crude or too conservative to imagine the pleasures of sexual positions other than the normative "missionary" man on top? Would he still be fixated with the image of woman as man's mattress?

By comparison to songs about the city, Fela composed only a handful of racial/cultural nationalist songs during the second phase of his career. He obviously learned important lessons from the episode of his unanswered Black Power salute by the Lagos audience on his return from the United States in the first half of 1970. He could not impose contemporary black American racial consciousness, a variation of what he called his own ideology of "Blackism" or "Africanism," on Nigerians, even if it made sense and was feasible, without patient reeducation.[44] But he also could not give up all that education in militant racialism and racial nationalism that he had received in the United States. He changed the name of his nightclub from Afro-Spot to Africa Shrine. Fela's compromise was to interpret the global politics of Euro-American racial hegemony in terms of its particular local manifestations; this should have been his position in the first place. Thus, he found that singing about Nigerians in three-piece suits in steaming tropical Lagos had far greater resonance with his audience than singing about how whites came to enslave Africans centuries ago. The distance between the two stances is the distance between racial nationalism and cultural nationalism. The two are not necessarily mutually exclusive and often do imply one another, but "race" is not "culture." In the matter at hand, "culture" is at best thought of as a subset of "race" in which a group of people may be united by "race," a larger universal category determined by some obvious human phenotypical features but nevertheless divided by "culture," the set of practices and meaning systems formed by a community bound by space and time. And second, in a racially homogenous Nigerian context where Euro-American racial hegemony, political or cultural, is transmitted through locally anchored agents and practices, it only made sense that resistance to that hegemony should be primarily, though not exclusively, anchored in the local, in both imagery and target. Among Fela's racial/cultural nationalist songs, the more racially coded ones such as "Black Man's Cry," "Why Black Man Dey Suffer," "Who No Know Go Know," and "Buy Africa" were far less successful than the more culturally themed songs such as "Lady" or "Gentleman."

"Why Black Man Dey Suffer" presents an originary scene of African Eden—"We dey sit down for our land jeje" (We were living peacefully in our land)—when, suddenly, "some people come from faraway land" and "fight us and take away our land" and "our culture" from us. That, in a nutshell, is the origin of the African crisis: "Na since then trouble start" (That's when our troubles started). "Buy Africa," which borrows the topic of economic nationalism and self-sufficiency that was an integral part of Black Power, is a patriotic call to Africans to buy goods made in Africa. But the theme has its own authentic local provenance in the many "trade fairs" embarked upon by many African governments to showcase goods produced locally or in alliance with foreign partners. Fela and his Nigeria 70 represented Nigeria at Ghana's Second International Trade Fair in 1971, and "Buy Africa" was part of that patriotic enterprise. In discussing "Viva Nigeria," I suggested that Fela would have made an excellent government propagandist; to listen to "Buy Africa" is to further confirm that speculative judgment. We can just imagine propaganda managers of various Nigerian regimes over the years shaking their heads sadly at the enormous talent lost when Fela crossed to the people's side! "Who No Know Go Know" is a lament about the ignorance of Africans who know next to nothing about their racial heroes. The song gives us a roster: Nkrumah, Sekou Toure, Idi Amin. Fela would again list Idi Amin favorably in "Underground System," released in 1992. Idi Amin was the crudest African dictator and had no redeeming feature, unlike the intellectuals Nkrumah and Toure, who went bad with the help of local sycophants and Cold War scheming by superpowers. Fela should have known this, but we know that ideological consistency was not one of his strong points. Even so, it does sound like irresponsible sensationalism for the writer of the entry on Fela in the 2002–2003 edition of the Microsoft Encarta Encyclopedia to have space, in a mere nine lines on the whole of the musician's life and work, to say that Fela "held up Idi Amin as a role model."[45]

"Black Man's Cry," recorded live with Ginger Baker, serves well to explain why Fela's more racially coded songs were not very successful. Like the rest of them, this track is not necessarily a musical lightweight. The horns are still vintage Fela, and the drums and percussion still make it clear that they stand ready to do the master's bidding. But the arrangement is comparatively conventional, a flat plateau. The horns sometimes sound lost or bored as they weave around Fela's energetic scat singing. Occasionally when Fela is silent, a riveting solo flares up and wakes us up from our near-slumber—we can indeed fall into that in this nearly twelve-minute track whose leisurely pace seems to be on autopilot throughout—but the whole track is not made of such solos, sadly. The drums do nothing extraordinary at any point; they are merely content with their supporting functions, which is a bad thing indeed. Even the classic *juju* tempo that this track recalls—that of Chief Commander Ebenezer Obey, for instance —sprays such tempos with strategically placed arousing wrinkles that are missing here. To make matters worse, the trademark Fela humor—graphic, sardonic, and always memorable—is completely absent. All we are left with is the pseudo-uplifting "Black Is Beautiful" lyrics, off-putting in their directness, preaching blackness to those who have never lost or doubted theirs, whatever that is:

| | |
|---|---|
| Ijo wo la ma bo o, loko eru? | When are we going to be free from slavery? |
| A o bo njokan o, loko eru! | We will be free one day, from slavery! |
| Ta lo so funmi pe awo dudu ti mo gbe sara mi o daa o? | Who says my black skin is not beautiful? |

| E mu wa ki nri o | Bring the person here before me |
| Ta lo so fun yin pe awo dudu ti e gbe sara yi o daa o | Who says your black skin is not beautiful? |
| E mu wa ke ri o | Let the person come out |
| Ko s'oun to dara to awo dudu ti e gbe sara yin o o | There is no better than this your beautiful black skin |
| Ewo yin dada | Look at yourselves closely |
| Ko s'oun to dara to awo dudu ti mo gbe sara mi a a | There is no better than this my beautiful black skin |
| Ewo mi dada o | Look at me closely |

Fela screams "yeeeeeeeeeh!" several times toward the end and says that is "the black man's cry."

The more specifically cultural nationalist songs are, on the other hand, much more successful. "Gentleman" is a satire against overly westernized African men, but the more wildly popular is the earlier "Lady," a satire against overly westernized African women and a most eloquent manifesto that gave many boys of my generation our first popular and pleasurable language of male chauvinism. The structure follows a classic Fela tripartite pattern of instrumentals, song, and instrumentals. An extended instrumental introduction opens the mid-tempo track—more than six minutes of the track's nearly fourteen. The ensemble horns, guitars, keyboards, drums, and percussion begin at once to define the theme. A bass guitar solo leads the pack with short riffs that are answered by the underlining horns, while the drums keep their warm consistency below. Then the horns abruptly withdraw, and the sonic range and pitch plummet. For a provoking and provocative twenty-four seconds, all we hear are the stout guitar, sizzling maracas, lushly ricocheting congas, and ever-so-slight cymbals. If you are not already on the dance floor after these three minutes of the track, this is a call you cannot resist. The horns rejoin just as abruptly. A horn solo improvises on the earlier guitar pattern in a call and response with the rest. This arrangement is repeated several times in a consummate version with supple, lilting, underlying percussion. There is an overall intoxicating sumptuousness in the track's soundscape. A longer horn solo purposefully explores several directions for over a minute before being called back by the others into the main call-and-response pattern for a while. Then Fela's parade commandant's voice enters haughtily:

| If you call am "woman," African woman no go 'gree | If you call her "woman," an African woman will not agree |
| She go say, she go say "I be lady o" | She will say "I be Lady o" |
| Chorus: She go say "I be lady o!" | Chorus: She will say "I be Lady o" |
| She go say I no be "woman" | She will say "I am not a woman" |
| She go say market-woman na "woman" | She will say market woman is a "woman" |
| I wan tell you about "LADY" | I want to tell you about "lady" |
| She go say she equal to man | She says she is equal to man |

| | |
|---|---|
| She go say im get power like man | She says she is as powerful as man |
| She go say anything man do inself fit do am | She says she can do anything a man can do |
| | |
| I never tell you finish! | I am not finished telling you yet! |
| She go wan take cigar before anybody | She wants to be the first to pick cigar to smoke |
| | |
| She go wan make you open door for am | She wants you to open doors for her |
| | |
| She go wan make man wash plates for am for kitchen | She wants a man to wash plates for her in the kitchen |
| She wan salute man she go sit down for chair | She won't stand up to greet a man but remains seated |
| She wan sit down for table before anybody | She wants to sit at table before everybody |
| She wan take piece of meat before anybody | She wants to eat piece of meat before everybody |
| Call am for dance, she go dance "lady" dance | Ask her for a dance, she would dance "lady" dance |
| African woman go dance, she go dance "fire" dance | African woman will dance "fire" dance |
| She know im man na master | She recognizes her man as master |
| She go cook for am | She will cook for him |
| She go do anything he say | She will do anything he says |
| But "lady" no be so | But "lady" won't do all that |
| Lady na MASTER | Lady is MASTER |

I have seen revelers have a swell time disputing interminably what are or are not "lady" and "fire" dances and the "really correct" way to dance them. The music is captivating, surely. But that is only half the source of the track's power with the audience. "Lady" is not just fine music and a charming satirical song; it is a musical theatre complete with dialogue, different characters in conflict, a surfeit of scenes, and of course, music. Perhaps the most theatrical element is Fela's own voice. He shouts, yells, and hollers in both high and low tones. He addresses the audience directly, "I wan tell you about lady," both conspiratorially and in market-square pitch. "I never tell you finish!" he snaps, as if his audience interrupts him, in a popular gesture that signifies deep engagement in the matter under discussion but that is also self-subverting because it indicates that you now know that others are tired of whatever you have been saying. Fela takes the people's idioms and mannerisms, transforms them, and gives them back in a most sensuous form. These are a few of the small details that glue the Fela mystique together in the perception of his core audience. The song's narrated case against our prudish Nigerian Victorian "lady" is a stereotype of westernized middle-class values that remains a target of barbs by a whole spectrum: the lower classes, those who are not western educated, and conservative sections of the educated middle class. But we know how often it is that a "defense" of "traditional African culture" is a vulgar cover for the promotion of all sorts of inequity such as, in this case, sexual domination and gender discrimination.

Appropriated folk tunes constitute the third and final group of Fela's songs in this second phase of his career. There are not many of them: only two major songs were published, but they are significant in that they are direct borrowings by Fela from the nonurban folk culture. They are from the repertoire of classic Yoruba moonlight tales. "Alu Jon Jonki Jon" is a story of how in the animal kingdom during a severe famine, every animal killed its mother to eat as the collective had agreed, but the dog deceptively hides its own mother in heaven. "Gbagada Gbagada Gbogodo Gbogodo" is an elliptical sung tale of a mythical war, heroism, and retreat, but it is more a reflexive song about singing in which both the lead and chorus repeat exactly the same lines all through but with varying pitch and timbre as skill and imagination permits. Musically, both tracks are similar to "Je'Nwi Temi" and are also party favorites.

## The Libertine Moralist

Fela's afrobeat took its definitive form during this second phase; all he would be doing later would be minor tweaking here and improvising there. Here then in more portable form are the main features of the music. Unlike highlife jazz, which often makes you wonder whether the musician ever listened to himself, afrobeat sounded infinitely more organized. This was at the same time that the sonic field increased tremendously with a range of theatrical voicing in addition to the lyrics: delivered lines, simulated dialogues, whoops, yells, yodels, hisses, ahems, and more conventional scat singing in all sorts of tones and tone clusters. Somehow they all seemed to fit in convincingly. The relationship between the main instrumental groups, the horns and the drums, became more rationalized. Apparently freed of his jazz anxiety, Fela could now make both groups mutually regard one another. The horns became more patient, more willing to share and even yield the spotlight to the drums. As I noted earlier, Fela never used talking drums, a canonical Yoruba musical instrument group, but he transformed the horns to now and then perform at least one of its most exciting functions: they "talked" as they drew out known tunes in recognizable Yoruba cadence, accompanied vocally by the audience in an interactive manner. The drums and percussion, no longer feeling second-class in the ensemble, blossomed in inventing catchy creative variations on their main job of supplying steady rhythmic, propulsive intensity. They, after all, would have been the royals in a much less westernized orchestra in that cultural context. It was as if Fela's new dexterous and confident arrangement needed a larger exhibition hall to display. The music as a whole became more corporeal, calling for much physicality in dancing. The tracks became longer. He jettisoned the older commercial highlife jazz format of three or five minutes for extended plays of between seven and fifteen minutes, to the chagrin of commercial radio programmers everywhere. But they would get used to it, as they would to compositions of similar length by other Nigerian musicians. Perhaps one of the main contributions of the latter to global music production and marketing is that they actually literalized the meaning of LP; "long playing" should, after all, really mean that. A direct dictate of the local urban culture was that dance numbers go on for nearly an hour at a stretch.

Fela's newly acquired ideology made him give up the highlife jazz love songs, and the panegyric form, or singing in praise of rich people—the mainstay of the post-1970s Nigerian popular music scene—was never his forte. He searched and found in the hidden underbelly of the postcolonial city a wealth of creative inspiration in lives and experiences never thought worthy of a line of song except as objects of condescension and vilification. The songs were mostly in Yoruba or pidgin English, gradually more pidgin English than Yoruba toward the end of this middle period as Fela began to more consistently think of a much wider audience. That thinking is reflected in the change of the band name during this period from Nigeria 70 to Africa 70 (or sometimes Afrika 70). Both Yoruba and pidgin English are widely used in urban Lagos, pidgin more so in the larger contexts of Nigeria and West Africa. Thus, in the language understood by the majority, afrobeat introduced into the Nigerian musical landscape new and offbeat themes of an unabashedly class-partisan character. The style of presentation was original too, highly theatrical and full of sarcastic humor. These two features—new themes and new modes of presentation—contributed immensely to consolidating in the mind of the audience the impression of afrobeat as a distinct, new, indeed revolutionary, musical genre and experience.

The theatricality extends to the album jacket. More than that of any other musician, Fela's typical LP became a jumble of at least two discourses—the musical and the visual—in a complementary relationship. This particular feature would become more prominent in the next phase of his career. The album cover became not just decorative but another terrain, extrasonic, to send out the musician's message; a terrain which, because it is visual, is more easily and cheaply accessible than the musical, which requires expensive electronic equipment. Indeed, during new releases, many people would go to record stores neither to buy nor even to listen but just to look at another outrageous cover design. Much of that design was composed early on with dramatic and sensational photographs. *Shakara* features kneeling bare-breasted young girls arranged in the shape of the map of Africa with "70" behind it. *Na Poi* shows the naked torsos of a man and a woman in the act of an embrace, the woman resting her head sensuously on the man's broad shoulder. *Gentleman* shows a supposedly well-dressed—in a European suit—male figure but with a monkey head. The sensational cover design and art had the effect of underwriting mass accessibility.

Ideologically, Fela at this stage was not someone we could call, using his own standard, a "political" musician; that is, a musician who uses her or his music to intervene in and pronounce judgments on the partisan social and institutional-political arrangements of his or her society. As shown in the metro songs, he was quite aware of the broad divisions of the society into classes of haves and have-nots, and his sympathies were clearly with the latter. But he did not hold any individual or the government or the structure of the system responsible for their plight. He was not opposed to the Nigerian government and in fact once represented it abroad in Ghana. He immersed himself in the people's idioms and language and produced sensuous musical representations therefrom. Those representations often had the effect of boosting the people's dignity and self-confidence as they saw their circumstances monumentalized by this middle-class musician, but that is the closest Fela came—and then only implicitly—to imagining a different circumstance for them. Fela interpreted most of postcolonial Nigeria's problems in individualist, personalist terms in which the solutions, by implication, lay in individual uprightness. Hence the predominance of the socio-moral crusading in his repertoire in this phase: against boastfulness ("Shakara"), gluttony ("Jeun Ko Ku"), the ever-present traffic jams on Lagos streets ("Go Slow"), witlessness and stupidity ("He Miss Road"), foolishness ("Swegbe and Pako"), skin bleaching ("Yellow Fever"), the supposed aping of European ways ("Lady"), the craze for imported goods ("Buy Africa"), and more.

Fela was also conscious of the much larger determinants of Nigeria's, and Africa's, contemporary circumstances in the history of European enslavement of Africans and subsequent colonization of the continent. To be aware of all of these issues and to sing about them, however, is not necessarily to be "political" about them in the sense that even Fela himself would accept. Fela sang about Europeans coming to enslave peaceful Africans, but every potbellied comprador bourgeoisie in Gambia, Kenya, or Cameroon was saying exactly the same thing, after which they would drive off from the political rally in their custom-built bulletproof Mercedes-Benz cars, with European mercenaries in tow as bodyguards. Fela was at this stage what one could call a moralist at best. As a moralist, he took the foundational structures of the society for granted but pointed out the bad behaviors and social disorderliness all around him. He had no doubt that things could be made better under the same arrangements, if only—and this was all done by implication—people would behave better at points of social interaction and whoever is responsible would build more roads and erect better traffic signs. In other words, he interpreted the numerous problems of the society as having their source in a general moral turpitude; moral rearmament through satire was Fela's solution. But there was one gaping incongruity. Throughout this period, Fela was consolidating his reputation as a countercultural figure. That was evident enough in the music, but there was also the harem of girls—with fathers' charges of abduction flying around in the courts—and open marijuana smoking, which was expressly against the law. Fela cared for social orderliness and the gap between the rich and the poor, but he was also a libertarian, indeed, a libertine, who wanted to be left alone to do as he pleased. A libertine moral crusader no less, even if that is a grating contradiction.

Other musical forms such as *juju* and *fuji* flourished in the 1970s, but it was afrobeat—so refined (the obvious skill and professionalism in the sound arrangements) and yet so earthy (the lyric themes), so local (it is the undeniable soundtrack of post–civil war urban Nigeria) and yet so foreign (all those brassy horns and keyboards of European origin),[46] so Nigerian and yet so the world, like Lagos itself, which got its name from a port in southern Portugal—that unequivocally captured the spirit of the age in all its mind-numbing contradictions. It remained the quintessential music of that condition of botched decolonization and ambiguous modernity known as postcoloniality.[47]

# 4 Dissident Tunes: The Political Afrobeat

## "I play music as a weapon"

In 1982, Fela recalled for Carlos Moore his immediate goals on return from his famous American trip: "I came back home with the intent to change the whole system. I didn't know I was going to have . . . such horrors! I didn't know they were going to give me such opposition because of my new African-ism. How could I have known? As soon as I got back home, I started to preach. I had decided to change my music. And my music did start changing according to how I experienced the life and culture of my people."[1] Fela stretched the details somewhat; he did not return home in 1970 determined to "change the system," as the preceding chapter has shown. However, it is true that by the time he spoke to Moore in the early 1980s, he had experienced enough persecution by agents of the Nigerian state for us to excuse his conceptual subsumption of the specifics of the past into the momentous present. His first antistate composition was "Alagbon Close" in 1974, and he would not actually begin the consistently politically combative and outspoken phase of his career that I call "political afrobeat" until 1976 with the famous song "Upside Down," recorded with Sandra Isidore.

The circumstance of the composition of "Alagbon Close" is a classic example of the transformation of a social rebel, a mere nonconformist with an ego as gigantic as that of most pop stars and then some, to an astute and indefatigable militant political artist who would be a major thorn in the flesh of six Nigerian governments, military and civilian, over a span of more than twenty years. General Murtala Mohammed of Nigeria (July 1975–February 1976) and Captain Thomas Sankara of Burkina Faso (August 1983–October 1987) were killed in military coups precisely for the pragmatism and steadfast vision that Fela so admired in them. As a musician, Fela had by 1974 become a phenomenon both in the unique kind of music he had invented and in his shepherding of that genre to commercial success. He had no less than five hit songs a year from 1971 to 1973 and twelve each in 1975 and 1976. He was a musicians' musician, as musicians far and wide acknowledged his originality and associated with him.[2] He performed to filled stadiums all over the country and all along the West African coast. He was the indisputable voice of the urban masses, students, and youth generally, who saw him as a fresh alternative to the ethnically an-chored local panegyric forms and their thoughtless celebration of the corrupt nouveaux riches and the mindlessness of American-derived disco pop. The oil boom was on and class distinctions, determined largely and crudely by one's closeness or distance to the center of power that distributed the proceeds, were sharpening faster than ever.

As a pop culture figure, Fela was in a category all his own. Perhaps he might have been able to postpone or at least reshape the nature of his encounters with the repressive arm of the state had he been famous and controversial solely for his atypical music. But by the mid-1970s, Fela had become a countercultural icon the likes of which had never been seen before. He was brash and outspoken. His immediate public platform was his nightclub, which he called Africa Shrine, with himself as "Chief Priest." During the *yabis* (idiomatically, "abuse," but more appropriately, "roasting") sessions that were a routine part of his shows, he would launch running commentaries on local and global headlines as they affected Africans in general and Nigerians in particular and withering satires against public institutions or officials whose actions or policies he considered untoward. To reach a larger audience, he would buy space in newspapers to run "Chief Priest Say" columns, essentially extensions of Africa Shrine *yabis*. His residence was a sort of commune with no less than seventy persons at a time, composed of Africa 70 band members, bouncers, visitors, admirers, hangers-on, bodyguards, individuals doing all sorts of work in the household and with the organization, and a bevy of young girls who were dancers, chorus singers, cooks, girlfriends, or a configuration of two or more of these. Fela was the center of this beehive of activity. Both his house and the Africa Shrine, one across the street from the other, became notorious as havens for illegal drug use, especially marijuana smoking. Messengers, bodyguards, and sundry characters connected with Africa 70 had a reputation for thuggish and intimidating behavior and appearing in public stoned, arrogant, and disorderly. Routine brushes with the police, often over traffic violations, were not uncommon. It was not as if Fela condoned these behaviors, but they derived authority from his image as a charismatic antisocial rebel, and in turn such events consolidated that image in the eyes of the public. He was beloved by the teeming masses in his largely lower-class neighborhood, but many were also exasperated by the habitual outrageous behavior of the man and his retinue.

But by far the most explosive public issue was that of "the girls." Since "Let's Start" (let's start to do what we have come into the room to do) in 1971, Fela had insistently thematized sexuality in his songs, and very few were unaware of his public boasts about his own generous sexual appetite and his comments about the supposed therapeutic effects of regular "fucking." But musical representations of, and rhetorical claims about, sexuality, are not exactly the same thing as bringing it into the public's field of vision. Fela lived openly with women in his household. Everyone knew he was legally married and had taken vows of monogamy yet lived in a separate household from his wife. The women were always the most spectacular part of his entourage—smoking, heavily made up, and skimpily dressed. On his album covers, he would feature himself and the girls semi-nude and in provocative situations. The dancers among them were famous for the eroticism of their acts during performances at the Africa Shrine and in concerts. Fela's image, which was fastened erotically to the musician on stage in the briefest of bikinis pumping away at the saxophone, was that of a veritable playboy. Although most of the girls sought out Fela after they dropped out of school or ran away from home, angry parents repeatedly complained to the police about Fela "abducting" their daughters. It was clear to everyone that a major confrontation between the Africa 70 counterculture and the police was inevitable and only a matter of time.

On April 30, 1974, more than fifty heavily armed officers of the Nigerian police showed up at Fela's residence. They said they were there to investigate reports of "hemp peddling, drug addiction, and underage girls on the premises."[3] More than sixty of the occupants were arrested and sent to jail. Most of them were released the next day, while many of the girls were sent to a juvenile welfare home. The girls escaped back to Fela soon after. Fela spent eight days in jail in the dreaded Police Central Intelligence Division at Alagbon Close, Lagos. Barely a day after his release on bail, however, the police returned. They apparently were not sure that the evidence they had collected during the first visit would hold up in court, so they came seeking an ironclad guarantee this time. Fela had done his job well and they could not find marijuana anywhere. But no matter, they produced a wrap all the same, pretending they had found it during their search. They showed it to Fela triumphantly, who no doubt saw ten years of his life behind bars flashing before him: "I looked at it. I was thinking fast, man. Then suddenly, in split second—really fast!—I went for the paper, grabbed it and put it in my mouth and jumped on my bed, man. I'd swallowed it! I took the whisky bottle by my bed, put it to my mouth and washed the shit down."[4]

The police, after fruitless efforts to procure the evidence from wherever they thought it would be in Fela's anatomy, which included hiring the services of a doctor, locked him up with strict orders to defecate only in a special chamber pot. Aided by his mother, who passed fresh vegetables to him regularly, and fellow prisoners who schemed for him to use the communal toilet unseen, Fela's "shit . . . was clean like a baby's" by the third day when he finally agreed to provide the "evidence."[5] Commencing what would later become the musician's characteristic hallmark of transforming immediate personal experience into memorable art, Fela produced two hit recordings, "Alagbon Close" and "Expensive Shit," based on the encounter. Although the two were released months apart—the latter in 1975—they share similar instrumental patterns. There is a certain urgency to the sound, a brisk, near-frenetic pace with a short, angular rhythmic theme anchored by drums that chug on with an unnerving regularity. There is no humor here, and the anger is palpable. It was as if the self-indulgent veil of the bohemian hippie had been violently torn off and he was now seeing for the first time the harshness of reality; in the evocative baroque language of Lagosians, it was as if Fela had been given a "dirty slap" that forcefully awakened him to reality. Indeed, Fela himself implied as much in reflecting on the memorable first encounter with the law:

That . . . first time I was taken to jail . . . it's a funny feeling. . . . You know how people are brought up thinking that jail is just for criminals, man. For people who've "gone against society." . . . You know what I mean? That "law and order" shit. But after they put me in that cell with people they call "criminals," I started thinking: "Who the fuck is Society? Who jails society when it does horrors to people? Why Society does nothing to help beggars; to provide jobs and keep people from having to steal just to *chop* [eat]? Why don't Society fight against corruption, punish the powerful . . . ?" I concluded to myself: "Fuck society, man, it's unjust!"[5]

"Expensive Shit" is all abusive satire. Dignified people, including Fela, and even some animals such as goats and monkeys, would never tarry on the spot after defecating. But "no be so for some fools I know" (that is not true of some fools I know), some filthy "people who like to quench your soul." And the chorus in a croaky masculine voice that mocks the pretentious bigness of power, identifies such people: "Hen eeh, Alagbon o." To add the potent spice of taunt to the verbal abuse, the album cover features a photograph of Fela and his girls, all completely topless, beside his newly constructed barbed-wire fence, giving the defiant Black Power salute.

"Alagbon Close" is much more philosophical, as if to say, "your jail can only make me stronger, and you can't shut my mouth"—roughly what he had in fact said in the earlier, more playful tune "Je'Nwi Temi" ("Don't Gag Me") years before. The drums set up a feisty strutting rhythm over which aggressive horns, performing solos and as an ensemble, scornfully blare and whoop and the organ whirls and screeches for stretches on a single breath. At appointed intervals, the bass drum comes down heavily to accent the beat for haunting seconds, pumping more power into stomping feet or wriggling torsos. In the irresistible physicality in dancing the track calls for, it is simply unmistakable that this is a purposive, angry, and hearty celebration of "aliveness" in the face of—indeed to thump the nose of—the killjoys. As if the latter would miss the message in this instrumental arrangement, the first words we hear from Fela, the very first vocal of the song which takes place seven minutes into its sixteen minutes' duration, is an ominous warning call, "Now listen!" From the extensive analogies Fela draws, we get an accurate picture of how he perceived himself and his role in society. In our different capacities, we all contribute to the well-being of society, he theorized. If the night-soil man does not do his job, an unbearable stench will envelop Lagos. Civil servants, lawyers, doctors, magistrates, singers, painters, and dancers all have similarly indispensable jobs to do. Without singers, for instance, there can be no happiness. But some people in Alagbon have made it their job to arrest people, beat doctors, pummel lawyers, deceive magistrates, and jail painters, singers, and dancers. In a brief moment of lightness in this grim song, Fela ridicules: "Alagbon dey roll like one yeye ball wey one yeye wind dey blow from one yeye corner" (See Alagbon roll like a useless ball blown around by some aimless wind from some rubbishy corner), and then cackles infectiously to himself. Meaningless, of course, but not when you consider the potential effect of so affectively broadcasting the idea of the central police security agency, the one that is supposed to strike fear into criminals and keep the rest of us in line, as "*yeye*," stupid, a laughable fluffy soccer ball at the mercy of a purposeless wind. But he returns most stridently to the serious business at hand and goes for the jugular in his concluding lines:

| | |
|---|---|
| For Alagbon | In Alagbon |
| Dem no get respect for human being | They have no respect for human beings |
| Dem no know say you get blood like them | They don't know you are a person like them |
| Dem go send dem dog to bite you | They will send their dogs to bite you |
| Dem go put dem gun for your face | They will point guns at you |
| The gun wey dem take your money buy | The guns they bought with your money [taxes] |
| Dem go torture you and take your statement from you | They will torture you to make a statement |
| Dem go lock you for months | They will imprison you for months |
| Dem dey call am "investigation" | They call it "investigation" |
| If you know dem for Alagbon | If you know them in Alagbon |
| Make you tell dem make dem hear | Tell them loud and clear |
| Uniform na cloth, na tailor dey sew am | Their uniform is ordinary cloth, sewn by a tailor |
| Tailor dey sew am like your dress | Sewn by a tailor just like your dress |
| Tailor dey sew am like my dress | Sewn by a tailor just like my dress |
| Nothing special about uniform | There is nothing special about a uniform |

The Nigerian civil war and the massive recruitments on both sides to prosecute that effort implanted in the nation's consciousness a particular cachet for the "uniform," by which is meant the ubiquitous military uniform but also, more generally, the uniform of any coercive agency of the state. After the war in 1970, it was not just cities and towns that were saturated with men—mostly men—in uniform; even remote villages got their share of wounded, returning, or visiting sons, husbands, and fathers. The men in uniform felt and acted special, and society obliged by granting that recognition, perhaps because of the soldiers' demonstrated courage and sacrifice or civilian fear of the gun, or both. A liberated nation is also, after all, a cowed one. But there were no established limits. Apart from skipping bus or taxi fares in the city, for instance, it was not uncommon for someone in uniform to take intercity or interstate trips and refuse to pay at the end. Small violent clashes between civilians and soldiers would flare up now and then; in spite of the leadership's usual iteration of "military discipline," the military's institutional attitude toward the civilian populace was a condescending one. "Bloody civilians" was the rank-and-file's crude dismissive term for the population at large.[6] The uniform was supposed to be a perpetual badge of honor, even when that honor had been soiled several times over, and of privilege, even when that too had been abused beyond forgiveness. It is this backlog of civilian discontent with erstwhile "deliverers"-turned-tyrants that we hear in Fela's most scathing deconstruction of the military uniform as no more than ordinary cloth sewn by a common tailor.

*Alagbon Close.* Album-cover art.
Courtesy of Lemi Ghariokwu.

"Alagbon Close" was an instant hit. Fela became more popular than ever. He stood up to the "uniform" and publicly and contemptuously spat—or, to use the actual language understandably spiteful Lagosians would use, pissed—on it. He appeared invincible to the people, to the horror of the police. Even if specific instructions to deal decisively with Fela did not come from military despot General Yakubu Gowon, his ruthless inspector general of police, Sunday Adewusi, knew what would please his master. Convinced they were going to lose the court case against Fela due for judgment in a few days, the police returned again on November 23, 1974. This time, they showed in no ambiguous terms that they were fed up with Fela as well as with the slow, overly rational wheels of justice; so they came with their own brand of the latter: "[T]hey almost . . . killed me! . . . That was the first violent attack I experienced. . . . I was beaten by the police!

So much. . . . How can a human being stand so much beating with clubs and not die? I was cut, bleeding profusely. Couldn't even stand up, or walk. This time I was taken to hospital, not jail. I was there for three days. Later, I was taken to court."[7] He survived but, predictably, the experience only made him more belligerent, convinced of the righteousness of his position. He christened his commune Kalakuta Republic, a name he got from one of the many police cells he had made home. The prisoners told him that the name in Swahili means "Rascal's Republic," so Fela reasoned that "if rascality is going to get us what we want we will use that name, because we are dealing with corrupt people so we have to deal rascally with them."[8] Kalakuta was supposedly independent of the Nigerian republic, with Fela himself as president. Fela's hubris, if this needs saying, had no limit. He fortified the security of his republic and electrified the fence. Meanwhile, Fela again seized on this last brutal experience in the hands of the police to compose the popular "Kalakuta Show" in 1976, a sort of musical news report on the raid.

Fela's first major musical success had been his invention of the commercially successful afrobeat formula with "Jeun Ko Ku" in 1971. With "Alagbon Close," "Expensive Shit," and "Kalakuta Show," it appeared, once again, that Fela had reached another significant milestone and found a winning formula for a new kind of afrobeat music that is oppositional in a directly confrontational way. By the end of 1976, that had become his unvarying distinctive trademark; most of the twelve songs he released that year dealt in one way or the other with attacking authoritarianism and the many forms of its manifestation. His afrobeat remained stylistically unchanged, except that the compositions began to be quite expansive, the tempo more varied, and the mood highly modulated, capable of shifting effortlessly from seriousness to horseplay or buffoonery without losing its critical punch against particular identified targets. The rhythm became more adventurous even within the same composition, now sharp and angular, now smooth and graceful, now more complex and interactive. The lyrics became more confrontational and sensational. Fela composed a sort of formal public declaration of his new uncompromising stance against injustice and tyranny in the deeply poignant and unusually solemn track "No Agreement" in 1977:

No agreement today
No agreement tomorrow

I no go gree
make my brother hungry
make I no talk
I no go gree
make my brother homeless
make I no talk

I won't agree
to see my brother go hungry
and be silent
I won't agree
to see my brother homeless
and keep quiet

No agreement now, later, never, never,
    and never.

Fela could not bear to see the masses of the people homeless or hungry, he declared, and not complain on their behalf; as long as those dire situations remained, there would be no agreement between him and the governing authorities. This is the self-chosen mantle of the voice of the voiceless that Fela would wear—many times heroically but also oftentimes comically—for the next twenty years until his death in 1997.[9] This is the third and last phase of Fela's career that most people worldwide are familiar with. Ideologically, he began to conceptualize postcolonial African problems in less personalist and more structural terms, often historicizing particular institutions to locate their colonial origins as one way of understanding their woeful performances in the contemporary period. He emphasized class relations and the need for the oppressed to overthrow their oppressors.

Fela composed prolifically, especially when one considers that he was a musician working under incredibly harrowing conditions of constant state harassment, intimidation, imprisonment, and physical violence on his person. He transformed the adverse circumstances into a creative resource. He sang about a vast array of subjects, from the quotidian to the arcane, all of them about the peoples of Nigeria, Africa, and the African world and their relations among themselves as well as with the rest of the world. It is not impossible but it would be difficult to find any other musician anywhere, popular or not, with a corpus that is such a painstaking documentation and unrelenting critical commentary on humanity's large social processes of self-organization, in both their local and global forms. He was particularly adept at popularizing the most abstract topics of transnational processes and relations into bits that were digestible by the bulk of his proletariat and lumpen-proletariat audience. Even so, there are few popular musicians anywhere dead or alive whose works exhibit such a high cerebral content.

It is impossible to detail all the specific issues addressed by Fela in his songs, but we can begin to have a glimpse of the depth and breadth of his concerns during this final phase from a brief sampling of some of the better-known recordings. "Ikoyi Blindness" and "Mister Follow Follow," both released in 1976, lampoon the class snobbishness and lack of imagination of the Nigerian middle class. "Zombie," released in the same year, gave the youth of Africa a handy concept that dramatized the intellectual shallowness of the military dictatorships rampaging the continent. "Upside Down" (1976), "Original Sufferhead" (1982), and "Confusion Break Bones" (1990) chronicle the disorganized state of the infrastructure and delivery of social services in many African countries. The African inferiority complex and debilitating psychological thralldom to European values is addressed in "Yellow Fever" (1976), which ridicules skin bleaching; "Mr. Grammartologylisation Is the Boss" (1976) protests the hegemony of European languages, especially English; and "Colonial Mentality" (1977) and "Shuffering and Shmiling" (1978) deal with mental servitude and religious charlatanism and exploitation of the masses by Christianity and Islam. The poignant "Sorrow Tears and Blood" (1977) reveals to the world what the true "trademark" of African dictatorial regimes really is, the main ware they sell to their people. "V.I.P." (1979) is a patient explanation of what disqualifies African leaders from being regarded as "Very Important Persons" and why they really are "Vagabonds in Power." Economic imperialism and endemic local abuse of office to privately appropriate public wealth are the general themes of "I.T.T." ("International Thief Thief"; 1979), "Authority Stealing" (1980), and "Chop and Clean Mouth: New Name for Stealing" (1990s). Bureaucratic corruption and nepotism are assailed in "Power Show" (1982), "Custom Check Point" (1984), and "Underground System" (1992). The process of musical chairs in which rogues replace rogues as leaders is exposed in "Army Arrangement" (1985), "O.D.O.O." ("Overtake Don Overtake Overtake"; 1989), and "B.B.C.: Big Blind Country" (1990s). This sampling is for no more than heuristic purpose only; to be found in any one of these recordings are themes that encompass most of the categories I have outlined. To demonstrate the much more robust nature of the archive of political afrobeat, I have selected for extended attention two particularly suggestive songs from about a dozen that I would call Fela's "political classics"[10]: "Shuffering and Shmiling" and "Original Sufferhead." They are in the front ranks of his most potent weapons:

> What makes me sad today is to see people pushed around in life by other human beings. . . . And the work that has to be done in Africa for Africans to progress. . . . To think of how many Africans are so unaware, how they suffer in oblivion. That makes me sad. . . . Despite my sadness I create joyful rhythms. . . . I want to change sadness. I want people to be happy. And I can do it by playing happy music. And through happy music I tell you about the sadness of others. So they will come to realize that, "Oh, we *can* be happy!" With my music, I create a change. I see it. So really I am using my music as a weapon. I play music as a weapon. The music is not coming from me as a subconscious thing. It's conscious.[11]

## "Shuffering and Shmiling": The Profiteering Business(men) of God

> This state, this society, produce religion which is an *inverted world consciousness,* because they are an *inverted world.* . . . Religion is the sigh of the oppressed creature, the sentiment of a heartless world, and the soul of soulless conditions. It is the *opium* of the people. The abolition of religion as the *illusory* happiness of men, is a demand for their *real* happiness. The call to abandon their illusions about their condition is a *call to abandon a condition which requires illusions.* The criticism of religion is, therefore, *the embryonic criticism of this vale of tears* of which religion is the *halo.*
>
> Karl Marx[12]

Perhaps the wellspring of religious faith within families is not inexhaustible, contrary to what zealous catechists and evangelists would have us believe. It seemed that after grandfather and father had taken their fill and achieved both national and international fame in the use of that faith to do various noteworthy deeds, the well was dry by the time it was son and grandson Fela's turn. All through Fela's adolescence and the Koola Lobitos years, his attitude toward religion in general and Christianity in particular was one of casual indifference. That changed dramatically to antagonism after he returned from his eventful first American trip in 1970. There should be no surprise at this. We know what Fela's newfound hero, Malcolm X, had said about Christianity in *The Autobiography* and how mind-altering that book had been to Fela. In his own African-American context, Malcolm X had substituted Islam for Christianity, a supposedly nondiscriminating religion for one that supplied endless justifications for the enslavement of Africans and institutionalized racial discrimination. He had confused facade for reality and waxed eloquent about the supposed egalitarianism of Islam, simply because of the communal mode of worship he saw in which teeming, modestly dressed millions of Muslims of all races and backgrounds in Mecca prayed together without distinction. The hierarchical mode of social organization that subtends that facade in many Islamic countries, including Saudi Arabia itself, he could not see. And very uncharacteristically for Malcolm the stickler for history, he seemed in that book to be unaware of the equally violent history of Islam in Africa. Fela did not bother with this quarrel between Christianity and Islam that animated his diasporic idol. As an African for whom indigenous religions were a real presence even if his Christian upbringing had circumscribed his involvement in them, he could not but be aware of the alien character of *both* Islam and Christianity to Africa. His perspective was "a plague on both your houses!"

We can deduce three major reasons for Fela's venomous opposition to Christianity and Islam. The first is the simple reason that he considered them foreign to Africa. Since his conversion to blackness, "Africanism," as he called it, had become his main measure of value. By Africanism he meant a privileging of autochthonous African values, virtues, actions, and processes. His logic had a charming simplicity: there were no Arabs or Europeans running around proclaiming themselves to be Ogun or Obatala worshippers, so why would any African be proud to say he or she is a Muslim or Christian? The second reason is that the symbolic trappings of the two religions are, in the status-crazy Nigerian context, instruments for securing often-undeserved advantages. A "reverend" or an "alhaji" or "alhaja" (the latter two are honorific titles for a man or a woman who has performed the pilgrimage to Mecca) before one's name could open doors regardless of merit. Religion thus becomes merely another tool of economic competition and accumulation in a desacralizing dependent capitalism. And then, of course, there are the many public holidays to honor this or that Christian or Islamic occasion; there are none at all for any of the indigenous religions; this in a country with more nominal than actual Christians or Muslims and in which the majority of the population is animist. The third and final reason is what Fela read as the submissive theologies of the religions—the opium they dole out—in their promise of paradise in heaven as solace for hard times on earth, even as the priests jostle with soldiers, businessmen, and bureau-crats for the grand prize for acquisitive venality.

Fela and Nigeria 70 had barely settled back into Lagos in 1970 when the bandleader's new attitude toward Islam and Christianity began to appear in the music. The catalyst for "Who're You" was an incident with an alhaji, and rever-ends and bishops were mocked in "Na Fight O," both of which were released in 1970.[13] Scurrilous criticisms of the religions, mainly in the form of derision, became a staple of Fela's performances both in his club and during concerts. Some of those would appear now and then as classified advertisements in Ni-gerian newspapers. "The church is an ideological centre for the spreading of European and American cultural and political awareness," one of the advertise-ments asserted, while Fela's own club, the "Afrika" Shrine was "an ideological centre for the spreading of Afrikan cultural and political awareness." More-over, "[t]he Church is a place where they practice foreign religion," while "[t]he Shrine is a place where we practice Afrikan religion."[14] In another advertise-ment, he argued that since the pope's country is full of assorted criminals such as thieves, robbers, and rapists and thousands die yearly of alcoholism, the pope had nothing to teach Nigeria. Tapping into the scornful plebeian idiomatic cri-tique of hypocrisy, he concluded: "Make him repair him own country first!!"[15] In yet another published *yabis,* he reasoned: "If expenses of 80,000 pilgrims who go to Mecca is at least 600 naira each, then Nigeria spends 48 million in Saudi Arabia this year for religious pilgrimage. What do we get in return: sick pilgrims and brainwashed Africans. For me it's not worth it."[16]

All of these were scandalous in Nigeria but not particularly unheard of; es-pecially in the class dimension Fela often introduced to his critiques, they ap-proximated the unspoken thoughts of millions of his fans. But Fela said such things everywhere he went, including the United States, where a sizeable per-centage of African Americans have a slightly different relationship to Islam. Fela's biographer, Michael Veal, reported that many African Americans were of-fended at a performance in Brooklyn, New York, in 1990 when Fela took the stage for his noted song "M.A.S.S." ("Movement Against Second Slavery"). Fela cannot but be Fela, Veal said as he described what happened: "'I'm disappointed. Americans don't know what is happening, man—African Americans especially. The Muslim religion is not for Africans at all.' As the song faded, he contin-ued his tirade, imitating the call to prayer: 'Allaaaaahu Akbar!' What the fuck is that, man? I'm African, man, I don't understand that shit! Our ancestors can throw away Allah away with one little finger."[17] In another version of the song titled "Stranger: Allahaji, Allahaji," the derisive attack was more sensational: "Allaaaaahu Akbar na Shaitani! Allaaaaahu Akbar na motherfucker! Allaaaaahu Akbar na bullshit! . . . For Africa, Allaaaaahu Akbar na hunger." African gov-ernments have sold the continent to Europe and Arabia for an epoch of second slavery, Fela theorizes in the song. The proof is the undue influence in African affairs today of the "white man" of Europe and his Christianity and the "white man" of Arabia and his Islam. Employing the decidedly crude and tasteless metaphor of cannibalism, he declares that the religions and their bearers, with the wars they bring and the divisions they sow (his audience would not have missed this reference to the endless violent clashes between Christians and Muslims in Nigeria) would soon "chop us away" (eat us all up). The song's second section is devoted to evacuating the honorific "alhaji" of whatever last remnant of respectability might still be lurking in it after all the years of Fela's relentless assault on it. He has traveled the world over, he suggests, but only Nigerian Muslims bear the name "alhaji," which is a strange thing indeed. But it gets worse. "Alhaji" is an Arabic word, he has discovered, which means "stranger." This means that all those powerful people who are alhajis. . . . He briskly begins a long list of them—heads of state, Muslims leaders, businessmen, and bureaucrats—while the chorus shrilly translates his accented prefix "Alhaji" into an equally accented "Stranger." As Fela reels out the names, the crowd roars in recognition. Fela's clincher here—he calls it "a revelation of our ancestors"—is presented as simultaneously an answer to the mystery of Nigeria's underdevelopment and a rhetorical question: How can a country ever develop when it is ruled by strangers?

| | |
|---|---|
| This na revelation | This is a revelation |
| A revelation of our ancestors | |
| Offender dey point at himself | The offender shows himself [by his title] |
| Brothers and sisters hear me | |
| Mothers and fathers hear me | |
| Na strangers dey rule our country | Strangers are ruling our country |
| Na strangers dey dominate us | Strangers are dominating us |
| *Chorus*: For inside police | *Chorus*: Inside the police |
| For inside air force | Inside the air force |
| For inside navy | Inside the navy |
| For inside army | Inside the army |
| For inside government | Inside the government |

But Fela's most astute commentary on the two religions is to be found in his classic song "Shuffering and Shmiling." I say most astute in part because it is not directed at all toward crooked and hypocritical religious leaders but to the victims, who are responsible for alleviating whatever unbearable condition they are in. The song is an unapologetic satirical assault on the suffering masses who run to all kinds of religious charlatans and illusions for comfort rather than fight their oppressors. But the song is also a consummate love poem, perhaps Fela's most tender offering—if *any* of Fela's songs could be described as such, given the harsh, high tessitura of the voice that dominates his corpus—to the masses of African working people whose unrelievedly squalid conditions gave his career its ironclad legitimacy.

The bass guitar leads the drums and percussion in constructing the main rhythmic theme. The ambience is unusually mellow, which can deceive one into thinking that the mid-tempo beat is actually a notch slower, but this is only apparent. Even when the bellowing horns enter more than two minutes later, the reflective tone already in place is not much disturbed. The thin wailing guitar solos that the horns respond to now and then assure that. One could mistake these transactions for a classical wake: not too mournful and not too boisterous, but a measured, energetic sturdiness. A horn solo begins most tentatively, but deliberately so; it gets more vigorous as the rest of the horns back it up in a call-and-response fashion. It reaches the height of its performance when it suggestively riffs the opening four lines of the song proper, twice. It tries to get excited after this by going in bursts of short quick notes, as if in self-congratulation, but the weighty mood remains in the air until Fela's voice comes to the foreground, clearly enunciating his prefatory spoken lines:

> You Africans, please listen to me as Africans
> And you non-Africans, listen to me with open minds

How do Africans listen? Or how does one listen as an African? What is or why the need for Africans to listen in a particular way? And is that way different from the "open minds" non-Africans are supposed to listen with? Only this hint of a serious business at hand could justify the tight rein on the sonic arrangement so far, exuding so much oomph but also so much restraint. Fela's humorous nonsense syllables before and after the first four lines of the song proper begin to gradually lighten the mood. The percussion takes his example and become busier. The song needs the lift to counterbalance the weightiness of its subject:

*Fela, sings:*

| | |
|---|---|
| Suffer, suffer, suffer suffer for world | If you suffer in this world |
| na your fault be that | that is your own fault |
| Me I say: | I say: |
| na your fault be that | that is your fault |

*Fela, speaks:*

| | |
|---|---|
| I want you all to please take your minds out of this musical contraption | |
| And you put your minds into any god-damn church | |
| Any goddamn mosque | |
| Any goddamn Celestical, including Sera-phoom & Cheraboom! | Any goddamn Celestial, including Sera-phim & Cherubim! [Evangelical Christian churches] |
| We are all there now, our minds are in those places | |
| Here we go: | |

| | |
|---|---|
| *Fela*: Suffer suffer for world | Suffer in this world |
| *Chorus*: Amen! | *Chorus*: Amen! |
| Enjoy for heaven | And enjoy in heaven |
| Christians go dey yab | Christians will fool you: |
| "In spiritus hevinus" | "In spiritus hevinus" |
| Moslems go dey call | Moslems will dupe you: |
| "Alaahu Akbar" | "Alaahu Akbar" |

Open your eye everywhere
Archbishop na miliki
Pope na enjoyment
Imam na gbaladun

*Chorus, in call and response with
    repeated horn pattern*
Archbishop dey enjoy
Pope himself dey enjoy
Imam self dey enjoy
Oga na wetin you say?
My brother wetin you say?

*Fela:*
My sister wetin you go hear?
Archbishop dey for London
Pope dey for Rome
Imam dey for Mecca

*Fela:* My people dem go dey follow
    bishop

*Chorus:* Amen!
Dem go follow Pope
Dem go follow Imam
Dem go go for London
Dem go go for Rome
Dem go go for Mecca
Dem go carry all the money
Dem go juba bishop
    juba Pope
    juba Imam dem
Dem go start to yab demselves
"In spiritus hevinus"
*Fela: Extended scat imitation of Latin
    and Arabic*

*Fela, sings:*
Everyday for house
Everyday for road
Everyday for bus
Everyday for work

*Fela, speaks:*
My people, my people, my people
We now have to carry our minds
Out of those goddamn places
Back into this musical contraption
Right opposite you
Now we are back here

Wake up and see reality
Archbishop lives lavishly
Pope basks in opulence
Imam revels in abundance

Archbishop lives in luxury
And pope in maximum comfort
Imam too in great splendor
Master, what do you say to that?
My brother, what do you say?

*Fela:*
My sister what do you hear?
Archbishop lives in London
Pope lives in Rome
Imam lives in Mecca

*Fela:* My people follow bishop

*Chorus:* Amen!
They follow pope
They follow imam
They flock to London
They swarm to Rome
They troop to Mecca
They carry all their money
They worship bishop
worship pope
worship imam
They begin to delude themselves
"In spiritus hevinus"

*Fela, sings:*
Every day at home
Every day on the road
Every day on the bus
Every day at work

| | |
|---|---|
| This is what happens to we Africans<br>  every day [In an exaggerated conspira-<br>  torial whisper]: | |
| Now, wetin I wan tell you | Now, what I want to tell you |
| na secret o | is a secret |
| Na confidential matter | It's a confidential matter |
| Don't tell anybody outside | |
| Na between ME and YOU! | It's between ME and YOU! |
| Now, listen! | |
| As I dey say before | As I have been saying |
| e dey happen to all of us everyday | it happens to all of us every day |
| | |
| We Africans all over the world | |
| Now listen. | |

*Fela, sings:*

| | |
|---|---|
| *Fela*: Everyday my people dey inside bus | Every day my people ride the bus |
| *Chorus*: Suffering and Smiling! | *Chorus*: Suffering and Smiling! |
| 49 sitting 99 standing | |
| Dem pack themselves in like sardine | They pack themselves in like sardines |
| Dem dey faint, dem dey wake like cock | They faint and wake like chickens |
| Dem go reach house water no dey | They get home, no water |
| Dem go reach bed power no dey | They get to bed, totally burned out |
| Dem go reach road go-slow go come | Back on the road, traffic hold-ups |
| Dem do reach road police go slap | On the road, police slaps |
| Dem go reach road army go whip | On the road, army whips |
| Dem go look pocket money no dey | They look into their pockets, no money |
| Dem go reach work query ready | They get to work, only to meet summons<br>  [for being late] |
| | |
| Everyday na the sametin | Every day is the same! |

Fela is far more than a singer. In the manner of accomplished raconteurs, he speaks, declaims, shouts, sings, whispers, scats, and hmhmms and ahems—all those vocal resources that written language is woefully inadequate to represent but are nevertheless indispensable parts of the auditory and emotional experience. The climax, a most exciting moment for audiences, is Fela's spectacular one-minute scat singing supposedly in Latin and Arabic during which one can hear him heaving and breathing heavily to keep up with the rhythm. The clean mellifluous high-pitched tone of the all-female chorus provides a dramatic counterpoint to Fela's gruff voice. I noted earlier the restraint of the instruments; it is not difficult now to see why. There is an accomplished sarcastic wit throughout the lyrics, but nobody is laughing; the lyrics stop just short of the ability to call up any hilarity. Who or what is there to laugh at here—"my people" who flock to the pope in Rome or "my people" who in utter tiredness daily faint and wake like chickens? There is no laughter here, only a pitiful head-shaking gesture. The noted sonic restraint is the instrumental correlation to this lyrical transformation of the would-be humorous to the unmistakably poignant.

Structurally, the track is divided into nearly two equal parts: an extended instrumental introduction of nearly ten minutes and the remaining eleven-and-a-half minutes of song. But I think we can more usefully reconfigure the track as having three sections. First, the instrumental introduction, with what I describe as its uncharacteristic composure, up to the heraldic "Here we go," spoken by Fela. The second section begins from that point to narrate the story of "my people" who need to wake up and see reality but instead carry all their money and troop to Mecca and Rome and London. They are the Christians and Muslims who "*yab*" "in spiritus hevinus" and "Alaahu Akbar!" Fela rhetorically cordons off this middle section with his beginning advice to us to take our minds out of the music we are hearing "into" "those goddamn places" and, later, to take our minds "out of" "those goddamn places" back into the music. This middle part is like a tableau banished "out there," away from "here." But we know, of course, that extradiegesis is not necessarily out of representational control, since representation calls it into being in the first place. The third and final section is devoted to the narrative of the harrowing lives of "my people"— beaten and battered on the road to work and queried when they arrive late— who daily dip into their pockets but always come up empty. I suggest we see the first section as a processional to an agon, or a major structural conflict between the other two sections. The conflict is Fela's particular use of the hackneyed category "my people"; its meaning in the second part appears to dramatically contradict its meaning in the third. Sadly, Fela's track does not have another section that could have been a recessional which might have hidden a resolution, but it is just like Fela to be iconoclastic against everything, even a classic ritual form so closely mimicked by the structure of this song. A close attention to the agon will serve as my commentary on the ideological makeup and significance of the song.

So who exactly are "my people" in the song? At beginning Fela urges Africans to listen to him "as Africans"; even if decoding how to "listen as Africans" is a fruitless exercise, it is impossible to make sense of the song without determining who his "people" are. This is because the group we would be right to consider as his default "people"—the working masses—certainly are not the ones "carrying all the money" to the pope in Rome and the imam in Mecca. Their poverty, after all, precludes such generosity, though they are surely part of those who worship, or *juba,* the earthly representatives of godhead. We can only conclude then that Fela's "people" are the rich African alhajis, imams, reverends, pastors, and myriad others in the cluttered hierarchy of God's gatekeepers who do the overseer work in Africa for the pope in Rome, the bishop in London, and the imam in Mecca, the three foreign head gatekeepers. This interpretation is quite odd—Could Fela really consider those people his "people"? —though logically, the appeal to listen as Africans should include without prejudice Africans of all classes. However, when Fela a short while later again invoke "my people" and movingly details how they are brutalized every day on the roads and end up with empty pockets, he certainly cannot be referring to the rich Africans who carry all the money to Rome-London-Mecca. Indeed, the garish cartoon on the album cover shows two groups of Africans: the rich and ro-bust reverends and imams grinning broadly over bags of money and the poor and emaciated ordinary people, either looking on in dazed vacuity or hanging dangerously on the side of an overcrowded bus or being whipped on the road by a soldier. Those who are suffering are *not* smiling, very contrary to the song's title.

It is not just that Fela is apparently deploying two registers of "my people"; he is engaged in the more complicated maneuver of deploying both simultane-ously as mutually inclusive and exclusive. The goal appears to be to speak in the names of race and class at the same time under the general thematic of foreign cultural, specifically religious, domination. The "my people" who swarm to Rome and Mecca with all the money is racially coded, while class is the operative factor in the other "my people" who pack themselves like sardines on commuter buses. The former allows Fela to critique European and Arab religious imperi-alism as aided by African underlings, while the latter focuses on the burden-some weight of such privileged underlings on their own common people. Thus both groups of "my people" are victims, though unequally so. The religious underlings actually benefit from their own subjection, while there is no relief in sight for those who get slapped in the face by the police every day. This is why Fela represents his people the religious cronies as having quite a lot of agency in their subjection: it is they, without obvious compulsion, who "follow" pope-bishop-imam, "carry" all the money, and "go" to Rome-London-Mecca—to great lengths indeed—to "*juba*" them, the holy trinity. But this agency-in-subjection only serves to condemn them in the song. On the other hand, Fela represents his people the working masses as harassed and traumatized, with little control over their lives. True, Fela does not say "they are packed in like sardines"—he says "they packed *themselves* in like sardines"—but it is unlikely that anyone can suggest that this is a sign of agency. It is not difficult to suggest that these are Fela's real "people." They are the "people" foregrounded in the spatio-temporal frame of the song, while the other "people" are rhetorically banished to "those goddamn places." The poor are more sympathetically drawn, but they are also uncompromisingly derided. With derisive imagery so graphic and culturally resonant as "dem dey faint, dem dey wake like cock," Fela's love is a tough, merciless one indeed. But to make his choice so clear, Fela needs to claim the other "people" too as his "people." There is no other Fela song where there is such a complicated interplay of his much-used and -abused category, "people."

But "Shuffering and Shmiling" rests on ideologically wobbly legs. It tanta-lizingly raises a sharp critique of the use of religion to exploit the masses of the African working people, but Fela is not against religious consciousness as such. I have borrowed the epigraph to this section from Karl Marx to indi-cate the far-reaching critique of religion that the song aims for but fails to reach. Fela simply wanted to replace alien religions in Africa with indigenous Afri-can religions. But whatever happens to the exploitive illusion sold by *all* reli-gions?

## "Original Sufferhead": The Scarce Bounty; or, Thrilling Notes on a False Enigma

> The people stagnate in unbearable poverty; slowly they awaken to the unutterable treason of their leaders.
>
> Frantz Fanon[18]

African artists cannot and do not choose their subject matter; they are, on the contrary, chosen by their subjects. This is indeed as circumscriptive as it sounds: while it structurally frees the artists from the heavy burden of a head-scratching search for *what* on earth to create their art about, it imposes on them the much heavier burden of *how* on earth to fashion from that surfeit of "what" an imaginative sublimation worthy of the label "art." This has been the contemporary African artist's greatest challenge, more so than artists in other climes.[19] To borrow from Fanon in the preceding epigraph, when an artist's main obsessions—such as, for Fela, the immiseration of the people and the irresponsibility of the leadership that rules—have become unbearably quotidian, they are transformed into the "unutterable." But "unutterable" is just polemical hyperbole; what it really means is that the overbearing nature of the "treason" requires more inventive tools and orders of articulation than the ordinary. By 1982, when Fela released "Original Sufferhead," he apparently felt he had covered enough ground to warrant a sort of catalog, a summative recasting of the core issues that had preoccupied him since 1974 but consistently since 1976. But part of the morbid symptoms of the postcolonial African condition—the postcolonial incredible—is the unyielding remorselessness of atavistic time. That time would later compel Fela to repeat himself—and he apparently got used to this dreary nature of postcolonial African time—and released not one but three more such summative "catalogs" before his death: "O.D.O.O." ("Overtake Don Overtake Overtake") in 1989, "Confusion Break Bones" in 1990, and "Chop and Clean Mouth: New Name for Stealing" later in the 1990s. Like the truly great artist that he was, he did it each time with all the novelty he could muster, marshaling it valiantly against the equally determined corrosive numbness of time. "Original Sufferhead," the first, is also the touchstone of the set.

The song is a list of what Fela obviously considers the most basic existential needs of the common people, a dramatization of the gaping inadequacy of those things, a clear identification and censure of the leadership class as culpable, and an explicit call to the people to take up arms against their oppressors. But after "No Buredi" (1976), "Upside Down" (1976), "V.I.P." (1979), "I.T.T." (1979), and "Authority Stealing" (1980), to cite just a few, what is new for Fela to say? Or, more appropriately, *how* is he going to make new, thoughtful, and pleasurable what we already know he is going to say? Fela's overarching strategy follows Fanon's polemical hyperbole of the "unutterable" and orchestrates his subject as an enigma, a conundrum. We know, of course, that every claim of a mystery is a call for attention; nothing arouses our curiosity faster.

Fela's mountaintop bellow, not to mention the choking string of repetitive questions in which the politely interrogative is answered with the reproachfully rhetorical, engages with the chorus in a dizzying whiplash manner:

*Fela*: Waaater—Lighttti—Foooodu—
   Houseee!!!
Yeparipa o!

| | |
|---|---|
| *Chorus*: Wetin do dem? | What about them? |
| *Fela*: Wetin do dem ehen? | What about them, ehen? |
| *Chorus*: Wetin do them? | What about them? |
| *Fela*: You mean you no no? | You mean you don't know? |
| *Chorus*: Wetin do dem? | What about them? |
| *Fela*: A go tell you | I will tell you |
| *Chorus*: Wetin do dem? | What about them? |
| *Fela*: When I tell you | When I tell you |
| *Chorus*: Wetin do dem? | What about them? |
| *Fela*: You go hear am! | You will know it! |

Fela is simply an accomplished sensationalist and rabble-rouser, and frequently one does not even need the lyrics to reach that conclusion. Like the Shrine itself, the sonic arrangement exudes a carefree festival ambience, but here it is mere playacting, for it is a rehearsed carefreeness. The extended instrumental introduction that is usually cleanly instrumental is in this track sprinkled and busied with all kinds of extrainstrumental sounds: casual small talk to the listener ("You see, at the Shrine, Afrika Shrine in Lagos, you have to go with the music"), conductor's one-liners and phrases ("Now ready," "it's coming now," "one more time," "ready to go"), casual nonspeech vocalizations to accent or counterpoint the beat, and whoops and yells by seemingly everyone in the band. Even the chorus comes in to riff on the vocal cliché "la." All of these businesses are going on while the drums dig deeper into the main rhythm groove and other percussion sounds frill the interstices and edges. Horn solos prance, bleat, and face off with the others and then collectively string out repeated patterns. And finally, ten minutes into the 21-minute track, when Fela formally begins with "Let's sing a nice song together," a horn solo picks up the line and creates a tune with it through varied repetition. It turns out that that is in fact what the horns have been "saying" with their primary pattern since their first entrance. In a low, casual, friendly voice, Fela invites us to what he describes as his "nice song." I am not quite sure that "nice" is the best way to describe the high-decibel "Water—Light—Food—House!!!" that follows.

Fela shouts out the names of certain essential human needs and expects that that alone should fully convey to his listeners, without any doubt remaining, what he means. Or perhaps it is his unusual clamorous mode of uttering those needs that he expects should signify so transparently and accurately to listeners. But it does not, and so he not only crafts disapproving rhetorical questions that make you regret voicing your lack of awareness but also concludes in a derisive accusatory tone that you must be alien to Nigeria and Africa not to know what he means:

| | |
|---|---|
| That means to say you no dey for Nigeria be that | That means you don't live in Nigeria |
| You see yourself you no dey for Africa at all | You see, you don't live in Africa at all |
| You must dey come from London | You must be coming from London |
| From New York, from Brazil | |
| From Germany, from Frankfurt | |
| From Rome, from Italy, from Spanish, from Portugal | |
| From Arabia, from Moscow, and Chicago! | |
| That means to say you no dey for Nigeria be that ahaha | You see, you just don't live in Nigeria |
| If you dey for Africa where we dey | If you live in Africa where we live |
| You go no! | You will know! |
| *Chorus*: A go no wetin? | I will know what? |
| *Fela*: Plenty! | Plenty! |
| *Chorus*: A go no wetin? | I will know what? |
| *Fela*: About waaater—lighttti—foooodu—houseee!!! | |

The "ignorant" listener, African or otherwise, has obviously not been listening as an African or with an open mind, as "Shuffering and Shmiling" recommends. The ignorant listener must be from those places outside Africa where no one, especially a musician, would need to shout "water, light, food, house" on record. Without the requisite experience, the listener is intimidated into acknowledging simultaneously his or her ignorance *and* the authority of the intimidating voice. It is a winning pedagogical contrivance, and the pedagogue can now begin his lessons. It works well structurally, too: a first part prefacing the next four that address the song's stated four necessities, while a final part suggests a particular people's response to the dramatized inadequacies. As Fela proceeds methodically, the horns accentuate his gems of wisdom with bold vibrating strokes:

| | |
|---|---|
| Na so so water for Africa | Africa is full of water resources |
| Plenty plenty water for Africa | |
| Water underground, | |
| water overground, | |
| water in the air | |
| Na so so water for Africa | Africa is full of water resources |
| Ordinary water for man to drink for town nko o? | So where is ordinary water for the people to drink? |
| *Chorus*: E no dey! | There is none! |
| *Fela*: E no dey, e dey? | There is none, or there is? |
| Where you go see am? | Where will you see it? |
| Water for town? | Water in town? |
| Government self e dey? | Where is the government itself? |
| Look left and right? | |
| A no see dem there | I can't find it anywhere |
| Dem dey tell us now | They're telling us now |

| | |
|---|---|
| Na 1990 | That not until 1990 |
| Dem go give us water | Will they give us water |
| From United Nations | |
| "Special Program" | |
| for "Third World Countries" | |
| I wan die o! | I am dying of thirst! |
| Give me water drink! | Give me water to drink! |
| Where the government now? | Where is the government now? |
| Dem no dey, e dey? | They're nowhere, aren't they? |

The enigma is finally revealed—one strand of it, at least. And indeed, maybe the conundrum is so agonizing as to call for no less than the scream to "utter" it. For how can Africa be "full of water resources" and yet water for people to drink "there is none"? The chorus doggedly attempts to lace the enigma with outrage with its tendentiously prim, repetitive "E no dey!" after each of Fela's vigorous short lines.

The government, the entity supposed to mobilize the people for the provision of social amenities, is ineffectual to the point of nonexistence. To further confirm its "unutterable treason," if any such extra confirmation is needed, it degrades the people by hiding under the charitable "Special Program" of the United Nations for "Third World Countries" to proclaim that Nigerians will have water in 1990. I explained earlier how Fela and postcolonial African atavistic time were at loggerheads throughout the third phase of his career. "Original Sufferhead" provides painfully graphic examples of Fela's—and his people's—loss in that struggle. The song was released in 1982. Fela, always in the polemical mode, had obviously marshaled the greatest exaggeration he could about how long it would take the government to provide all Nigerians with safe, pipe-borne water: eight years. Fela's hyperbole sounded so utterly ludicrous to everyone then: eight years before all Nigerians would get drinking water? Impossible! That is an eternity; it just can't be that long. At several listening occasions in the year of its release and a few years after that, I saw fans thrilled to tears at a derision that masterfully hits the bull's eye whenever the song gets to Fela's graphic lines, "I wan die o! / Give me water drink," conjuring the image of a person crumpled on the floor dying of thirst right this moment in 1982 and being told to hold on until 1990 to get water to drink! They recognized the delicious hyperbole, guffawed with musical pleasure, and said with pompous, dismissive finality that, oh no, that's just an exaggeration. Twenty-two years later, most Nigerians still do not have drink-safe, pipe-borne water. Fanon is right after all about the unutterability of the treason.[20]

In between the parts are interludes of no more than fifteen seconds each. Even though they are very short and do not have lyrics, they are among the most memorable stretches of the track. They are filled with whoops, wails, screams, shrieks, and squeals by Fela and others, and the horns, in their unchanging pattern during the interlude, actually give legitimacy to these sounds. Just as in his politics, Fela's approach to musical sound is a very deconstructive, iconoclastic one. Because he takes music to be no more than organized sound,[21] he pushes the limits of what kind of sound can or cannot be made musical. The kind of affect this communicates to listeners is a very irreverent one: irreverent toward any conception of music that would mystify its fundamental reliance on every-one's favorite straw target called noise. The sounds Fela packs into the interludes are those associated with motor-park touts, hooligans, street gangs, and the un-couth generally; they exist within the narrow spectrum from the vulgar to the threatening. They are an assault on "decent" society. But then, what decent so-ciety would have so many energy resources and no electricity for its people?

| | |
|---|---|
| Na so so sunlight for Africa | Africa has abundant energy resources |
| Plenty plenty energy for Africa | |
| Energy for sun, energy for moon, energy for oil! | |
| Na so so energy for Africa | Africa has bountiful energy resources |
| Na the big big people dem go dey get electric | But only the rich people have electricity |
| If dem no get electric, dem go get plant | If they don't have electricity, they have power generators |
| Light for ordinary man for town now nko o? | What of electricity for the common people? |
| Chorus: E no dey! | There is none! |
| E no dey e dey? | There is none, or is there? |
| Where you go see am? | Where will you see it? |
| E dey go dey come | It goes off and comes on |
| E dey come dey go | It comes on and goes off |
| E go bright gaan | It brightens in a flash |
| E go bright small | And dims just as swiftly |
| If e no go | If it doesn't go off |
| e go come | then it comes on |
| If e no come | If it doesn't come on |
| e go go | then it goes off |
| E no dey e dey? | There is none, or is there? |
| E dey go dey come | It goes and comes |
| E dey come dey go | It comes and goes |

Although many of the political classics would serve the same purpose well, "Original Sufferhead" is particularly demonstrative of Fela's uniquely com-plex, sophisticated deployment of that central structural component of all mu-sic, repetition.[22]

Instrumentally, the short, repetitive ostinato pattern is important to Fela's, and indeed to most African, music. But a distinctively longer and more supple repetitive pattern also distinguishes afrobeat. The short repetitive patterns, while serving particular musical functions in themselves, are also articulated as part of a larger edifice that itself becomes part of a recursive structure. While the shorter repetitions are obviously associated with the rhythmic foundations of the music, the lengthier ones seem to serve more of a virtuosic or intellectual function, demonstrating calculated artistry and logic.[23] The effect is a particu-larly close interweaving of the affective and the cognitive. In "Original Sufferhead," this kind of relationship is reflected in the organization of the lyrics, too. Short repetitions are concentrated within each of the four middle sections on water, electricity, food, and housing in a very theatrical way, especially in the chorus subsections. Additionally, some of the "sentences" that are themselves repeated internally encompass short rapid repetitions: "Na so so water for Africa," or "Na the big big people dem go dey get electric." The structure of the whole section, complete with the "statement" sentences that lay out the case and the rapid dialogic intercourse with the chorus, is then repeated in more or less the same way in the next section. This wholesale repetition reflects and comments by implication upon the preceding sections. Especially when the "contents" of each succeeding section stand in a relationship of affirmation of or amplification of what is articulated in the preceding ones, the interweaving of both kinds of repetitions can create a powerful channeling effect of both affective and cognitive intensities. This is how Fela creates the "happy music" of his goal without compromising the decidedly unhappy expressive content he also steadfastly holds on to.[24]

Note the rhetorical redundancies that Fela employs in this section to great derisive effect: "E dey go dey come / E dey come dey go"; "if e no come / e go go / if e no go / e go come." There is virtually no one in Nigeria who has lived in a household with electricity service that would miss this most imaginative, incredibly apposite rib-cracking ridicule. Even the rich people with standby power generators are not spared this experience, since they too have to switch their generators on and off in response to the erratic service by the power company. The company is called National Electric Power Authority, but Nigerians long ago renamed it Never Expect Power Always. The story of its inefficiency, in spite of the millions of naira regularly poured into it, is "unutterable." The investment in food production is even greater, but with only mixed results: if it is available, is it affordable for many?

| | |
|---|---|
| We all know say plenty food for Africa | We all know that Africa has ample food resources |
| Plenty fertile land | There is so much fertile land in Africa |
| Na so so land dey for Africa | There is just so much land in Africa |
| Na the big big people dem go dey plant cocoa | The big people plant only cocoa [a cash crop for export] |
| If dem no plant cocoa dem go plant groundnut | If not cocoa, then they plant peanut [another cash crop] |
| Na the big big people dem go dey plant rubber | The big people plant rubber [another cash crop] |
| Operation Feed the Nation e plenty well | Operation Feed the Nation began with fanfare |
| Fertilizers in dey go and come | Imported fertilizers flood everywhere |
| Billion billion naira e dey follow am | Billions of naira down the drain |
| Now we dey go buy rice from America | Now we import rice from America |
| We dey make other rice from Brasilia | We import rice from Brazil |
| Dem dey send us rice from Thailand | We import rice from Thailand |

| | |
|---|---|
| Green Revolution in self don start well | The Green Revolution program started well |
| Ordinary food for man to chop for town nko o? | And after all that, where is food for the people? |
| Chorus: E no dey | Chorus: There is none! |
| E no dey e dey? | There is none, or is there? |
| Where you go see am? | Where will you see it? |
| Dodo nko? | What of dodo? |
| 10 kobo for one | It's 10 kobo for one |
| Akara nko? | And akara? |
| 20 kobo for one | It's 20 kobo for one |
| Orange nko? | What of orange? |
| 30 kobo for one | 30 kobo for one |
| Bread nko? | And bread? |
| 40 kobo for one | 40 kobo for one |
| Na konkolo e be! | It is very small! |
| Bread nko? | What of bread? |
| 50 kobo for one | 50 kobo for one |
| Na janjala e be! | It is extremely thin! |
| Where you go see am? | Where will you see even that? |
| E no dey e dey?[25] | There is none, or is there? |

Until a few years before his death, when he fell silent due to ill health, Fela was virtually a one-man countergovernment in the popular realm, rhetorically redressing with vitriolic scorn various government policies launched with fanfare and utmost seriousness and passing them on to the people—through the great power of his music—completely tattered and dripping with ridicule. It is merely an accident of fate that he did not die in one of the many state-sponsored violent repressions he was subjected to in retaliation.

Operation Feed the Nation (OFN) was launched by General Olusegun Obasanjo's regime (1976–1979[26]) in May 1976. It was designed to mobilize the nation for self-sufficiency in food production. Everyone was advised to create a garden in the backyard, while radio and television advertisements attempted to rehabilitate the lowly image of the farmer and the profession of farming in the consciousness of Nigerians who had already been corrupted by the oil boom. University students were engaged during summer vacations to work on farms for a stipend. Perhaps this is the "laudable" inward-looking part of the program. Chief Commander Ebenezer Obey, the distinguished popular *juju* musician, composed a hit record, "Operation Feed the Nation," in support of the government's efforts. But it was Fela who got things right. Contractors—who were, of course, connected to centers of power—made millions of naira importing fertilizers, farm equipment, and food.[27] Some Nigerians with overactive imaginations later insisted that the real meaning of OFN all along was "Operation Fool the Nation." The civilian government of Alhaji Shehu Shagari (1979–1983) changed the name of the program to Green Revolution—a name fashioned in the hallowed halls of Harvard University, street-corner humorists insisted—but the results were even poorer, as Shagari's cabal of most inept and venal elected leaders emptied the treasury into their pockets. The government was so embarrassed at its own moral degeneracy, corruption, and mismanagement of the economy that it launched an "Ethical Revolution" for itself. The reality was so much stranger than fiction that even the country's foremost and globally recognized fictionalists, Nobel Prize laureate Wole Soyinka, and Chinua Achebe, had to resort to a satirical musical recording, *Unlimited Liability Company,* and nonfiction prose, *The Trouble with Nigeria,* respectively, to publicly intervene. As to Fela's "grocery list" lament of 1982's supposedly astronomical prices, the less said about it in relation to today the better; that is because the situation is really "unutterable." If bread then was 50K or half a naira and considered expensive in 1982, what is one to say or think when the same bread twenty years later costs 100 naira in the context of not a rise but a real drop in earnings? Although Fela says below that housing matters are "different," it is clear the difference is in kind, not in substance:

| | |
|---|---|
| House matter na different matter | Housing is a different case |
| Those wey dey for London dey live like lords | Those in London live like lords |
| Those wey dey for New York dem dey live like kings | Those in New York live like kings |
| We wey dey for Africa we dey live like servants | We in Africa live like servants |
| United Nations get name for us | The UN has a name for us |
| Dem go call us "Underdeveloped Nations" | They call us "Underdeveloped Nations" |
| We must be "underdeveloped" to dey stay 10-10 in one room | We must be "underdeveloped" to be living ten in a room |
| First and second day dem go call us "Third World" | Another time they will call us "Third World" |
| We must be "third world" to dey sleep inside dustbin | We must be "Third World" to be sleeping in dustbins |
| Dem go call us "Non-Aligned Nations" | They will call us "Non-Aligned Nations" |
| We must dey craze for head to dey sleep under bridge | We must be crazy to be sleeping under bridges [unseemly places] |
| Ordinary things for man to enjoy for town nko o? | What of the means of good life for the people? |
| *Chorus*: E no dey! | There are none! |

Fela has this charming pedestrianism that unfailingly cloaks gleaming deconstructive spikes. With it, he verbally caresses all the pet and well-embroidered foreign-policy commitments of successive Nigerian governments and completely perforates them, making them look ridiculous to the people. If the world is really as "united" as the name "United Nations" is meant to indicate, why is there such an unspeakable disparity in the standards of living across different regions and countries? Why are New Yorkers living "like kings" and Lagosians living "like servants"? It is an enigma. He pushes the logic farther in the 1989 release, "Beasts of No Nation," ridiculing the "unity" of the "United Nations," where "one veto is equal to 92." The cover art by Lemi Ghariokwu features Nigerian and African dictators and Margaret Thatcher, Ronald Reagan, and apartheid leader P. Botha, all with devil horns on their heads and bloodied fangs for teeth; radical African youth protesting with defiant fists in the air refuse to be cowed by the police shooting at them. As to the Non-Aligned Movement[28] that embodied one of the nation's, and Africa's, ideological cornerstones, Fela would say curtly in an interview that "Africa could not be non-aligned because Africa was the *center* of the world. Not its south. Nor its north. Nor its east. Nor its west."[29]

As Fela concludes the song, he ratchets up the dialectic between him and the chorus, obviously borrowing the structure of a popular Yoruba folk game, *kin ni nleje?*, which tests verbal dexterity and mental alertness by requiring an interlocutor to respond appropriately to a series of rapidly uttered alternating or contradictory cues:

| | |
|---|---|
| *Fela:* Trouble? | Trouble? |
| *Chorus:* Iyen dey! | Plenty of that! |
| *Fela:* Food? | Food? |
| *Chorus:* E no dey! | There is none! |
| *Fela:* Problem? | Problem? |
| *Chorus:* Iyen dey! | A lot! |
| *Fela:* Light? | Light? |
| *Chorus:* E no dey! | Not available! |
| *Fela:* Water? | Water? |
| *Chorus:* E no dey! | Scarce! |
| *Fela:* Wahala? | Suffering? |
| *Chorus:* Iyen dey! | Plentiful! |
| *etc. etc. etc.* | |
| *Fela:* Don't turn us to sufferhead | Don't turn us to slaves |
| *Chorus:* Original sufferhead! | |
| It's time for jeffahead | It's time for our liberation |
| Me I say sufferhead must go | I say our suffering must end |
| Jeffahead must come! | Enjoyment must come! |
| I want to tell you my brothers one bitter truth | |
| I want to knock some truth right into your heads | |
| Before we all have to jeffahead | Before we can enjoy |
| We must be ready to fight for am | We must be ready to fight for it |
| Why e no go go sef? It must go! | Why won't oppression end? It must! |
| Why not? Jeffahead must come! | Why not? Freedom must come! |

Fela maintains to the end that "water, light, food, house" in the African context can only be talked about in the enigmatic mode; this allows him to declare with justification that the only way the oppressed can explode the enigma and turn "sufferhead" into "jeffahead" is through struggle against their oppressors. One would suppose too that it is this "fight" that will loosen the tongues of the people and make the treason of their leaders "utterable," nameable, and therefore defeatable.

Fela obviously designs "Original Sufferhead" as a bravura epic of the dispossessed. The presentation is meticulous and the conclusion logical. Musically, the track is a party classic—the touchstone of success, let us agree, for any contemporary commercial popular music. I say this to underscore the fact that the song answers again the pedantic question that Fela had long made redundant: whether "politics" is compatible with "art." The song's elaborate conceit of the enigmatic works well structurally but, as I hinted in the subtitle to this subsection, it is precisely that, a conceit, a false enigma. And Fela knew it. Two years earlier, he had himself supplied the answer to the question of why there are such bountiful resources in Africa and yet its people live in such abundant scarcity in a famous song whose title says it all—"Authority Stealing." But the physical and mental thrill that "Original Sufferhead" provides is not false at all.

## Ideologies of Politics

It is clear from the preceding sections that Fela was a musician of strong convictions. Even if he had not done such extraordinary things as invent a musical genre and then wholly dedicate it and his professional life to active intervention in the political life of his country, it would still be crucial to explore those convictions—the catalytic ideological matrix of his musical practice. We can identify three broad streams of thought in this matrix. First, there is the radical black nationalism that Fela absorbed during his 1969–1970 American trip. This opened out to a much more expansive pan-Africanism and Afrocentrism as Fela adjusted to the specificities of his immediate sociopolitical context. These variants of strongly racially inflected ideologies of the African world are related but not conflatable. Second, there is the sturdy partisanship for the oppressed lower classes that could be described as socialist in orientation. And third, there is the irrepressible libertarianism that frequently tries to be the anchor and articulator of the other two.

I have examined in detail Fela's indebtedness to African-American nationalism of the 1960s. Fela quickly discovered on his return that radical African-American nationalism, deeply marked as it is by racialism, could not be simply transposed to Nigerian soil. This was 1970, a whole decade after independence from colonial rule in Nigeria and many African countries. Race was a far distant specter, both at the macrolevel of social and political organization and at the microlevel of individual personal experience. At the same time, however, Fela would be ideologically vapid if he were to give up black nationalism. That the early 1970s were ideologically experimental years for Fela is shown in the two simultaneous directions that nationalism took in his work. First, there was the explicit racialism of such songs as "Buy Africa" (1970), "Black Man's Cry" (1971), and "Why Black Man Dey Suffer" (1971). This direction is closer in spirit to the thematic of African-American nationalism that influenced him. Second, there was the cultural nationalism laced with racialism of "Lady"

(1972) and "Gentleman" (1973). This direction is a genuinely inventive compromise to continue fidelity to racialism but through the only channel in which it can make more immediate sense in the Nigerian context: the local culture. Fela apparently learned from the comparative success of these two directions with the audience and worked more within the second than the first direction for the rest of his career. This is so in spite of occasional returns such as the 1980 releases with Roy Ayers, the African-American vibraphonist: "2000 Blacks Got to Be Free," a hopeful desire for the unity of the African world by the year 2000, and "Africa Centre of the World," Fela's account of an instance of the racism he experienced during his student years in England. Predictably, these songs, like the earlier ones in the same category of direct racialism, were barely noticed by the audience.

The successful ideological formula of cultural nationalism allowed Fela to, as it were, hit two targets with the same shot: his explicit attacks on locally recognizable attitudes and behaviors that he judged to be "un-Nigerian" or "un-African" *also* implicitly critiqued Euro-American racial and cultural imperialism. In addition, because those behaviors were often connotatively associated with the middle and upper classes or with higher social status in general, Fela's critique also took on a class dimension. Thus Fela discovered in cultural nationalism, defined as the defense and preservation of a threatened national or ethnic culture, a seemingly coherent and especially flexible ideology that simultaneously suggested and nourished the many dimensions of his growing critical consciousness: the nation, the continent, diasporic Africa, and class. By 1976, with such songs as "J.J.D." ("Johnny Just Drop"), "Mister Follow Follow," and especially "Upside Down," Fela had clearly expanded his cultural nationalism to what we could describe as pan-Africanism.

Pan-Africanism, a philosophical creed based on the conviction that peoples of African descent share common bonds, historical experience, and goals and therefore should unite to achieve those goals, is inherently political in orientation and articulation. From the various Pan-African Congresses from 1900 to the activities of figures such as Edward Wilmot Blyden (1832–1912), Marcus Garvey (1887–1940), and W. E. B. DuBois (1868–1963) and especially to the widespread influence of the indefatigable George Padmore and his classic book, *Pan-Africanism or Communism* (1956), the emphasis of pan-Africanism was politics qua politics; that is, the struggle for independence from colonial rule, for statehood, and beyond that, for the invention of institutions and techniques of effective governance directed toward advancing the interests of blacks in modernity. On the African continent, canonical figures include Sekou Toure, first president of Guinea, and Kwame Nkrumah, first president of Ghana. Nkrumah's most famous proclamation is often remembered by many to be "Seek ye first the political kingdom, and everything else shall be added on to it." In spite of the World Black Festivals of Art and Culture in Dakar in 1966, Algiers in 1969, and Lagos in 1972, pan-Africanism has never shed its image as basically a "political" philosophy.[30] Fela did not give up his cultural nationalism but simply expanded it to incorporate matters of political arrangements and institutions. In this sense, his position remained actually more robust than historical pan-Africanism and its negligible attention to the cultural dimension of the Afro-world struggle.

The immediate shepherds of Fela's pan-Africanism were radical intellectual activists and leaders such as Kwame Nkrumah, Frantz Fanon, and Walter Rodney. Fanon's emphasis on the psychological subjection of Africans to European norms and values and his astute reading of the tragedy that the newly emergent class of post-independence African leaders would become are themes strewn all over Fela's work. From Rodney, Fela learned the enormous contribution of Africa, through slavery and colonialism, to European civilization generally and industrialization in particular. On the front cover of *V.I.P.* (*Vagabonds in Power*) (1979), there was a picture of Fela reading Rodney's classic book *How Europe Underdeveloped Africa* (1972) with what looks like an undisturbable concentration. Fela sang in "Perambulator" (1983) that "Oyinbo no teach us nothing / Na we open dem eye / Na 500 years slavery cause am" (Europeans taught us nothing / It is we who civilized them / with 500 years of our slave labor); we know where the rigorous conceptual and ideological support for such sentiments came from.

The case of Nkrumah is like a return of the repressed for Fela. Here is a long-time family friend who meant little to young Fela other than as an occasional source of racial pride to a lonely black African college student in London in the late 1950s. In the 1970s, Nkrumah returned to Fela's consciousness, and as is typical of repressed returns, it was with a vengeance. Nkrumah, the charismatic leader who led Ghana to become the first independent African country in 1957 and thereby inspired (and actively supported) an anticolonial revolution that saw most of African countries independent by the mid-1960s, Nkrumah, who once proposed a United States of Africa and was instrumental in the establishment of the epochal Organization of African Unity (now defunct; replaced by the African Union in 2002), became a hero to Fela. A prolific author, Nkrumah's widely circulated books include *Africa Must Unite* (1963), *Neo-Colonialism: The Last Stage of Imperialism* (1965), and *Class Struggle in Africa* (1973). Fela kept a bust of Nkrumah, along with photographs of Malcolm X, Patrice Lumumba, and his mother at the "altar" in the Shrine and poured libations to them before each performance. Books and published speeches by these and other notable pan-African leaders were also sold at the Shrine. He even formed a pan-African–oriented think tank, the Nigerian Association of Patriotic Writers and Artistes, as an ideological resource pool. By the end of the 1970s, Fela was talking more continentally than nationally and would switch from "Nigeria" to "Africa" in his speeches and songs, as if they mean exactly the same thing. His pan-Africanism assumed a staunchly antinationalist bent. At a lecture he gave at the University of Ife in 1979, Fela said derisively about Nigerian nationalism: "In 1884–1885, the white European and American leaders got together and cut-up Africa for themselves. That was how Nigeria came about. . . . Bearing in mind that our V.I.Ps go overseas and they go about boasting 'I am a Nigerian'. However, the

whiteman he is talking to knows the history of the Nigeria he is proud about—
he will say inside him 'Welcome another certified slave.'"[31]

When Fela came across the canonical texts that prefigure the movement
known as Afrocentrism, he added that too to the mix. Afrocentrism is a movement for the reformation of the consciousness of both blacks and whites—
but particularly of blacks—perceived to be hamstrung by centuries of racist
European thinking, teaching, and general ideas. It is an "escape to sanity," as
Molefi K. Asante, the African-American scholar and chief popularizer of Afrocentrism in the United States, puts it.[32] It gathered steam in the late 1970s in
the United States and flaunts its genealogy in the great African empires and
kingdoms, the many slave revolts, pan-Africanism, Negritude, the independence of African countries from colonial rule, and the Black Power/black aesthetics movement. Unlike pan-Africanism, which takes the political as its primary terrain, Afrocentrism locates itself squarely in the cultural; and unlike the
earlier black cultural nationalism, Afrocentrism's focus on culture is more in-
tensive and extensive.[33] Afrocentrism sets about its daunting task of the reformation of minds by adopting two approaches often deployed simultaneously,
deconstructive and reconstructive: a rebuttal of the whole archive of European
ideological racism and a bold and passionate restitutive act of inscribing authentic (because self-constructed and not blatantly imposed) African—most
often meaning black—subjectivity. Without this framework, it would be difficult to fully appreciate the significance of some texts that have become favorites
with Afrocentrists such as *The Stolen Legacy* (1954) by George G. M. James, *The
Black Man of the Nile* (1972) by Y. Ben-Jochannan, *They Came Before Columbus*
(1976) by Ivan Van Sertima, *Black Folk Here and There* (1991) by St. Clair Drake,
*The Destruction of Black Civilization* (1974) by Chancellor Williams, *The African Origins of Civilization: Myth or Reality* (1974) by Cheikh Anta Diop, *Black
Athena: The Afroasiatic Roots of Classical Civilization* (1987) by Martin Bernal,
and *Yurugu: An African-Centered Critique of European Cultural Thought and Behavior*, by Marimba Ani. Ani's 672-page book was first published in January
1994; by July of the same year, it had gone into its fourth printing. One of the
more polemical objectives of the Afrocentrists is the reclamation of the Africanness of ancient Egypt, with its—more obviously—breathtaking material
culture and the civilizational sophistication that implies, against entrenched
racist traditions of European scholarship and public opinion that interpret it
otherwise. The album cover art of Fela's *Shuffering and Shmiling* features ancient Egyptian motifs in the representation of African deities beckoning futilely
to morose Africans apparently zombified by Christianity and Islam who are
carting all their wealth to joyful bishops and imams. I argued earlier that "Shuffering and Shmiling" has a wobbly ideological focus; the mixture of this Afrocentric cultural nationalism with the class-inflected critique of foreign religions
is responsible for that haziness. In the song "Don't Worry About My Mouth O"
("African Message"; 1977), he insists that his listeners must go and read Ben-
Jochanan's *The Black Man of the Nile* for the truth instead of the lies they have

been told about Africa's past. Fela's band, Africa 70, became Egypt 80 as the new decade began.

This is the complex of cultural nationalism, pan-Africanism, and Afrocentrism that Fela liked to call his "Africanism." It sponsored his change of surname at the end of 1975 from "Ransome-Kuti" to the more "culturally African" "Anikulapo-Kuti," meaning one who holds death in a pouch. It served him as a polemical counterdiscourse against a generalized Euro-American domination of Africa; with it, Fela was able to challenge the truth-claims of that domination and short-circuit their process of "catching" his people. With his inventive rhetoric, sarcastic humor, and irresistible rhythms, he makes his people feel ashamed to succumb to the glitters of Europe and proud to be Africans in spite of their poverty. The claims of Eurocentrism to be the norm and to seamlessly account for all experience is, in Africanism, embarrassed by a force and passion that is not only disconcerting and negative but also practically ectopic. This subversive thrust authorizes dreams beyond existing boundaries and is thus a propeller of the dynamism of history.

But if Fela's Africanism exhibits the strengths of counterdiscourses, it also cannot but bear their weaknesses. It is an irony that the abhorrent racialization of thought and culture that is the cornerstone of Euro-American hegemony that Fela opposes is a main crutch of Africanism too. After Fela became "African," his obsessive search was for everything "authentically African," from how to think to toileting procedures. Fela's quest for self-authentication was driven by the need to flaunt something original against an overwhelming Europe, not out of deep conviction. Fela gave dictators who made the headlines regularly by mouthing shallow Africanisms against Europe the benefit of the doubt; this is the reason he was duped by the repugnant Idi Amin. Eurocentrism and Africanism are both locked in an intricate specular embrace in which difference resides more in the "visible" paraphernalia than in the "invisible" supporting structures. For every Roman aqueduct and Gothic cathedral, there must be found parallel African feats. This explains the undue fixation of Afrocentrism on the Africanization of Egypt of antiquity, with its pyramids and sphinxes. No, it is not shunning the execrable monumentalization of history that is important but merely adding one's *own* monuments; it is not how history is represented that matters but simply a question of additional representations. Fela once said polemically: "If Europe and America used capitalism to develop, Russians used Marxism and Leninism, China used Maoism and Arabs used Mohamedanism to develop, why can't Africans use NKRUMAISM?"[34] Even if this makes sense as argument, whatever happened to Fanon's stirring appeal against such "nauseating mimicry"?[35]

Because a counterdiscourse is very often fixated on what it opposes and idealizes its position as an underdog, it is frequently incapable of imagining itself as probably composed of structures of inequity. Africanism, which is engaged in a laudable war against oppressive Eurocentrism, is itself the bearer of oppression in its crude conception of gender relations. Fashioned in the name of Africanism, Fela's unreconstructed sexism and crass masculinism is globally infamous. In the haste to defend some vaguely defined "African culture" against Euro-American cultural imperialism, the internal dynamism of Africa is repressed and its cultures atrophied.[36] And those who benefit the most from this African self-abuse are the men: those who have the resources and power to define and proclaim what is or is not culturally African. In spite of the attenuating factor of pan-Africanism that is more political in orientation, the fundamental cultural nationalism in the complex of Fela's Africanism remained not just dominant but often extremist. It degenerated once into his cavorting for a while with a magician called Professor Hindu, presenting the latter's tricks as authentic African spirituality; he even sang about it in "Just Like That" (1990). He thought he was striving for mystical sublimity, but all we get is woolly thought.[37] What is more significant, that cultural nationalism is the ideological prop of his vulgar and dominative male chauvinism that emerged so graphically early on in "Lady" (1972).

But as I have suggested, Africanism is just one component of Fela's ideological matrix. The second is his solidarity with the oppressed lower classes, irrespective of gender, that could be described as socialist. If true solidarity means sharing the same risks, as the radical slogan theorizes, then Fela's was steadfast and unimpeachable. He lived in their midst, trumpeted their sounds to national attention, experienced their brutalization at the hands of official lawlessness, and even shared their poverty. He did not belong to them by birth, but he belonged by self-resocialization. Only a conceptual idealist would contest that this is as consummate an example of class suicide as we can get in the world of actual social struggles. In spite of the fact that he was the child of an internationally known left-leaning mother who was one of the few women in the world to win the Lenin Peace Prize, necessity forced Fela to turn to the people after his return from his ten-month American trip in 1970. He no longer could bring himself to sing love songs; he never seriously tried the panegyric form but even if he wanted to now, his new critical consciousness firmly disqualified that option. He turned to the idioms, foibles, joys, and sorrows of the exploding urban population of the lower classes and found his own voice. They shaped him as much as he shaped them for the world in his music. As class distinctions sharpened with the oil boom, with their attendant vicious competition, violence, and crude accumulative ethics, he began to also articulate the people's class interests.

Without the committed class dimension, Fela would have been just another Afro-cultural nationalist musician like Sonny Okosun, who after a track or two against apartheid and cultural imperialism ran out of steam and became a Christian evangelist, like one of those peddlers of mystification savaged by Fela in "Shuffering and Shmiling."[38] It is the class partisanship that usefully complicates Fela's cultural nationalism and pan-Africanism and put him *always* at odds with successive Nigerian governments whose staple visions were also cultural nationalist and pan-Africanist. The government-sponsored Second World Black Festival of Arts and Culture held in Lagos in 1977 was a gargantuan event to showcase world black arts and therefore celebrate black pride. One would expect that Fela and the government would have been on the same page for once. As a leading Nigerian artist, he was duly invited to the planning stages. Fela submitted to the army general chairing the committee a nine-point program of which the first called for the "participation of the people."[39] The relationship unraveled rapidly thereafter and Fela ended up in his usual position of critical antagonist.

I will give just one more instance of Fela's uncompromising class partisanship here, and only its suggestive profundity necessitates the extended quote below. In 1978, Fela encountered Sam Nujoma, then head of the South West Africa People's Organization (SWAPO), the main antiapartheid movement fighting for the liberation of Namibia, and first president of independent Namibia. It was at the airport in East Berlin, and Fela and the Afrika 70 were returning from the Berlin Jazz Festival. Someone in the group engaged Nujoma in a chat and asked about the ongoing struggle. Fela overheard Nujoma's reply:

"Certainly, the struggle for the liberation of Africa will continue for a long time. Our children will have to continue where we stop. But *a lutta continua, a victoria e certa.*"

Minutes later, we all proceeded to board our plane and you know what happened? Well, Sam Nujoma and his group went towards the front of the plane, to the *first-class* passengers' section! And us? All seventy of us went into the economy class. . . . What do you think of that? I'll tell you what I think. Sam Nujoma could have saved the extra money he was spending on first-class tickets to buy a gun for the freedom fighters who don't have the opportunity to take a plane, let alone travel in first class. Their homes, their permanent homes are in the trenches. It's them, man, who are fighting for the total liberation of Africa.

*A lutta continua.* . . . *A lutta continua.* . . . *A lutta continua.* . . . Those words kept turning over and over in my mind. At first I didn't understand because it was Portuguese language. One of the boys finally translated it as "the struggle *continues!*" I said to myself: How can a responsible leader ever want the struggle to *continue?* Who can want war to continue? War is massacring . . . and killing. How can anyone want that to go on indefinitely? Those were the things I kept turning round in my head on the flight back from Berlin to Nigeria. That's when I said to myself: "No! It must not continue. The struggle *must* STOP!" Since then, that's been my slogan. . . .

Back in Lagos. What do I see at the airport? Mr. Sam Nujoma and his group, escorted by Nigerian officials, leaving in a long line of Mercedes-Benz. I asked myself: "And how about the poor, ragged, barefoot, hungry guerilla who is fighting on the front, exposing his life every day to the deadly bullets of the enemy? Suppose he showed up right now at this airport and walked up to those same top officials who welcome Nujoma? Would they receive him as they received Nujoma?" That day I understood the whole shit. *A lutta continua* was the slogan of the . . . leaders. Those who will be eating the pie, not those who are getting killed to get the pie. I understood why it's Generals—leaders—who write their memoirs. And not the poor motherfucker who gets killed in their name![40]

The soldiers kill one another while the generals salute one another: sounds like a sentiment right out of the famous political parable *The Caucasian Chalk Circle* by the late distinguished Marxist dramatist, Bertolt Brecht. But even the unconventionally radical Brecht was not radical enough to make such mincemeat of hallowed "in-group" slogans. It would be difficult to find a more far-reaching deconstruction of the radical world's most preeminent rallying cry, "*A luta continua, a vitória e certa!*" by someone who cannot in any way be dismissed as an apologist for oppression and conservatism. The last part about generals writing their memoirs is a barely veiled critique of the recently published *My Command: An Account of the Nigerian Civil War, 1967–1970* by General Olusegun Obasanjo, the dictator under whose reign Fela's Kalakuta Republic was sacked in broad daylight. Obasanjo's memoir opened the floodgate to many more by retired Nigerian generals.

Fela's Africanism and class partisanship frequently speak through a third ideological component: an irrepressible libertarianism that is frequently at odds with the collective sacrifice, unity, and individual discipline demanded by the politics of Africanism and class. The result is an explosive mix, and commentators have mistaken this to mean that Fela is basically anarchic in ideology. Indeed, in his high school days, he set up a Planless Society with like-minded friends and published *The Planless Times* to broadcast their goal, which was "Disobedience."[41] But these teenage antics were no more than psychologically liberating attempts to coerce some space of freedom from a strictly regimented adolescent and colonial missionary-school life. Fela was not opposed to order or rule as such. In fact, all his exertions implied a yearning for order, a different kind of order that would be more responsive to the people. Fela believed that part of the responsibility of such an order is to guarantee the widest realm of freedom possible for the individual and to impose little or no constraints. That is why, for him, smoking marijuana should not necessarily and automatically be a "crime," nor should the fact that many young girls, none of whom were under age, lived in his household, especially since he had never kidnapped anyone. He lived as an autocrat in his household and organization, but he never held anyone there against his or her will. As he expostulates in the song "V.I.P.," just as the country's president has power over the nation, the truck-pusher too has his or her own power over the truck, and he himself, the "Kalakuta president," has his power over his Kalakuta empire. Fela pointedly ignores the nonequivalence that links these examples and goes on to heavily pontificate that what is really detestable is when any of the power holders uses that power to do bad things, such as the country's president and his cabinet of powerful people; for that, they become "vagabonds in power." I discussed earlier what I describe as Fela's "charming pedestrianism"; it is now time to name the opposite, which is equally prevalent in his work and pronouncements: an utterly repellent pedestrianism. Frequently, they are sides of the same coin.

It would have been odd if such a volatile ideological matrix had not yielded irreconcilable contradictions in practice. These have riled both Fela's admirers and detractors to no end. But in spite of the high intellectual content of his work, Fela was no professional intellectual or scholar. More important, he was just another musician aiming at pop stardom first and foremost before he became a political musician. He lived commonly, but the egotism of the pop star, the kind that lives through contradictions as if they were part of the perks of stardom, never left him. Fela himself provides us with a suggestive conceptual handle to assess him. "I am not Ph.D. Economics," he declared polemically in one of his many attacks at intellectuals for having failed the nation, "but I can say conveniently I am Ph.D. Commonsense. My own commonsense is not written in any book, but it is something any right thinking, honest African man's brain should think about."[42] Fela did not know it, but that is precisely the problem, his self-immolation on the altar of "common sense."

"Common sense" is that sedimented habitual, unconscious, and therefore largely areflexive perception of the world that has become conventional, traditional—that is, "common"—in a given society or epoch. That it is conventional does not mean it is unchanging; common sense is flexible and continually adapts itself to the changing conditions of its context, for which it is supposed to provide explanations. It even has a probing, incisive edge with which it identifies the unusual and abnormal and could be a quite useful though limited weapon against the disease of normalization of crisis that currently afflicts most postcolonial countries. But common sense is often worn down quickly by difficulties and complexities. What is "right thinking" under common sense is frequently shallow thinking. It may make "common sense" to say à la Fela, and without humorous intentions, that Nigeria cannot be united because it is divided into too many states, but that is really a useless sense. As an overall erratic, contradictory set of commonly held beliefs and assumptions, common sense customarily comforts itself with the existing, the seemingly obvious, and the most easily available—of visions, definitions, solutions, and rationalizations. This is why common sense is most often very conservative. Although Antonio Gramsci, the most perceptive theorist of common sense, invests the broad masses with this outlook, the specifics of the sociohistorical context I am dealing with demand that I be much less absolute about its class character. Nevertheless, I do agree with Gramsci that it is generally the case that common sense is "fragmentary, incoherent and inconsequential, in conformity with the social and cultural position of those masses whose philosophy it is."[43] Fela may have not belonged to the "broad masses" by birth, education, and the breadth of his knowledge about global affairs, but he shared to a large extent their commonsensical perspectives on the conundrums of postcolonial existence, which is why they understood him so well. If we are not purist, we could, to some extent, invest him with the title of an "organic intellectual."

We certainly cannot overemphasize the need for ideological clarity in any program designed to effect social change, but we also need to be wary of turning ideological clarity into a fetish. After all, in times of great social ferment such as the one that produced Fela, which we are still living through, resistance against domination will not necessarily follow the "theoretically sound," "politically correct," and "revolutionary" plans fashioned in our jargon-filled books and interminably dreary and routinized back-patting seminars and lectures. Retired General Olusegun Obasanjo, during his first session as dictatorial head of state of Nigeria, once accused Fela of "destroying the lives of Nigerian youth." Fela, who cannot be defeated in rhetorical combat, retorted that Obasanjo had "destroyed the lives of an entire nation."[44] Let us ignore the exchange as such and focus on Obasanjo's statement. It is actually a compliment, an acknowledgment, albeit negative, of Fela's profound influence on the country. That influence is, Obasanjo's condemnation and Fela's demonstrated ideological contradictions notwithstanding, on the whole very salutary.

What Obasanjo actually meant to say was that Fela, through his music, ideas, and even his lifestyle, successfully broadcast to young people totally new, rebellious, and impatient desires that completely pushed out of their hearts and minds any affection for the state. For twenty years, both Fela and the state battled epically for the soul of the youth, but the trophy in the end went to Fela. This is shown in his enormous influence among that most articulate section of the youth—and indeed, of Nigerian civil society in general—students.[45] Obasanjo had every reason to be resentful. He remained number one on the Nigerian students' list of infamy for the 1978 student crisis he caused that led to the deaths of several students at the hands of his antiriot police. This took place one year after he sent a battalion of soldiers to sack and raze Fela's Kalakuta Republic in the middle of Lagos. That they were battling a common tyranny was not lost on both Fela and the students, and Fela would later memorialize both events in the political classic, "Coffin for Head of State" (1981). Fela was even more popular with students after these events, and during the 1980/1981 academic year alone, he, by invitation, delivered more than sixty lectures on campuses nationwide.[46] We know that postcolonial states rule more by direct domination than by moral authority.[47] The goal of every regime is to be able to rule by moral authority, to win the consent of the people, to make the people believe in it. It is ironic, but Obasanjo actually thought that his regime, a tyrannical military regime, could succeed in that. It took on the antiapartheid cause boldly and even nationalized British Petroleum, actions that would otherwise have endeared it to the vocal populace and students, but the latter were not deceived, thanks, in no small part, to the likes of the self-described "leaking basket mouth," Fela. If the white apartheid regime is killing unarmed students and the black African Nigerian regime is also killing unarmed students, Fela would argue, what is the difference? With his simple deconstructive insights, sardonic humor, and exhilarating sounds, he taught young people to see the state as fundamentally illegitimate, selfish, dictatorial, even unpatriotic and un-African and to see many of its policies as irredeemably foolish. Through his unconventional lifestyle, he liberated tabooed desires that the system needed to understand if it hoped to contain them; and through his committed radical politics, he served as a model to follow. As a composite phenomenon, he helped to democratize thinking by constantly pushing the boundaries of what can be thought and imagined. Obasanjo was right, after all: Fela destroyed the Nigerian youth, but only the kind of mindless, pliant youth a dictator craves. Many of those students later graduated to become fearless journalists, educators, civil rights lawyers, and social activists; they were the bulwark of opposition to the hideous dictators General Ibrahim Babangida and General Sani Abacha; even Obasanjo's second coming as elected president (1999–2003; 2003–2007) has not been spared critical scrutiny by that first socially conscious and restless generation molded by Fela. Fela's music did not overthrow any government. His overall contribution was much more far-reaching: his potent detachment of the power of truth from any putative hegemony that the state might profess. This was, and remains, his central political effect and significance.

# 5 Fela, Lagos, and the Postcolonial State

## Lagos, Civis

In the entirety of its sonic repertoire, the language of its lyrics, the imagery in its soundscape, the countercultural mode of life within which it was created, and its implied and actual audience, the afrobeat of Fela Anikulapo-Kuti is the quintessential music of the postcolonial megalopolis. Lagos, Nigeria, is the sprawling conurbation that served as the primary canvas upon which Fela inscribed his gigantic creative will. But the city was not just a passive surface for Fela's inscription of all sorts of idiosyncrasies. It simultaneously enabled and circumscribed Fela's imagination and influence. It set the terms of engagement but also had to concede and absorb the endless and unpredictable contractual revisions Fela routinely threw in. It is not surprising then that it has become difficult to think of Fela, both the music and the lifestyle, without Lagos or indeed to study postcolonial Lagos without considering Fela!

We know that musical talent ran deep in the family of Fela Anikulapo-Kuti. His grandfather, J. J. Ransome-Kuti, was a famous pioneer in the local production of Christian music in Nigeria; a biographer once labeled him "the singing minister of Nigeria." Fela's father, Reverend Israel Oludotun Ransome-Kuti, was also a music teacher and song composer. It was under his tutelage that Fela learned the piano. Fela himself once confessed that all he seemed to have any brains for during his high school days was music. My conceptual argument here is that had Fela remained in his native Abeokuta, a sleepy town fifty miles north of Lagos, he perhaps would still have been a musician but a musician of a very different kind—certainly not the devout hymn master and cultural nationalist committed to the radical task of indigenizing colonial Christianity that his grandfather and father were, for Fela never showed any such religious inclination or seriousness of purpose in his adolescent years. And in any case, the battle for the decolonization of Christianity was more or less won by the time Fela was setting out on his own. Fela would also certainly not have been the inventor of afrobeat music and a counterculture world famous in its controversial composition and organization, for Abeokuta was much too small, too conservative in values, too homogenous in population, and too provincial to support such a quintessentially urban musical practice. My point, then, is that only a postcolonial metropolis such as Lagos could have produced Fela; he could hardly have thrived the way he did in any other Nigerian city.

Even before the end of his high school years, Fela discovered he could not

*Lagos Shity.*
Courtesy of Lemi Ghariokwu.

resist the lure of nearby enchanting Lagos. This was the 1950s. The most significant thing happening then in Lagos was primarily political: the decolonization struggle, of which the city was the prime center, but this was not what Fela responded to. Lagos has always been like the accomplished magician with a bagful of tricks: you may not like many of them, but you surely will succumb to one. It was that other most significant phenomenon, primarily cultural, which ensnared Fela: the glitzy highlife music scene. Along with his more streetwise and citywise lifelong friend J. K. Braimah, Fela spent the last years of high school immersed in this exciting Lagos highlife scene.

For over a century before that time, Lagos had been Nigeria's premier political and cultural center. The city had started much more humbly in the sixteenth century as a small fishing and farming village. While its small islands proved ideal for the early inhabitants from the point of view of defense from hostile neighbors in the hinterland, the area's few square miles of arable land could hardly be expected to support a large population. From early on, it was clear that outsiders would play a decisive role in the development of the settlement. Since naming is so significant to the Yorubas, it is important to note that what is widely known today as the indigenous name for the city, "Eko," is actually not autochthonous at all but a corruption, introduced by Benin invaders in the seventeenth century, of what the original inhabitants called "*oko*," a farm. And

"Lagos," the name by which the world knows the city today, was imposed by the Portuguese in the eighteenth century after a port in southern Portugal. At the end of that century, the population of the town was no more than 5,000 people. That number doubled in the next fifty years, due mainly to waves of immigration by three groups of people: slaves and slavers, especially after 1821 when the town became an important slaving port; the "Brazilians"; and the "Sierra Leoneans." The so-called Brazilians were actually former slaves shipped to Brazil who worked hard to buy their freedom and returned to where they were originally captured. The "Sierra Leoneans" were those rescued on the high seas by British ships enforcing the antislavery act passed by the British Parliament in 1807. Known as "recaptives," these lucky slaves, so to speak, were settled in Freetown, Sierra Leone, from where they later found their way to Lagos, the entry point to their homeland in the Yoruba country. Such immigrations would continue until late in the century; by 1850, the enduring identity of Lagos as an immigrant city composed of people of widely differing ethnic, racial, and class backgrounds, life experiences, and degrees of westernization was solidly in place. Active British involvement in the affairs of the city began in 1851 when it deposed the reigning King Kosoko and restored Akintoye, the uncle Kosoko had deposed and exiled, to the throne, all in the name of the "humanitarian" goal of blocking the trade in slaves being fed then by the widespread intra-Yoruba wars of the nineteenth century. European merchants and missionaries began to settle in the city after that. Britain richly rewarded itself for its supposed humanitarianism when it formally annexed Lagos as a colony in 1861; humanitarianism, after all, need not be unprofitable. That action marked the beginning of Lagos as the premier commercial, administrative, and political center of the country that would later in 1914 be known as "Nigeria." The excellent harbor as well as the later construction of a railway line liking it and the north of the country gave Lagos an advantage as a magnet for commerce and people that very few other Nigerian cities had. The obvious was formally affirmed when in 1960 the city was made the capital of the newly independent nation; it would remain that until December 12, 1991, when the seat of government was moved inland to Abuja, ending a tenure of 130 years.[1]

By the time Fela settled in Lagos on his return from college in Britain in 1963, the distinctive character of the city in Nigerian public consciousness as the anonymous-neon-lights capital of immense opportunity and bottomless uncertainty was already formed. Of all the cities in the country, it was the most populous and the most heterogeneous in composition and the one in which modern class distinctions were sharpest and most visible, especially in its spatial arrangements. Extensive slums ring a few exclusive and rich neighborhoods. For the rich, there can be no better place on earth than Lagos, for it is not just that money will buy you all the material pleasures you wanted—the latest model custom-built Mercedes-Benzes and BMWs, all-leather Italian-made shoes, "gatored" suits directly from the West End of London, and special-issue wristwatches from Switzerland—it will also, and this is more important, buy you power in its rawest, uncorrupted form; that is, it will exempt you from all the formal rules and regulations that even the rich in other places must conform to. The roads are bad, but the shock absorbers of your comfy Range Rovers and Mercedes-Benzes will take care of that. There is no running water but you have your own private borehole and water processor in the yard. The electricity supply is unreliable, but your sitting-room–sized electricity generator is standing by. You are in control, at least according to the particularly crass nose-length vision of wealthy Lagosians. Other things that you cannot control, such as traffic gridlock and armed robbery, you just accept and pray that they won't happen to you.[2] For the aggressive aspirants to the status of the wealthy, Lagos is a Mecca to flock to, for class distinctions there may be sharpest but they are infinitely permeable. As the classic embodiment of the nation's raucous and freewheeling dependent capitalist economy in which rabid acquisitiveness, swindling, cozening, corner-cutting, and cleverness are the primary currencies of exchange, even the barely solvent today could become a millionaire tomorrow, "just like that," to borrow the title of a famous song by Fela. All you need to do is win one building contract from a local, state, or the federal government and, as Nobel laureate Soyinka put it, "You are made forever, no more worry / play the game and you won't be sorry."[3] For the wretched of the city as they shunt from joblessness to underemployment to nonpaying jobs to stinking ghettoes without electricity or pipe-borne water, where, as Fela graphically puts it in "Original Sufferhead," they live "10-10 in one room," Lagos is the pitiless incubus that feeds on their most valuable possession, dreams, which it endlessly defers and derides.

This then is Lagos, Fela's city. Bitten by the bug of modern jazz which he came in contact with while he was a student in London, Fela returned home dissatisfied with the dominant musical culture of highlife he had been strongly attracted to a few years earlier. He began to distance himself from highlife and move closer to jazz. He was determined to change the popular musical taste of Lagos. There was no audience for jazz to support a musician, much less make that musician widely popular. Fela coined the name "highlife jazz" for his music, which was supposed to be a hybrid of the two forms. But Lagosians were not deceived, for the so-called hybrid sounded to them more like jazz than a hybrid and certainly not quite like the highlife they wanted to hear from him. The city studiedly ignored him. Fela was unsuccessful in Lagos throughout the 1960s. The degree of his alienation from the popular musical and cultural life of the city is evident in one of the statements he made in 1968 about transforming highlife: he said that Nigerian popular music would be really great if only the musicians were able to read and write music, supposedly like himself. He said: "You will soon find that it will be a very great asset for Nigerian musicians to be able to read and write music. When it reaches that stage, you will see the wonderful brand of highlife they will be playing. I personally am on a crusade to rejuvenate the style."[4] Of course, the feeling was mutual: if he did not think much of the music the people, across class, consumed avidly because the musicians did not have Trinity College degrees, the people too did not think much of what he, Trinity-certified, had to offer. The statement was actually a cover for his desperation in failing to have the ear of Lagos. And part of that desperation was his risky calculation in 1969 that a badge of acceptance from a successful tour of the United States of America would make Lagos listen to him.

Fela returned the next year not with the expected success but with the ingredients for it. Even so, he found that Lagosians simply refused to be coerced by any "been-to" musician merely on account of a trip abroad. His earliest recordings made only a little blip on the radar screen of popular acceptance, and those ones directly inspired by American-type racialism made decisively smaller blips. Lagos finally forced Fela to come down from his high horse. He began to really listen to the heartbeats of the city. And the heartbeats he heard, because they were the most distinctive and loudest and also because Fela's ears now were favorably disposed to hearing them, were those of the laboring millions without whose daily toil there would have been no Lagos to speak of; they are the city. He lived in their midst and immersed himself in their idioms, hopes, joys, and sorrows. He acquired their peerless sense of humor, without which their poverty-ridden city lives would have been most unbearable. He absorbed their streetwise philosophy with all its egalitarian strivings, critical insights into the nature of big-city social relations, intractable contradictions, ambiguities, and even blundering self-subverting conservatism. Ingeniously creative, Fela transmuted all of these into a musical discourse the likes of which had never been heard before. At the level of pure instrumental sound, the aggressive, blaring horns and deeply pulsating drums express an unmistakable belligerence that is simultaneously mere city braggadocio and substantive accumulated resentments and frustrations of the lowly as they scrape and scrimp at the bottom of the city hierarchy. And at the level of vocal sound, there could hardly be a better convergence of form and content than Fela's hard, gruff voice that gave distinctive articulation to both the profundities and inanities of Lagos life as the poor—who were considered loud and uncouth—experienced it. He became the voice of the voiceless. He brought them into musical representation outside the condescension and negativity that was typical of the *juju* music that overthrew highlife in prominence beginning in the 1970s. The people embraced him and gave him the rare privilege of making money not only without having to sing in praise of the wealthy and the powerful but actually by abusing and singing against them, a merit very rare in Yorubaland Nigeria, where the panegyric is usually the form of the most successful popular musics. We usually credit Fela with the patent for afrobeat, but to speak truly, it was a joint invention with the teeming masses of Lagos and their kind in similar locations elsewhere in the country and in Africa generally.

It makes all the sense in the world then that Lagos is imprinted all over Fela's musical corpus. In a fundamental way, it engendered and supplied the language without which afrobeat would never have been what it is today. Fela began the first phase of his musical career singing mostly in his native language, Yoruba. But Lagos, as a cosmopolis that is Yoruba in origin but multiethnic and transnational in evolution, demanded more from him. In addition, the genre of music he chose from the menu that Lagos offered, highlife jazz, was the least ethnic in association; highlife was quintessentially urban, even if the lyrics were in this or that particular language. Therefore, Fela would now and then sing in Yoruba and English, sometimes in the same track, translating from one language to the other. At the critical juncture when Fela finally figured out a working sonic formula for afrobeat in the early 1970s, he also hit upon a most contextually appropriate lyrical language: the language of the multiethnic masses on the streets of Lagos, pidgin English.

Pidgin is formed by and located in the interstitial space where English meets an indigenous language or languages. As a potent denativizing and transethnic mass language, it disciplines both the foreign and the local languages within the seething cauldron of sprawling urbanization, where only self-conscious and heroic periodic renewals are able to shore up—and even then, in reshaped "modernized" forms—ethnic loyalties. Pidgin's syntax is more African, while its vocabulary is more English; in spite of this indebtedness to the foreign, it nevertheless provides a comfortable, less-threatening psychological space between English and the diverse indigenous languages. It is experienced—and welcomed —as a language of a cosmopolis that is larger than the domains of one's native tongue but that nevertheless bears the imprint of local agency, unlike English, which has yet to shed its image as an imposed alien language.[5] But pidgin also bears an unmistakable class stamp as the language of the working masses who often need help filling out the endless forms—in English, of course—of an alienating, labyrinthine city bureaucracy. Here then is the lyrical language of afrobeat; Fela may have originally resorted to it out of commercial expediency in a competitive Lagos city environment, but the language so fitted his later propeople and antistate politics that it became quite difficult to imagine that the language was not chosen for, but was already there before, the "politics."

Lagos and its landmarks or specific events that happened there are the subjects of a large corpus of Fela songs such as "Eko," "Eko Ile," "Monday Morning in Lagos," "Ikoyi Mentality versus Mushin Mentality," "Ikoyi Blindness," "Alagbon Close" "Confusion," "Confusion Break Bones," "Coffin for Head of State," and "Unknown Soldier," to name just a few. "Metro songs," a category I identified as dominant in Fela's repertoire before 1974, actually traverse the musician's whole career. In other words, even in the songs that contain no definite references to the city, it is impossible to know the city and not recognize it in the imagery of the lyrics. I mean songs such as "Go Slow," "Who're You," "Lady," "Shakara," "Yellow Fever," "Zombie," "Sorrow, Tears and Blood," "Upside Down," "Shuffering and Shmiling," "Original Sufferhead," "Perambulator," and more. Lagos exercised a powerfully determining influence on Fela's imagination, but Fela also actively sought to reshape the city in his own image, compel it to accommodate his eccentricities, and firmly imprint his footprint on it. He musically represents the city from as many different perspectives as the number of his songs, but I suggest that there is one overarching conceptual anchor that governs the representations. From the vulgar and humorous tracks to the grave and heart-rending, Fela's underlying conception of Lagos in his songs is as an aborted civis.

"Civis" is an archaic word with origins that implicate cities, citizens, citizenship, and civilization or community. This is probably an excess of significations, but the conceptual service I am pressing the word into demands no less.[6] Cities everywhere have historically been centers where citizens are made, where citizenship is conferred, negotiated, and renegotiated. This was more obviously so during colonial rule in Africa, as Mahmood Mamdani made eloquently clear in his book *Citizen and Subject: Contemporary Africa and the Legacy of Late Colonialism*. And cities have always been centers of civilization, of "every great burst of creativity in human history," as Peter Hall puts it in his massive volume *Cities in Civilization*.[7] In fact, cities have not just been centers of civilization but have also at the same time been held as markers of the quality of the community and civilization of its inhabitants. The depth of Fela's critique is clear, then, when I say that the idea of Lagos he circulates in his works is that of the city as an aborted civis. But the critique is shot through with ambivalence; this hardly could have been otherwise, since Fela loved Lagos profoundly. But he was also convinced, like everyone else, that the city could be much better than it is. Simultaneous affirmation and disavowal, therefore, were the vehicles of his critique. This remained so even though his warm, charming, and humorous critique became quickly and progressively somber as he became politicized and entangled in a web of repeated persecution by that other major city resident: the postcolonial state and its security agencies. This is why the distance between "Eko Ile" (1973) and "Alagbon Close" (1974) is so great indeed, not to mention between "Eko Ile" and others such as "Sorrow, Tears and Blood" (1977) or "Confusion Break Bones" (1990).

I have attended in substantive detail to the vivacious metro songs that were the signature mark of Fela during the early 1970s. "Eko Ile," as paradigmatic of those songs, is built, both lyrically and sonically, upon a playful cheekiness and self-ironizing that bespeaks of Lagos as a problem, yes, but a problem of *known* dimensions; Lagos is a familiar, unsurprising problem, and therefore one could be comfortable with it. It is for this reason that Fela's attitude toward the city was always one of jabbing geniality, a prodding, prickly affection. London and New York are more organized and traffic there flows smoothly. But in Lagos, topsy-turvydom reigns. If you are an expert driver in London or New York, you must learn driving anew in Lagos, for "Turn Right" really means "Turn Left," so you had better open your eyes and learn fast. Yes, yes, this civis is far less civilized and civil than it could be, but it is home, and after traveling all over the world, there is still no place like homey Lagos. The lyrics call for some reflection, but the bubbly pounding rhythm and the hypnotic repetitive chorus of "Eko Ile" say something dramatically other: don't reflect, just dance! Lagos is an aborted civis, but Fela is hardly complaining. At a fundamental level, Fela was more honest in this than he realized. Topsy-turvy Lagos, after all, was the ideal home of the counterculture he was setting up then, with the open marijuana smoking, the train of runaway girls, the arrant sexualization of his own image, and, of course, the antisocial, even criminal, reputation of his hangers-on, which included driving in the wrong direction down one-way streets! Fela's friend and collaborator on some songs comments:

> He didn't have any competitors [laughs]. There was nobody doing what Fela was doing. . . . One stunt he used to do . . . when the Shrine was on the opposite side of the main Lagos road, they would close the road before the gig, and cause a traffic jam for miles in both directions [laughs]. Completely block up Lagos. When Fela was ready to go to the gig he'd go across the road on a donkey, with all the girls and the band in a procession. And every time he did a gig they'd stop Lagos' traffic from moving. Completely. The whole of Lagos. This was a couple of times a week.[8]

Above all, the chaos of Lagos provided Fela with subjects to creatively sing about. He contributed to the disorder even as he sang derisively about it. Afrobeat, in short, needed a chaotic Lagos as ducks need water.

Lagos may be disorganized, but Fela would soon learn the hard way that that did not mean it was outside of any supervisory power. Cities, after all, have always been the most policed, the most regulated, and the most intensively governed territory since their emergence. Lagos was no different. For most of the three decades of Fela's residence in Lagos, the city was the seat of several governments, each with its own bureaucracies and surveillance agencies: the federal, state, local, and municipal governments. It was not long before Fela bumped into one or the other of these many tentacles of the nation-state. And when that happened in a substantive way in 1974, the result, as we can see from "Alagbon Close," was very dramatic, not to say traumatic. Catalyzed by a newly discovered sense of vulnerability, Fela woke up to this other dimension or character of the city. Even comparatively innocuous songs such as "Monday Morning in Lagos," "It's No Possible," and "He Miss Road," all released in 1975, began to take on new meanings in their accents on recalcitrant, untamable aspects or experiences of the city. For the first and last time in his career, and perhaps in a desperate act to send a message to his tormentors in a language they would understand more viscerally, Fela actually borrowed the mystical formula of *juju* musicians who see enemies everywhere and rhetorically place themselves—and vicariously, their audience—on the winning side of every visible and invisible combat. This is in "Water No Get Enemy" (1975). Although it is a very popular track, no one has remarked on its ideological awkwardness in the afrobeat corpus. As the city confronted Fela with a new, life-threatening experience courtesy of that other co-resident, the state, he resorted to the comforting popular Yoruba habit of steeling oneself against adversity through iterations of meaningful sayings and proverbs that cast one in a saintly or powerful light against one's enemies. In the track, Fela is water that no one can do without; you cannot not like water, and you cannot have a relationship of enmity with it. Although the literal logic of the song's title is "Fela has no enemy," the intended meaning is actually the metaphorical one: "You cannot be an enemy of Fela, just as you cannot hate water," for it is we who have to seek out water for use, not the other way around. Most meaningfully, that was the song booming from the speakers as Fela was laid to final rest in 1997.

By 1976, Fela's genial humor would vanish altogether and be replaced by a dark, scorching sarcasm and outright verbal abuse directed at the state, its security agencies, and the entire middle to upper classes that benefit from its rule and its "order." He could no longer comment on Lagos, in song or speech, without dragging the state into it. And any time he commented on the state, his remarks were, implicitly or explicitly, about how it is experienced in the city. As state harassments and intimidations led to more determinedly antistate compositions and then to more harassments, what was at stake in the cyclic movement was no less than a struggle for the redefinition of the soul of Lagos and therefore of the civis—a place of citizenship, of "civilization," as distinguished poet Odia Ofeimun, puts it—that it represents. "Zombie," "Kalakuta Show," "Ikoyi Blindness," and "J.J.D." are a few examples of Fela's expressions of antistatism. "Sorrow, Tears and Blood" was originally composed as a critique of the atrocities of the South African apartheid regime against black Africans in the townships. Before the song was released, events in Nigeria overtook that immediate goal. The Kalakuta raid of February 18, 1977, had happened, during which all forms of unspeakable official violence were visited not just on the residents of the house but also on the people living in the vicinity. By the time the song was released later in the year, it had become, without Lagos being mentioned at all, a critique of savage official tyranny rampant in the postcolonial city. Who is that Lagosian—or indeed that resident of any other big city in Africa—who has not witnessed, been a victim of, read about, or heard from someone, an event similar to the following:

Everybody run run run!
*Chorus:* Hey yah!
Everybody scatter scatter
Some people lost some bread                Some people lost money
Someone nearly die
Someone just die
Police dey come, army dey come             Police and army are on a rampage
Confusion everywhere.

Huh, huh, seven minutes later
All don cool down brother                  All is quiet again
Police don go away                         Police has gone
Army don disappear                         Army has disappeared
Dem leave sorrow, tears and blood.         But they leave sorrow, tears and blood
*Chorus:* Dem regular trademark.           *Chorus:* Their regular trademark.

In "Confusion Break Bones," the absolute chaos of the major Lagos traffic junction of Ojuelegba, where motorists jumble for passage without the help of traffic lights or traffic wardens, becomes for Fela a metaphor for a country with collapsed institutions, from law enforcement to health care. The slow, even ponderous, tempo of this very long track is an indication of the tamed exasperation of a musician who over the years had shouted himself hoarse over social problems that just wouldn't go away or were getting worse:

| | |
|---|---|
| I sing about one street for Lagos | I sing about a street in Lagos |
| Dem call am Ojuelegba | They call it Ojuelegba |
| I think I compare how Nigeria be | I compare it to Nigeria |
| One crossroad in center of town | |
| *Chorus:* Larudu repeke | |
| For Ojuelegba | At Ojuelegba |
| Moto dey come from east | Vehicles approach from east |
| Moto dey come from west | From west |
| Moto dey come from north | From north |
| Moto dey come from south | From south |
| And policeman no dey for centre. | And no policeman to direct the traffic |
| Na confusion be that oh-o | The result is utter confusion! |
| *Chorus:* Pafuka na quench | It is utter confusion |

These are typical samplings, and what this means is that Fela found it extremely difficult to think of the state and Lagos city outside of facts and suppositions of official brutality and social anarchy. Fela backgrounds these features a little bit in the song that remains his most astute and widely suggestive in thinking about the postcolonial African state and its capital city. This is "Perambulator," released in 1983.

## The Perambulating State

Fela applies the term "perambulator" to individual representatives of institutions, victims of named systems or institutions, and to systems and institutions themselves. It is clear that the immediate target of the song is the political state, the structure of authority and those who rule. But beyond this narrow target, the song also ropes in the general social circumstances subtending the structure of rule. We could say then that Fela is playing implicitly upon two senses of the word "state": as a structure of rule operated by "officialized" individuals *and* as a condition, a state of things. According to the logic of the song, only "perambulation" best describes the Nigerian political state as well as the state, the condition, of Nigeria. And given the way that Fela typically interweaves the national and the continental, the concept is also no doubt meant to apply to both the postcolonial African political state and the postcolonial African condition as sociopolitical genres. We know that as a matter of routine, Fela wears hubris like a second skin, but he is at his most conceptually daring here. The postcolonial African state, he theorizes, is a "perambulator" state.

From the heights of hope at independence in the 1960s—hope of reversing a colonially induced African dependency on the global economy and of creating prosperous, politically stable, and socially cohesive entities; in short, hopes of "rapid modernization," to borrow the popular nationalist rallying cry—most African nations had by the 1980s sunk into depths of destitution and despair. Since the 1970s, there has been no shortage of "specialist" explanations of the crisis from all hues of the ideological spectrum. One generally acknowledged source of the predicament is the undecolonized nature of the postcolonial African state, resulting in an unending crisis of legitimacy.[9] Social scientists have produced tomes proposing one grand concept or the other to understand the state: the "Praetorian State," the "Predatory State," the "Prebendal State," "personalist rule," the "politics of the belly," the "Bula Matari state," and so on. To the extent that explanations have a concrete materiality to them—that is, in their ultimate transformation to (or basis of) social actions—the crisis today ought to be considered as much social as epistemological.[10] Fela's song "Perambulator" is an early and vigorous intervention in this effort to understand and describe the African state as a preamble to arresting its crisis of legitimacy. Given the pervasiveness of the crisis, it is only mildly significant that in 1983, the year Fela released "Perambulator," another experiment by Nigeria at electoral governance collapsed as monumentally corrupt soldiers, yet again, filed out of the barracks to overthrow the monumentally corrupt elected civilian regime of Alhaji Shehu Shagari. Change, but no progress; motion, but no movement. Musical chairs.[11]

"Perambulator" begins with a deep bass guitar whose dull thud, chopped into brief short patterns, seems more important than its fifteen-second duration would suggest. But this is the sharp head of the shuttle that would soon enter the loom to create an ornate sonic fabric. The sound of Fela's hands join in, clapping the rhythmic outline. Then piano sounds enter, shrill and sumptuous and at the same time heating up the pace to an explosive climax, counted down "1–2–3–4!" by Fela. All of this happens in the first thirty seconds of a track of fourteen-and-a-half minutes; the climax ushered in a dramatic, high-octane barrage of ensemble sounds—roaring horns, cavernous rumbling percussion, guitars, maracas, and sticks—that is Ogunian in its frenzied tempo.[12] The horns wail, scrape, and lope in hypnotic repetitive formations; solo efforts of contrasting sounds—baritone sax, alto sax, and trumpet—skitter creatively but purposively and then engage in theatrical call-and-response configurations with the rest of the horns; all of these are built upon a rhythmic edifice pillared by a muscular percussion that is mesmerizing in its unfailing regularity. For a song that is about perambulation, this is a very ordered, unperambulating sonic arrangement. Perhaps that is precisely the point: to construct order in the context of, and as a critique of, disorder. Fela does not begin singing until nearly six minutes into the track:

*Fela:* Perambuuu!
*Chorus:* Perambulator!
Perambulator dey come        Perambulator is coming
Perambulator dey go          Perambulator is going

*Fela:* He must to turn, turn right; turn
   right for nothing
*Chorus:* Turn, turn right
He must to turn, turn left; turn left for
   nothing
   :Turn, turn left

He must start to go; start to go for
  nothing
   :Start to go
He must to come, come down; come
  down for nothing
   :Come, come down
He must to turn, turn round; turn round
  for nothing
   :Turn, turn round

*Fela:* He must to turn right
*Chorus:* Perambulator!
And then turn left
He must start to go
And then come down
He must turn round
All for nothing
All no progress
All no profit, yes

The *Oxford English Dictionary* defines "perambulate" as to walk around or through an area or place for pleasure, especially in a leisurely way. Its origin is late Middle English: from Latin *perambulat-*, "walked about"; from the verb *perambulare* we have *per-*, "all over," + *ambulare*, "to walk." The word has a much more negative connotation in Nigerian idiomatic usage. To "perambulate" is to walk aimlessly about, to drift without purpose or direction. If you miss this meaning in the first two full lines of the lyrics above where the perambulator is simply "coming" and "going," you will not miss it in the next several lines with their unmistakable structuring by redundancies: "turn turn," "turn right, turn right," "start to go, start to go," "come, come," and so on, both by Fela and the chorus—another redundancy. Even when we know full well that repetition is the soul of music, it is still impossible not to be struck by Fela's dazzling ability to make redundancy so productive, at the levels of both sound and lyrical meaning. Like the perambulator himself[13] about whom they speak, the lyrics as transcribed into cold print simply perambulate, turning right, left, and around, and going and coming, all with the purpose of mimicking the purposeless perambulation—"All for nothing / All no progress / All no profit"—of the perambulator.

Earlier in "Alagbon Close," at the outset of his dangerous and volatile relations with the state, Fela had used a similar image of aimless drift to describe the state's top police headquarters and, by implication, the state itself. By the time of the composition of "Perambulator," the satiric yen had bloomed luxuriantly. The perambulator state is a rudderless, directionless state. There is a strong cultural resonance to this theoretical censure. Yoruba culture could be said to be literally obsessed with *irin iranu*, aimless walk or perambulation, so much so that it has all sorts of sanctions, sayings, and prayers against it. Perhaps this goes without saying, for a culture that conceives life as one long journey cannot but

"No Agreement Today, No Agreement Tomorrow." Singing against the tyranny and corruption of the postcolonial state.

be perpetually apprehensive about the nature of paths and directions: Are they purposive and do they advance the journey or are they purposeless and impede it? The stories of creation the culture tells itself are replete with momentous journeys by this or that deity or ancestor, between this or that place.[14] It is perhaps for this reason that roads and directions carry much symbolic significance for the Yoruba, for they are the stage upon which the drama of life is played; the journey of life taken. Because the risks on that journey are heightened dramatically at crossroads, the Yoruba made not just any of its many deities but the most radical and deconstructively self-reflexive one, Esu, the deity of aporia, to be the guardian of crossroads—the one to pray to for guidance and proper directions—and made the crossroad its shrine.[15] To perambulate, or *rin'rin iranu,* is to be short on Esu's good fortunes, to lack direction in the maze that is the journey of life; the misfortune is epic in proportion and none could be greater. One becomes literally a mad person, the cultural stereotype of the one who roams the streets aimlessly and, after making all lateral and vertical turns, is still on the same spot:

| | |
|---|---|
| *Fela:* if you look de man well, | Look at the man closely, |
| Na de same place he dey | He's still in the same place |
| *Chorus:* Same same place! | |
| Same place he dey | He's on the same spot |
| He no go anywhere | He's not gone anywhere |
| Perambulator! | |

Fela is the exemplary pedagogue. Having carefully sketched the conceptual handle, he then goes on to practical application by extracting examples from four areas that he invests with significance in both the operations and the experience of the Nigerian state and the state of Nigeria: the bureaucracy, public health, labor, and education.

The four subjects are sung about in separate sections; with the extended instrumental preface, the theoretical introduction just discussed, and a polemical conclusion that situates the perambulating condition of Africa within the context of its 500 years of unequal incorporation into the orbit of the West, we have seven parts in this tightly structured song. Within Fela's corpus of political classics, these are so many sections in a song of less than fifteen minutes. What Fela sacrificed here is the usually riveting instrumental bridge between the sections during which he would yell and whoop and grunt and scat in a variety of sounds against or with the flow of the rhythm. Functionally, the instrumental bridges are audience favorites and never fail to be greeted with roars of approval at concerts or parties. They draw the audience deeper into the music after each section of heavy-cudgel lyrics. While such bridges usually last anywhere from fifteen to over thirty seconds, only one such bridge in "Perambulator" is more than ten seconds. With six of the fourteen minutes already devoted to instrumentals only and so much yet to be said, Fela clogged the remaining minutes with lyrics.

Although Fela has always depended on topicality in subject matter to give his critiques their sharpest edges, he tries in this song to jettison topicality for, or at least transform it into, the archetypal. Derision is the primary mode of articulation. Here then is Nigeria's—Africa's—perambulating bureaucracy:

| | |
|---|---|
| Lagos full full of doti | Lagos is full of dirt |
| Town Council just dey take | The Town Council is getting |
| salary for nothing | paid for nothing |
| Commissioner wants to do something | |
| about it | |
| He call meeting for dustbin | He calls a meeting about dirt disposal |
| *Chorus:* No solution! | |
| He make announcement for radio | He broadcasts it on the radio |
| He make reshuffle for office | He reshuffles his office staff |
| Plenty money dem dey spend | They're spending a lot of money |
| Commissioner go for London | Commissioner is going to London |
| He make big press statement: | He calls a big press conference: |
| "I'm going over to London" | |
| "To learn how the English carry dustbin" | |
| Wetin Commissioner no know | What Commissioner does not know |
| be say other people dem go there | is that others go there |
| to learn atomic energy | to learn atomic energy |
| Our commissioner go to | Our commissioner is going there to |
| learn dustbin carrying | learn dustbin carrying |
| You see, him just dey perambulate | You see, he's just perambulating |
| and him still dey | and is still on the same spot |
| *Chorus:* Same, same place | |
| Commissioner | |
| Dustbin | |
| And Town Council | |
| Perambulator. . . . | |

During the reign of the infamous dark-goggled tyrant General Sani Abacha (November 1993–June 1998), his propaganda machine produced a video, *Nigeria: World Citizen,* to burnish his image and the image of Nigeria he had dragged into the mud. The clips of Lagos that appeared in it were all high-angle shots of towering skyscrapers. The vertigo induced immediately tells you that something is amiss far before you are able to make sense of it: conventional eye-level shots that would have shown people on the streets are missing. Yes, the dirt on Lagos streets is so legendary that it subverts any attempt to perfume it over by propaganda. In the year "Perambulator" was released, the nation's leading dramatist and poet, Wole Soyinka, also released a satirical recording, *Unlimited Liability Company.* In the track "I Love My Country" is this, well, paean, to Lagos dirt:

> The Russian astronauts flying in space
> Radioed a puzzle to their Moscow base
> They said we are flying over Nigeria
> And we see high mountains in built-up area
> Right in the middle of heavy traffic

Is this space madness, tell us quick
The facts were fed to their master computer
Which soon analyzed the mystery factor
"That ain't no mountain," the computer said, snappish!
It's just a load of their national rubbish!

Part of what makes Lagos an aborted civis is precisely its mountains of dirt in built-up areas, which virtually take over the streets in many neighborhoods. The city town council bureaucracy is bloated, but Lagos is dirtier than ever. The commissioner, of the higher-level state authority or even the highest-level federal authority, decides to take charge; Lagos is, after all, the state and the federal capital. He wants to be seen to be active and determined to rid Lagos of dirt. He reshuffles his office staff and with gusto calls a press conference to announce, in the stereotypical "big man" voice that Fela mimics with consummate derision, that he is going to London to learn "dustbin carrying." In well-known songs such as "Gentleman," "J.J.D.," "Follow Follow," and "Colonial Mentality," Fela had lampooned the social extraversion that he saw as defining feature of the mentality of the formerly colonized. As in all other things from governance to sartorial habits, the commissioner, agent of the Nigerian state, must go to London to learn how to clear Lagos of dirt.[16] Fela could at least understand a Nigerian going to London to learn "atomic energy"—that sounds relevant enough and not likely to be locally available—but about how to clean the streets? Fela makes it sound extremely ridiculous; his derisive tone is unmistakable, especially in mimicking the commissioner in the stereotypical "big voice" of the wealthy and powerful. However, the irony is that in the management of large cities, it is precisely in the area of waste disposal—Fela insists on calling it the evocatively demeaning "dustbin carrying"—that Lagos and Nigeria need to learn a lot from London. But for Fela, that is perambulation, another means of wasting public funds on unproductive ventures. In the final analysis, he is probably right, since he could point to scores of similar ventures in which bureaucrats junketed round the world, supposedly to learn from successful examples elsewhere, only for the targeted problems to remain as insoluble as ever. Again, there is much motion but no movement.

Fela reads a similar extraversion in the areas of medical care and public health—both the development of medicine and the administration of treatment —in the country:

| | |
|---|---|
| English man go say "pile" | The English calls it "piles" |
| Yoruba man go say "jedi-jedi" | The Yoruba calls it "*jedi-jedi*" |
| Doctors want to do something about it | |
| Doctors must give you "capsule" | |
| *Chorus:* No solution! | |
| Doctor must give you "tablet" | Doctor will prescribe tablets |
| Doctor must give you "mixture" | Doctor will recommend potions |
| Injection must enter your nyash | Your butt must be injected |
| Doctor carry you go theater | Or you will be carried to the [operating] theater |

| him take de knife slice your nyash | so the doctor can operate on your butt |
| I say solution dey for African medicine | I say solution is in African medicine |
| In one week jedi-jedi go start to run away | You are cured in a week! |
| We must learn to respect our African medicine | |
| Our doctors must go to learn how to make research | |
| but, but, dem go dey perambulate | but they will be perambulating |
| and dem still dey, same same place | and so are still on the same spot |
| *Chorus:* Same same place! | |
| See jedi | See piles |
| Malaria | |
| Gonorrhea | |
| And syphilis | |
| Dem no fit do dem | They can't cure them |
| Me, I dey tell dem | I keep telling them |
| Our medicine better | Our medicine is better |
| They get name for am | There is a name for it: |
| "herbal medicine" | |

Like his counterpart the bureaucrat, the medical doctor is also afflicted with the colonial disease of cultural extraversion and therefore stands aloof from African healing practices and indigenous knowledges in general.[17] Again, Fela's logic is unimpeachably simple: How can contemporary Africa not perambulate in its journey of life if it is so utterly dependent on foreign healing systems for its people? If "our medicine better" but those charged with health care in the current dispensation, the "doctors"—western-trained, of course, ignore it for ineffectual "capsules" and "tablets" and "mixtures" and "*nyash*"-slashing operations, is not this both perambulation and a guarantee of its perpetuity?

Fela does not specify what "African medicine" will make "*jedi-jedi*" disappear in one week. I raise the issue not to doubt that there is such medicine—I can be his witness on this score—but to draw attention to one of the repressions he must make to construct a seemingly tight commonsensical argument. That he could easily identify "capsules" and "tablets" but only an amorphous "African medicine" is itself an indication of the serious limitation of "herbal medicine" in the context of health care delivery in the megalopolis—and in the nation at large—where serving the large populations seems to demand ever-greater medicinal specification and standardization. But of course, Fela would reply that he at least says that "Our doctors must go to learn how to make research," supposedly so the doctors can appropriately transform the indigenous system to fit contemporary needs. Fela's older brother, Olikoye Ransome-Kuti, who died in 2003, was a distinguished professor of medicine and a former minister of health. Younger brother Beko Ransome-Kuti is also a distinguished medical doctor and a former president of the Nigerian Medical Association (NMA). Fela's routine derisive attacks at the nation's "un-African" health care system apart, he denied to the end, even while dying of it, that there was such a thing as the dreaded acquired immune deficiency syndrome (AIDS). Condoms were unpleasurable and unnatural, and he sang about that. AIDS was no more than the usual Euro-American propaganda, circulated locally by, as usual, an overly westernized medical elite. Fela believed, said Olikoye, that "all doctors were fabricating AIDS, including myself."[18] Olikoye, in announcing Fela's death to a stunned populace, had the last word on the matter.

On Fela's evocation of the condition of the laboring masses of Africa, there can be no nitpicking; it is faultless in systematic articulation and consummately heartrending in its emotional tenor:

My father, your father
African fathers must start to work at the
   age of twenty
Comfort, success, riches are all his targets
Perambulator!
Then
*Chorus:* Perambulator
every morning
6 in the morning
going to work
6 in the evening
coming back home
Every month
Small salary
for 55 years

| | |
|---|---|
| Him go tire | He will be tired (worn out) |
| If he no tire | If he is not tired |
| dem go tire am | they will retire him |
| Dem go dash am | They will award him |
| one gold wrist watch | |
| for 55 years service | |
| All him property: one old bicycle | All his property: one old bicycle |

With the bureaucrat and the doctor who are presented as representatives, we are shown the sick—that is, perambulating—nature of African institutions, the bureaucracy, and the health care that they represent. In the third section, however, the figure we have is that of the representative victim: the African worker, presented as "father" in Fela's masculinist scheme. Since the component institutions of the entity-as-system have been shown to be so sick, is it reasonable to expect individuals upon whom they inflict their institutionality to be less than sick? Fela obviously does not think so, and all his sympathy is for the victim. All seventy-five years of the African worker's life, fifty-five of those in the most boring routine for the least pay, amount to no more than an old bicycle and a miserable palliative long-service award of a "gold wrist watch." From 6 A.M. to 6 P.M. for over half a century, the African worker perambulates on the same spot, making lots of motions but no movement or progress. S/he is thereafter worn out and drops dead or, if we prefer the euphemism of the language of bureaucracy, s/he "retires." It is not surprising at all that the expected derision in this section of the song is transformed to utter poignancy.

No doubt saving a most fundamental issue for the last, Fela in the fourth part returns to a staple theme of his nearly thirty years of oppositional musical practice: the miseducation of Africans. Much earlier in "Why Black Man Dey Suffer" (1971), he had constructed the origin of the tragedy, as he liked to regard it, in European enslavement of Africans. Rhetorically evoking the image of an Edenic precontact Africa, he sings: "We dey sit down for our land jeje" (We were living in our land peacefully) when some aliens from a far away land invaded and "take our people and spoil all our towns" (stole our people and despoiled our towns). "Na since then trouble start" (That's when our troubles started), he makes clear. Upon European invasion and enslavement came colonization and the forceful imposition of European culture on Africans. One result of the miseducation is the alienation of the African from her or his cultural background:

| | |
|---|---|
| Our riches dem take away to their land | They stole our riches |
| Dey return and give us their colony | They colonized us |
| Dem take our culture away from us | They suppressed our culture |
| Dem give us dem culture we no understand | They imposed on us their culture which we don't understand |
| Black people we no know ourselves | Black people we don't know ourselves |
| We no know our ancestral heritage | We don't know our ancestral heritage |

For Fela, this fundamental absence of self-knowledge lies at the heart of African perambulation in the contemporary world. This is why the informing spirit of the Fela corpus is that of the heroic pedagogue struggling for the reeducation of Africa away from the historical aimlessness imposed on it by Euro-America. Historical revisionism and venomous derision are just a few weapons of that pedagogy in the fourth section of "Perambulator":

| | |
|---|---|
| As him go to school before | If he's [the African] ever been to school |
| Dem go teach am plenty things | They will teach him a lot of things |
| Dem go teach am plenty English | They will teach him plenty of English |
| Dem no go teach am nothing for himself | but nothing about himself |
| Dem go give am certificate | They will give him a certificate |
| to go carry file for office | to be an office clerk |
| Dem go give am certificate | They will give him a certificate |
| to make am certified slave | to make him a certified slave |
| Dem go give am certificate | They will give him a certificate |
| to make am "civil servant" | to make him a "civil servant" |
| Dem go teach am for dem school | They will teach him at school |
| that Mungo Park discovered River Niger | that Mungo Park discovered River Niger |
| I say when Mungo Park him reach R. Niger | I say when Mungo Park reached River Niger |
| na African people | it was Africans |
| na dem show am de way | who showed him the way |
| you see him for dey perambulate | or else he would have been perambulating |
| and for still dey, same, same place | and still be on the same spot today |

*Fela, Lagos, and the Postcolonial State* 105

| | |
|---|---|
| He no discover am | He didn't discover it |
| Na him write am | Yes, he wrote about it |
| He write am for them | But he wrote it for them [his people, Europeans] |
| He no write am for us | He didn't write it for us |
| He no discover | He discovered nothing |

By the mid-1970s, fifteen years after Nigerian independence, the colonial curriculum savaged by Fela above had been all but flushed out of the schools. He went through the system in the 1940s and 1950s, nearly four decades before "Perambulator." If that was the memory he relied on for the composition of the song, then he remembered well.

My generation went through the same curriculum in the 1960s and early 1970s, and decades later, I can still remember passages and illustrations from the biased books. Perhaps there was something in the disjunctive nature of the curriculum in relation to students' experience that seared it permanently into their memories. In middle and high school, we wondered to no end how white people, born and raised in their own faraway land, could have "discovered" and renamed landmarks in Nigeria and elsewhere in Africa when Africans had been living by and using those landmarks and resources "from time immemorial," to quote our favorite expression. "Mungo Park discovered River Niger," "John Speke discovered Lake Victoria in East Africa"—the list is endless. As I was writing this, I remembered the Microsoft Encarta Reference Library 2003 I have on my computer and decided to try it. Here is a sample: "Baker, Sir Samuel White (1821–1893), British traveler and explorer, discoverer of Lake Albert in Africa, born in London, and educated in England and Germany. In 1859 and 1860. . . ."[19] I resisted the sense of déjà vu. If Fela seems to be too passionate, it is no doubt because he found that prejudice is unyielding in many quarters.

As an indication of the significance of the theme of the historical miseducation or, properly speaking, subjection of Africans, Fela concludes the song with it:

| | |
|---|---|
| Oyinbo no teach us | Europeans did not teach us |
| Oyinbo no teach us nothing | Europeans taught us nothing |
| *Chorus:* Na we open dem eye! | It is we who civilized them! |
| Na we open dem eye | It is we who civilized them |
| Na 500 years slavery cause am | Thanks to 500 years of slave labor |
| We teach dem how to do plenty things | We taught them plenty things |
| I say we teach dem plenty things | I say we taught them plenty things |
| No be me talk am | I am not making empty claims |
| Na books dey talk am | These are in authoritative books |
| No be de yeye books you dey read | Not the stupid books that you read |
| for de yeye schools for your town | in those stupid schools in your town |
| Those colonial schools from that London | |
| I'm telling you now, na we open dem eye | I tell you we civilized them |

Fela anchors any possibility of reversing African perambulation on the continent's self-reeducation or self-resubjectification. Only this critical "return to the source"[20] can return it to the path of a self-charted subjectivity. He hoped that the resulting disalienation would put the continent in touch with its "ancestral heritage" and, as a new beginning, return it to the crossroads to *know* and offer some sacrifice to Esu.

## Modality of Critique

If the postcolonial city is an aborted civis, look to the postcolonial state itself, the city resident with the almighty coercive powers. But the state is itself both overdetermined by and a perpetuator of a historical African condition, perambulation, that cannot but produce and reproduce the aborted civis everywhere. Fela's modality of critique, as deducible from the song, is infinitely more stimulating than his offered solution, which is only too obvious. He orchestrates two critical directions at the same time; I call these the *pragmatist* and *foundationalist*.[21] The pragmatist critique affirms the African state/condition as it is and insists that it could be much better if we could bring uncorrupted reason and commitment to bear on the business of government and learn and domesticate what was learned from any source. Fela foregrounds the necessity for managers of people and resources to be of unimpeachable character, the assumption being that the soul of any institution is people of integrity. When Fela lampoons the commissioner for going to London to learn "dustbin carrying" rather than "atomic energy" or the doctors who know nothing about African medicine and "must go to learn how to make research," he is stoking the pragmatist fire. But at the same time, Fela is also deeply invested in what I call the foundationalist critique. Here, he probes deep into the origin of the crisis under consideration and suggests, implicitly or explicitly, that the contemporary African state/condition is so compromised by centuries of unequal relations with Euro-America that only a thoroughgoing decolonization of social processes would do. The problem is at the foundations; in other words, the problem is structural or systemic. Poor management of human and material resources is not the root of the problem; it is only a symptom of the problem. Fela repeatedly intimates this deeper critique in his insistence on African miseducation as the primal scene, with the implication of a systemic overhauling. What would an African education in the contemporary world look like that did not include "capsules" and "tablets" and injections in the "*nyash*"? If Fela did not notice any aporia between the two critical directions, it is only because he was really a pragmatist at heart and needed the historical excursions as catalysts to pragmatist compromise. For our part, we ought to acknowledge the aporia and suggest that given the complexity of the issues at stake, coupled with the famed brashness of the thinker, we can expect no less than his willful, simultaneous orchestration of the two opposed modalities.

# 6　On the Shop Floor: The Social Production of Afrobeat

## Art as Practice

In this age of compact discs, MP3 players, and electronic music files exchanging hands on the Internet, the hegemonic conception of art as an object, a thing, a product, has never had seemingly better support. However, it is very unlikely that anyone would mistakenly apply that impoverished idea of art to Fela's afrobeat. This in itself is part of the theoretical significance of Fela's art; it *compels* us to follow the much more enriching conceptual direction of art as *process,* as practice imbricated in tangled, thoroughly social conditions and relations of production, dissemination, and consumption.[1] I stress "compel" because the conditions of production are more rather than less unhidden in afrobeat, and some of them are so transparent that they have become part of the public perception of the music itself. Technological mass reproduction notwithstanding, afrobeat is no "culinary" music completely finished and coded ready for passive consumption.[2] Unlike most genres, it comes unusually proofed against easy reification. This helps to advance my goal in this chapter, which is to examine some of the varieties and expenses of extrasonic labor that go into the social production of the enthralling sound and the gigantic image of its public face, Fela. With scores of instrumentalists, singers, dancers, and myriad other personnel—graphic artists, photographers, drivers, messengers, attorneys, security aides, and more—Fela ran what was easily the largest musical organization in Africa. Afrobeat is thus far more than the finished music.

## "The Boys"

In close to thirty years, nearly 120 musicians worked at various times for Fela on afrobeat as saxophonists, trumpeters, flugelhornists, guitarists, trombonists, pianists, drummers, conga players, *shekere* and maracas shakers, and stick hitters.[3] For a musical group that was organized around a permanent band rather than hired musicians for recordings and concerts, this is quite a large number. But Fela's band was always large; the horn section alone sometimes featured up to a dozen, and the whole band itself up to thirty, musicians. This is no doubt an indication of the fame and prestige of afrobeat and its power to continuously attract a stream of talent. Indeed, from the 1970s to early 1990s, there was no more original phenomenon on the African popular music scene than afrobeat or a bandleader with greater international reputation. Fela's band in its different incarnations, Africa 70 and Egypt 80, featured musicians not just from Nigeria but also from neighboring African countries and outside the continent. This was so in spite of the fact that though afrobeat remained a popular genre, there were no other bands playing exactly the same music that musicians could go to if they were to fall out with Fela. Very skilled individual instrumentalists could always get jobs with other bands playing other genres, but they would be working with entirely different sound arrangements and approaches to musical production. Since Fela's reputation was very well known, especially his controversial lifestyle, his political views and activities, and his regular encounters with the law and the risks that involved, only those committed enough to withstand all these risks ever worked with Fela. It is thus a sign of the wide acceptance of his vision and musical practice even among musicians that he was able to command so much professional attention.

But there are far less salutary aspects of the large size. For one thing, it hardly makes much economic sense, especially for a commercial outfit that was operating in a context where bootlegging and even official violations of copyright— by government radio and television stations—are endemic. Even in the very best of times, such as Afrika 70 had for most of the 1970s until the army invasion of Kalakuta Republic in 1977, all it meant was that each musician was paid only a little bit more than usual on a regular basis. Fela put his musicians on a salary, and it is indeed a tribute to his openness and perceived fairness in these matters that he was able to maintain a high degree of stability in his personnel for nearly a decade. Fela justified the large band size by referring to, as usual, "African culture." "To play African music, you cannot economize," he argued contentiously,

> The culture of Africa is not based on economy, it is based on naturalness, being natural. And if you try to put money first before the culture, then you will destroy the beauty of what you wanted to represent. I don't have any intention to destroy the beauty of African music for money. I will never do that.[4]

But it must be said that the large size, which makes for position duplications, was undoubtedly part of the calculations of a shrewd bandleader to guard against "untimely defections."[5]

The problematic of a large band was further complicated by the fact that the band itself was only part of a much larger organization of anywhere between fifty and seventy members at any time, most of whom were dependent on the proceeds from the music. When Kalakuta was sacked, Fela said there were "about *eighty* of us"[6] in the Afrika 70 organization. In addition, Fela was not just a musician but also a political activist, and that was not inexpensive. For a while, he bought space in newspapers regularly to broadcast his ideological positions and comment on government activities. In the second half of the 1970s, he bought a press to print *YAP News,* the broadsheet of the activist youth organization he founded, Young African Pioneers. He and the group distributed thousands of pages of, as he himself described it, "anti-government propaganda . . . [d]enouncing those corrupt, unprogressive politicians and military men to the people."[7] All of these activities drained the organization's resources. Even before Fela formally entered electoral politics in late 1978 with the formation of the party Movement of the People (MOP), of which he would be the presidential candidate, his unthinkingly selfish attitude had taken its toll on his band. The band was invited as the featured attraction at the September 1978 Berlin Jazz Festival, for which Fela was paid the hefty sum of $100,000. Most of the money paid for air tickets and hotel accommodations for the seventy members who went on the trip.[8] It was clear to the musicians that in spite of the tidy sum, not only would it be business as usual with Fela but also that he was planning to funnel whatever remained into his presidential bid in the next year's general elections. His own egotistic ambitions would take precedence over the welfare of the musicians. Fela's response to the grumbling among the band members was harsh: he sacked everyone and asked them to reapply for their old positions, but at lower salaries. Walter Benjamin was right, after all: "There is no document of civilization which is not at the same time a document of barbarism."[9]

Some of the musicians had been with Fela since the mid-1960s and had suffered with him—more than him, in fact—the hardships of the 1969–1970 U.S. trip. Of the likes of lead drummer and band director Tony Allen and lead trumpeter Tunde Williams, Fairfax writes: "In thirteen years with Fela's bands these musicians had never been able to achieve what might be called a comfortable living. During this time, their circumstances had often been determined more by political considerations than by professional musical ones."[10] They had been with Africa's most famous band for years but there had been little to show for it in terms of financial well-being. Insulted by Fela's action, almost all of the musicians refused to reapply and left. Here is Tony Allen on Fela's exploitative side:

> I discovered that this guy is a real slave driver. He never paid what he was supposed to pay his musicians. . . . I told Fela when we were in Berlin that I was going to resign when we got back to Nigeria. Fela went into politics. He was telling me that the money we make in Berlin, he was using on politics and he wants to be elected as the president of Nigeria. . . . I told him I am not a politician, I'm a musician. So I left.[11]

Of course, Fela had all the cultural capital on his side on the Nigerian and African musical scene, and he was soon able to successfully reconstitute the band with new and much younger musicians. But Michael Veal's assessment is apropos, nonetheless: "Despite the afrobeat classics to come and the outstanding musicians who would pass through his later groups, Fela was not subsequently able to maintain as stable or talented a group of musicians . . . [as] the original Afrika 70."[12]

Observers have pointed to Fela's usually stern onstage demeanor toward his musicians as an eloquent indication of his exploitative, authoritarian relations with them. This is indeed part of the equation. Except at the Shrine, one is likely to see nothing but a solemn relationship between him and the musicians during performances. Afrobeat is dance music, but the festive atmosphere concert attendants normally expect to radiate from the musicians to the audience was nearly always absent in Fela. He was always obsessive about staging a flawless performance and he never ceased to make an unseemly spectacle of himself in the way he communicated and demanded that from the band. At a perceived untoward sound, he would shoot a withering look at the offending section of the band, stamp his feet, and gesticulate agitatedly, with anger visible all over his face. For someone who made a career of criticizing tyrants, Fela's complete absence of self-consciousness about his style as a conductor is remarkable indeed. But he was not all dictatorial as a bandleader; he was a complex mixture of that *and* a genuine populism. He was without doubt the most accessible of popular bandleaders in Lagos. Either by air or road, he traveled at the same level of luxury, or lack of luxury, with the band. Most significant, he was the only leading popular bandleader in Lagos who lived in the same house with most of the members of the organization rather than in more opulent circumstances.

Fela was certainly selfish, but not in the sense of avariciousness. In fact, part of his fault was that because both by disposition and by ideology he cared little for personal possessions and could make do with far less than befitted his status, he assumed that anyone around him ought to be as self-sacrificing. He—and therefore his musicians too—could have been richer, of course, but then, who would Fela be without an idiosyncrasy or two to damn that possibility? When representatives of Polygram expressed an interest in signing him and raised the issue of song length, Fela not only refused to compromise but also assured them that his songs would actually get longer. "When I have so much to say, I cannot say it in a short time."[13] And that was that. At another time, Motown offered a multimillion-dollar contract for his previous releases, but Fela turned that down too, "on the advice of the spirits."[14] Anyone in the organization could see the openly social causes Fela was financing, including the large household and its unusual composition itself as a symbolic social and political statement. But what was undeniable was that *most* of the gains from those causes—and they were largely psychological—accrued to Fela alone in a substantive sense. Fela never acknowledged this grossly unequal nonmaterial advantage to the extent of making it a factor in the treatment of his musicians. As a rebellious scion of a solid middle-class family, Fela could turn away from material luxury and derive psychological satisfaction from that. But most of his musicians were from humbler backgrounds whose structural location in the social hierarchy had implanted in them an intuitive quest for upward mobility. The relationship between him and them could only look like one of enforced pauperization from their point of view. This is what Michael Veal means when he writes that "[w]hen class background, education, and economic advantage are factored in, it becomes apparent that Fela, despite his rhetoric, ultimately held some of the same disregard that African elites as a class hold for the underprivileged masses upon whose work and suffering their advancement is largely based."[15] The observation below by a Nigerian musician may sound harsh but it is to the point:

You can assess somebody by the people around him. For instance, Sunny Ade's con-gaist has his own personal house and rides a Mercedes Benz car. Onyeka has pro-duced some of the biggest stars in the country like Mike Okri, Chris Hanen, Stella Yamah, Ceceil Omohinmi. But I cannot pinpoint what Fela did for his band boys before he died. Music made Fela what he is, but he gave nothing back to it. Fela has no single investment, not even a recording studio or a demo studio. It is sad. Now that he is gone, his band boys are confused.[16]

But the "band boys," central as they were to the production of afrobeat as mu-sical sound, were by no means the only lubricants in the engine of Fela's mete-oric rise to enduring fame who toiled with only ambiguous recompense. There were the women, too.

## "The Girls"

It is impossible to have even a cursory familiarity with Fela's views on and practices of gender relations and not consider him an incorrigible sexist. That conclusion, however, would be missing some much-needed pathos if its many ironies were ignored. A close examination of Fela's relations with the women publicly associated with his life and career would tempt us to divide them into three hierarchical groups. His mother he held in the highest esteem. Those he had to treat with regard as if he considered them equals—indeed, be-cause they coerced such recognition from him through the force of quiet dig-nity, such as his first wife, Remi, or through defiant self-assertion, such as his African-American friend Sandra Smith Isidore—occupy the middle rung on the ladder. All the other women he harbored as chorus singers, dancers, cashiers, disc jockeys, and so on, and subsequently married, Fela towered over like a monarch.

In spite of the "thousand" cane strokes that Fela liked to say he received from his strict disciplinarian mother in his adolescent years, their closeness later on became legendary.[17] Apart from Fela's immersion in the London jazz scene, one other memorable experience of his student days was the ten-day vacation trip to communist East Germany his mother arranged.[18] She was his constant source of mental stimulation and psychological strength. She lived with him for a few years until her death in 1978, though Fela's household was the oddest and most controversial of all her children's, not to mention of any household in the country. She surprised everyone by following Fela in changing her name from Ransome-Kuti to Anikulapo-Kuti.[19] Fela shunned the popular panegyric mode, but his few songs that could be described as such are either acknowledgments of professional elders, such as "Araba's Delight," or tributes to his mother, such as "Alagbara" and "Iya Mi O Se O," all from the Koola Lobitos years. Of all the Africa 70 and Egypt 80 recordings, the only songs that could be interpretively stretched to be panegyric, aside from positive mentions of certain political fig-ures, are "Unknown Soldier" (1979) and "Coffin for Head of State" (1981), and both are, more properly speaking, memorials for his mother. It is a surprise indeed to hear the ever-boisterous voice of Fela crack and become deeply emotional as he sings about his mother in "Unknown Soldier":

| | |
|---|---|
| FELA: Dem throw my mama | They threw my mama |
| CHORUS: "Unknown Soldier" | |
| 78 year-old mama | |
| Political mama | |
| Ideological mama | |
| Influential mama | |
| Dem throw my mama | They threw my mama |
| Out of from window | Out of the window |
| Dem kill my mama | They killed my mama |
| . . . . | |
| I get some information for you | |
| That my mama wey you kill | That my mother you killed |
| She fought for universal adult suffrage | |
| That my mama wey you kill | That my mother you killed |
| Na the only mother of this country | She is the only mother of this country |

It is quite significant that the qualities Fela admired the most in his mother and emphasized in the song all revolve around her dedication to public service. This is the same Fela who had been preaching the subordination of women since the early 1970s in songs such as "Lady" (1972) and "Mattress" (1975), not to mention his many provocative public comments.

A much less public relationship existed between Fela and Remilekun (Remi) Anikulapo-Kuti, his first wife and mother of four of Fela's children.[20] But that is only because of the self-assured quiet dignity of Remi. Frequently people forget, in the sensational context of the stream of young women in Fela's household and his eventual marriage to twenty-seven of them, that Fela was already legally married and sworn to monogamy. Had Remi had a different temperament, she would have divorced Fela early in the marriage. In a sense, precisely because she was so much out of view and unheard from, she fits the stereotypical image of the oppressed housewife burdened by housework and caring for children and condemned to silence by the almighty husband. Nothing could be farther from the truth. Fiercely independent, she lived separately from Fela and the hustle and bustle of Kalakuta Republic for years. Carlos Moore writes that when she finally joined the residence, she "cultivate[d] an Olympian detachment borne out by her stately demeanour."[21] When Moore interviewed her in the early 1980s, about fourteen of Fela's wives were still in the household.

To those who think they know what women want in a marriage, Remi would make a good case study. The large communal living constituted an invasion of her monogamous marriage, but Remi took a larger view that few monogamous African families would fail to recognize: the number of persons in the household may be larger now, but people have always dropped in and lived with them, she said. On Fela's score-plus girlfriends—the amazing issue to every outsider—Remi answered dismissively, "'[H]e's always had them. He made me understand before I married him that he would always have them. I could take it or leave it."[22] She was worried more about what was fair and appropriate in the circumstances. When she was pressed about whether she wished the situation were otherwise or was just accommodating it, she replied,

> I don't think I am accommodating because he really didn't bother me. The only thing that bothered me was if any woman should come and try to act big over me. I wouldn't take that. It really didn't bother me because he had, you know, girlfriends outside. He never brought any woman to my house. And he wouldn't have done it anyway; whereas his friends, they took their women in whether the wife was in or not. He always respected me.[23]

Although Remi was the only wife who could confront Fela about his actions, we cannot discount her unwillingness to publicly criticize her husband. Even so, we must take seriously the revealing way she redirected her expectations and emotional investments. She insisted again that what would make her "unsatisfied" in her life with Fela was "[i]f I thought he was trying to treat someone better than me, which has happened on occasions."[24] She ignored the fact of the fundamental illegitimacy of Fela's other girls from the point of view of her monogamous marriage with him and instead focused on whether or not she was accorded the proper recognition—by Fela as well as by the other wives—as the most senior wife in the "new," questionable dispensation.

Remi cut the figure of the mature and infinitely resilient senior wife with a scrupulous sense of fairness about what should happen in her polygamous household. When Moore observed that "there is a paternal attitude that Fela has towards his other wives that he doesn't have towards you," Remi bent over backward to explain the observation away. "I think we are all treated individually," she insisted. "I don't think we're classed, like this is Remi, she is up and they are down or anything like that. And if I talk to him differently, it's because I'm more or less his same age and I've lived with him longer, so I know him more."[25] Fela did not consult her before the mass wedding, but she was sure that was because Fela was "afraid" of her because of his uncertainty of her response. This interpretation makes sense given the respectful space each gave the other, but it could also mean that Fela cared little for her opinions on the matter since he had already decided what he was going to do. What kept her with the man through two decades of turbulent living was his honesty and his obvious commitment to the common people. Repeatedly, she supplied public answers to private questions. What was negative in Fela and made her angry the most was his unthinking "generosity" to everyone, and one of the major disagreements with Fela she recalled was over the schooling of their children.[26] When she was asked about Fela's "authoritarianism," she responded only with conformist clichés: "That's how I think a husband should be. [Laughter.] I don't believe in women's lib at all. I mean I don't believe a man should tell me I'm lower than him, but I don't believe in me going to drive a bus. That's left to a man, you know. Just that type of thing. These women in Europe, I don't agree with at all."[27]

Perhaps Remi imagined herself in a polygynous household and adjusted on that account. Polygyny, after all, is a common practice in Nigeria, supported by cultural traditions as well as by the Islamic religion to which many belong. If this is indeed how she conceived her situation—and it appears that this is the case, from her insistence that she was not bothered by the girlfriends and wives as long as she was recognized as the first wife in the house—then that would explain her compromising silence on her own monogamous marriage with Fela and her search instead for some of the perquisites of being a senior wife in a polygynous family. This mindset would have helped her made her peace with the situation, but it is ultimately self-deception to imagine that polygyny alone adequately explains the relations between Fela and the women. If we believed that, we would have been hoodwinked by Fela as victims of his many justifications of his crass promiscuity under the banner of indigenous cultural traditions.

Fela did not say much publicly about his relationship with Remi. Apart from his mother, the only other woman Fela spoke about at any length is Sandra Smith Isidore, his friend and mentor in the United States. "Nothing about my life is complete without her,"[28] Fela once said of Sandra, a meaningful acknowledgment given Fela's own confession that he hated to give women any credit. When he said he had finally discovered his first real African tune and Sandra insisted he name it "My Lady Frustration" in her honor to mark the frustrations he had caused her, Fela balked, but he ultimately gave in:

> Oh, this woman, she helped me in America-o. She has fed me for five months. There are telephone bills I've run up; they've even cut one telephone line of their house. . . . I've almost made her family bankrupt. . . . I've spoiled their cars. . . . This was what was going on in my head, you know. So I said to myself, if I'm gonna sing about any one woman, I would sing about this one. At least to clear my conscience. That's how low I was at that time, man. I hated to give women any fucking credit, man. Everybody was singing about women. How could I sing about a woman in my tune? I didn't want to start singing about women.[29]

Fela's boasts at the end of the quote notwithstanding, it is clear that Sandra was not a woman he could lord it over. A feisty woman, she, unlike Remi, tolerated none of Fela's habitual philandering in their few months together in the United States. Her assertiveness put Fela in the uncomfortable situation of having to carefully plan to cover his tracks. Of course, she was formed by a different context in which monogamy, even in premarital relationships, was hegemonic and is subverted, even if routinely, only under the cover of darkness.[30] Both out of her love for Fela and as part of the return-to-roots consciousness of Africa among African Americans at the time, she arrived in Nigeria in 1970, hoping that the relationship would be permanent, but she left six months later in 1971. Her problems with immigration authorities paled in comparison with her experience in a house full of Fela's girlfriends: "Although like any other woman, not understanding African women, not understanding African culture, I had my jealousies. They were jealous of me and I was jealous of them, so we were jealous of each other. It was just natural. Everybody was jealous. But since everybody felt it was because of me, I caught more hell than anybody."[31] In spite of the disappointment of it all, she was the only one among the wives and girls who judged that she had a more or less equitable relationship with Fela. "He showed me something and, I guess, in turn I showed him something," she said reflectively.[32]

If Sandra supplied the political and intellectual catalyst for the invention of afrobeat, Remi supplied the quiet strength and stability on the home front while the hero managed the enterprise, and Funmilayo supplied the emotional, even metaphysical, pillar of it all. But the immediate propulsive force that sent afrobeat to the forefront—not just as a music, but as a phenomenon—was "the girls": the nearly forty young women who at various times featured in Fela's life and organization as chorus singers, dancers, wives, girlfriends, cashiers, disc jockeys, and many mixtures of all of these. More than the music itself, and certainly more than any other factor, it was these young women—the fact of so many of them living with one man with impunity, their flamboyant lifestyle, their skimpy dresses, their carefree smoking in public, their heavy makeup, and the general seductive ambience they evoked—who made Fela's and afrobeat's reputation in Nigeria spread—well, as Nigerians would say—like bush fire in the harmattan. Fela's girls triggered in men young and old lascivious and voyeuristic imaginations; in young girls, fanciful dreams—"misguided!" parents quickly sternly warned—of limitless freedom and pleasure in the city; and in parents of girls everywhere, dismay at an apparent lecher and enchanter on the loose. It was not as if expressions of sexuality were generally repressed, at least in Fela's immediate region of southwest Nigeria; erotic songs and dances could be found everywhere. But the seemingly programmatic flaunting of a sexualized image by Fela and the women—and consistently, as if they aimed to institute and normalize a regime of the erotic—was of a different order entirely. There is little doubt that it was this highly titillating, provocative aspect of Fela's fame that attracted police attention to him so early; this admission would not be found in any police log at Alagbon Close or anywhere, but we can surmise with a fair degree of accuracy that wild fantasies by the police about the interactions in Fela's house were in large part responsible for their unusual determination to actually do their duty by taking complaining fathers—who were otherwise ignored in other cases—very seriously. The presence of the women transformed afrobeat from just another musical genre to a whole new phenomenon. They constituted the core of Fela's controversial reputation from early on, and the practical effect was a furtherance of his fame and his music: whichever side you were on, you simply could not ignore Fela.

By default, the women functioned as a most effective advertisement for Fela and afrobeat. The dancers among them were famous for their erotic routines such as the "opening up," as Shrine fans imagine it, in which a dancer spins on one leg while raising the other high and wiggling her buttocks, or the "buttocks special," in which the dancer stands still while moving only her buttocks in many creative patterns to the beat, not unlike the Mapouka dance from Côte d'Ivoire that many francophone West African governments are currently pursuing with all sorts of legal prohibitions.[33] If the dancers served as dependable

Relaxation time with some wives.
Courtesy of Femi Osunla.

crowd-pleasers, the chorus and back-up singers introduced a no less distinctive sonic dimension to afrobeat. Their voices on records, shrill, businesslike, and penetrating, often set up a meaningful dramatic counterpoint to Fela's gruff bellows, playful yaks, and witty scat singing, all of which made for an enriched musical experience. We only need to listen to such tracks such as "Ariya" (1970) or "Shenshema" (1970), which were recorded with a male chorus before Fela began using the women, and "Shakara" (1972) or "Lady" (1972) to recognize the profound and inestimable impact of the introduction of the female chorus on the soundscape of afrobeat.

Most of the women joined Fela when they were in their teenage years. Carlos Moore profiled the remaining fourteen of the twenty-seven wives in 1982.[34] Some had finished high school and many had not. Most had not run away from home, as popular lore would have it, but simply left after their parents refused to give them permission to leave. A few actually said their parents agreed with their decision. Most sought out Fela on their own after hearing his music or hearing about him and his open household or after visiting the Shrine and deciding to be part of the sort of show-business life they had seen. Fela had others come to him. A few had no intention of being Fela's girlfriends; they just wanted to be informal employees in the organization. And although none said she came to Fela because of sex or marriage, all of them were happy to have sexual relations with him, even more so when the opportunity to formally marry him arose. Most were from polygynous families. From his interviews with them, Moore summarizes their hopes in casting their lot with Fela:

A recurring theme is that many of the queens, as young girls—often naïve, adventurous in spirit and suffocated by their family homes—went to Fela's as the place where they could fulfill their adolescent dreams. His door, they knew, was always open, for Fela was known never to turn anyone away from his house. To live at Fela's meant being free, as opposed to being held in strict check by their families. Smoking, drinking, fame, traveling, earning money, being with the man of their dreams. . . . Essentially, they found security in one man who was to become their husband, father, big brother, adviser and employer.[35]

Whatever their specific dreams and expectations were, all said they came and remained with Fela, in spite of the incessant police harassment and the Kalakuta tragedy, primarily because of Fela's ideas, his personality, and his obvious struggle for a better life for the people. Alake, whose father, a judge, has five wives and fourteen children, said it best, in language that clearly betrays evidence of Fela's ideological teachings:

My father is very strict. Then in Nigeria they didn't like colonial children going to Fela's; they think that Fela corrupts the youth and all sorts of things. People going there smoking hemp. In Fela's house they rape girls, all sorts of untrue rumours, untrue things. . . . All my friends they just got married. I don't move as these children, my brothers, their friends, they move around in the bourgeoisie, but me I love all the people because I don't like the way they (the bourgeois) treat the workers, the common people. I don't like it. Like in my family, the driver, the servants, they treat them badly. Even the way my stepmother treats our house, I don't like it . . . so I told my father that unless he explains why he doesn't like Fela—'cause I like him—and if he doesn't want me to stay in his house I can choose where I'll stay.[36]

Whether out of indoctrination or personal conviction or both, the consistency with which the women cited Fela's ideas as their core attraction—especially the class partisanship and Africa-centered cultural nationalism—has an aura of conviction in itself.

Although none of the women ever said she expected a life of luxury with Fela, life at the Kalakuta was far from being a bed of roses for them. The conditions were cramped, for instance, so that "[m]attresses are placed wherever there is space."[37] All the women worked, whether in the household or in the production of afrobeat in the Shrine. In addition to salaries that varied by job and seniority, they also received special allowances for concert tours and recording sessions. Household expenses came from a separate budget and were managed by anyone of Fela's choosing each month. To keep order, the women were subject to an established system of punishments and rewards; Fela fined offenders and occasionally slapped them, which all the women said they detested, or denied them sex time with him—being "edited" out of the schedule, they called this. Rewards for excellent job performance included gifts and more time with the husband.[38]

More than the human-relations challenge of negotiating the intricacies of Fela's household with over twenty fellow girlfriends, Fela's children, Fela's mother, musicians, friends, passers-by, and hangers-on, the biggest problem of the women for several years was the state security forces. They invaded the residence several times, arrested some of the women, and locked them up in a juvenile welfare home for weeks. There were also charges of abduction filed against Fela; some of the girls hid whenever an angry father came with agents of the law. The culmination of brushes with the law was the horrific incident of the sacking of the Kalakuta in 1977 by a battalion of soldiers. Virtually all of the women were wounded in the attack—broken heads, arms, legs, and noses. Some were raped, many were sexually assaulted with bottles and bayonets, and many were jailed for five days in the infamous maximum-security Kirikiri Prison instead of being rushed to the hospital emergency room. It is not a metaphor to say that afrobeat is music written in blood.

Given the prominence of women in Fela's life and art and their sacrifice alongside his in the production of afrobeat, Fela's unreconstructed crude, domineering, and masculinist views about women, gender, marriage, and sexuality is surprising indeed. The major source of Fela's views on these subjects is his racialist cultural nationalism in which everything he likes and does is "African" and "natural" while all the things he detests or simply does not understand are "foreign" and "unnatural." Around this fundamentalist self-centeredness he gathered thick chaff composed of inane positivisms, insipid reasonings, atavistic deductions, and general intellectual shallowness, with a few grains of possibly recoverable insights struggling into view now and then.

"What I think about women in general is a subject which calls for a colloquium," Fela once pronounced magisterially. He continued: "Women? Mmmmmm! You see, before I used to be afraid of them. That's how it started. After that, fear changed into understanding."[39] Given the honest, unvarnished vulgarity of his positions, and given his pop-star status, it is important that we take what appears to be a founding psychological explanation for his views seriously. Fela did not say when or how the fear started and he did not exclude any specific woman from the category "women." Remi said that she believed that Fela was "a little bit afraid of me."[40] This could be part of it, but the main evidence comes from Fela's relationship with his mother, which, as Fela himself described it, was governed by plenty of fear and some love in a sort of unequal dialectic.[41] But he had the same kind of relationship with his father. He would later attribute his parents' unusually stern "spare the rod and spoil the child" philosophy to their "English colonized mentality."[42] This understanding of his mother's strictness is not sexed or gendered. His father died when he was seventeen, and his mother did not beat him anymore after that. So his mother did not treat him more harshly or longer than his father. In any case, the "understanding" that Fela said the fear of women produced in him was momentous: "What do I understand about women? First, that they like to be slept with. They like you to make them do things for you."[43] Fearing women seems a great distance from wanting to sleep with and control them because those are the things you think they want. At the very least, it sounds illogical. However, we know from psycho-analysis that there is never a one-to-one correspondence between psychic processes and reality. In fact, there is an underlying intimate relationship between Fela's fear of women and his reading of women's desires. If women are a source of fear for him, then what better way to get rid of that fear than to pacify and dominate the source? For Fela, to "sleep with" women, to "make them do things" for him, were ways of quenching that deep-seated fear. And the psychological bonus for him was that all these acts supposedly required of him had nothing to do with him as an ethical being; no, no, it was the women who wanted to be slept with and ordered about. In his own mind, he was just stupid to have ever been afraid of women when all women were silently telling him that they wanted to sleep with him and be made to do things for him, for men. After he had the "understanding," everything fell into place. Fela's capacity for self-delusion was immense.

Fela argued vociferously about the idea of equality between men and women, armed with no more than his own personal prejudice and the power of conviction of the existing unequal arrangement: "No! Never! Impossible! Can never be! It seems the man must dominate. I don't want to say so, but it seems so." According to Fela, that was why men are stronger physically. Women are fragile, hence "[p]roducing babies is woman's job. It's more tender. The more vigorous job is man's. The tenderer one is woman's."[44] The radical who could imagine and campaign at great personal risk for social equality between the lowly and the high found it difficult to envision another system in which men and women would be equal. Yet we cannot rush to conclude on a philosophical note that interest is of necessity the handmaiden of vision. Fela went beyond and against his class origins and interests, but he remained happily and arrogantly mired in the muck of his gender interests. "It's part of the natural order for women to be submissive to man," he insisted, because, well, it is part of nature:

> Do I see man as being naturally superior to women? Naturally. Why? Well, I wouldn't say superior. I'd say *dominant*. Yes, dominant. Dominant is the word I want, not superior. Dominant means that there must be a master. Men are the masters, not women. When you say the "master of the house," you mean the head of the household: the father, not the woman, man. That's life, man. Natural life. Life is based on nature. The nature we don't see now. You can't ask me "Which nature?" 'cause you can't see nature. . . . What I am saying is that there is a natural order which says that man must be dominant. Yeah! The advantage is that one has more strength, can carry heavy loads. He can even carry the woman when she is tired.[45]

Fela would never have accepted this proposition, but he obviously must have watched one too many Hollywood romances in which the swooning petite bride is swept off her feet, literally, by her bare-chested hunky groom. But watching too many of those movies is not the problem; passing them off for "nature" certainly is.

Class liberation, an agenda he devoted all his creative efforts to advancing, is not against nature, but "women's lib" is. It is "against the natural order of the world." And, of course, it is un-African: "It comes from European religions. Their religions didn't teach them properly. They teach that man and woman are equal in the house, for better and for worse. No, man, that's bullshit! . . . Nobody can force a woman to stay with a man she don't want. Nobody can force a man to stay with a woman he don't want."[46] I hold no defense for "for better and for worse"—a historically culturally specific form of matrimony sponsored by Christian monotheistic absolutism—but this is vintage Fela in the use of polemics to cover astonishing ignorance and gross pedestrianism. Sometimes Fela abridged and then simplified ideas about human evolution, sociobiology, and sexuality picked up in journals or books and used them to serve urgent matters at hand such as, for instance, a defense of his having many wives. Monogamy is bad because it is "imposed by religion" and "against the natural order." On the other hand, "[P]olygamy is fantastic! 'Cause men just have to go for other women. Why? You explain it! Nobody can explain it. It's just natural phenomenon. But it's been proven that a woman can stay with one man if she likes him enough. A man with many wives is natural. A woman with many men is not. Yeah. The woman can be satisfied with one man. Besides, women can stay without sex. They can do it but men can't. Why? Go ask nature, man. Different sexual structures, that's all."[47] As to how he was able to cope with so many women, he advised that it was "not difficult at all. It's difficult if you don't think of them or deal with them as *women*." That did not include beating them, though "sometimes it is necessary to give [them] some *paf-paf-paf-paf-paf-paf*. . . . I slap 'em. Yeah." And that is only because that is what women want and will show gratitude to the husband for it all: "They need you to show authority, man. See what I mean? Then they'll say to themselves: 'Ah-aaaaaaaah! This na good husband-o! He don't care fo' no bullshit.' "[48] Fela's megalomania was simply bottomless.

It is important, however, not to cast the women as absolute victims of an egocentric musical genius. That would be a condescending relegation of the women's own desires and actions. Indeed, we have to steer clear of two opposite extremes: one that sees them either as victims of a "psychology of servitude"[49] that chains them to men or as exercising absolute choice in who they want to be with. Human beings do act against their own "objective" interests, but "objective" interests—the interests of one's particular location within established social relations—alone do not constitute the totality of the human person, nor are they exclusive generators of human actions and affinities. The "subjective" dimensions of dreams and desires are sometimes much more powerful as catalysts of social action. The women made their choice to cast their lot with Fela within the conditions in which they found themselves, and some tried it and left. Agency is produced by, and can only be exercised within, the structure of constraints and possibilities in which people live. Human beings make their own history, but not in the circumstances of their own choosing. Hence when the women said repeatedly that they would rather be with Fela than elsewhere, we must accept that and then acknowledge that we know that given different circumstances, they might have chosen differently. This clarification allows us to specify, without sounding crude, some of what the women actually gained in the relationship, apart from fame, travel, and so on. By an ironic logic of the women's patriarchal context, their mass wedding to Fela—the ambiguity of it all notwithstanding—actually rehabilitated their image, albeit grudgingly, in the eyes of many people who had considered them lost wayward children who were really no more than prostitutes. In a society that still believes a woman is incomplete until she is married, that even professional women with a string of academic degrees had better quickly add "Mrs." for proper recognition, even a questionable marriage becomes better than none. The women became Fela's "wives," not "girls"; he called them "queens." Those who used to sneer at them were now forced to reluctantly accord them the regard due to "wives." And given the great horror the women went through during the Kalakuta raid by the government, Fela's reason for marrying them touched even the most cynical; it is probably the most moving thing he said about them in public record:

> I was with my group travelling by road back to Nigeria [from Ghana]. I'd be looking at the fucking beautiful country and thinking how beautiful Africa is, man. My girls were tired. Most of them slept through that trip. Now and then I'd look at them sleeping. And I'd think: 'These girls have suffered plenty-plenty for me-o! For years. Some for eight years! Fearless women, these my girls. Good women, man!' And I said to myself: Fela, these na good women-o!' . . . So I married them.[50]

Carlos Moore noticed the dramatic effect of the marriage on the women themselves when he interviewed them: "Marriage has undoubtedly brought an even greater sense of security to the lives of the queens. Earlier bickering and rivalry has since slackened. There is a new willingness to cooperate."[51] All of these are no more than compromises under fundamental inequality, but insofar as they give the subject breathing space without obvious compulsion, no self-critical ideology in quest of egalitarian gender relations can afford to ignore or demean them.

It is may be tempting to invoke polygyny to explain away Fela's accumulation of girlfriends and wives. Indeed, this is an important part of the explanation. After all, it provides a ready and convincing framework because it is a common practice in Nigeria among men of all classes.[52] But polygyny alone does not adequately explain the Fela example. Apart from minor procedural matters such as the mode of acquisition of the women and the unusual mass wedding, Fela never cared about or committed to marriage, whether monogamy or polygamy. What he really cared about needed neither form for satisfaction, though polygamy serves better as a socially acceptable cover for it: sex. Fela himself made the point very clearly:

> What attracted me to each of them? *Sex!* I thought they were sexy and fuckable. That's what attracts me to a woman first. Some came to my house on their own.

Others, I had come. Why? 'Cause I wanted to fuck them. That was all. I wanted a house where I could be fucking and I had it. It *grew* into something else after though. Something special. But it just started with *sex*. The desire to fuck. Man, the one most important thing in the human being is that life-giving and pleasurable sensation: sexual orgasm. And that's what's being condemned the most. Yeah. Somebody was asking me, trying to put down my ideas, if I thought sex was politics. "No, I don't," I said. "*Sex is life.*" That's what I believe. Me, I fuck as often and as long as I can-o! Now, it's not even a matter of choice. When I married *twenty-seven* women I knew what I was doing-o![53]

Fela did not need any marriage to "fuck" as much and as many women as he wanted. In fact, it would appear that the practical effect of his marriages underwrote and socially legitimized his brazen promiscuousness. In any case, he disavowed marriage completely in the late 1980s. "I condemn the institution of marriage," he proclaimed, "I just don't agree to possess a woman. I just don't want to say: 'This woman is mine, so she shouldn't go out with other men.'"[54] This was after his release from jail on a dubious charge of foreign currency trafficking. Given the difficulties of living in such an unwieldy household without the one person who had a key to its order, some of the wives had left; the fact that only two of the wives had had a child for Fela made the decision easier for those who wanted to leave. Fela affirmed their right to leave and offered divorce to free them from any obligation. As to the rumors he heard while in jail about the infidelity of his wives, he blamed neither the women nor himself but the institution of marriage that expects fidelity between the wife and husband at all costs. He again reiterated his disavowal of marriage:

> After I got married [to Remi] and we separated, I thought I was free from marriage, and I was enjoying myself. I went to marry twenty-seven women again. . . . For me to have called it marriage at that time was very wrong. . . . When I married them, they became possessive. They never wanted me to meet any other women. . . . In prison I decided not to marry again. I will have an association with women but not marriage.[55]

First a monogamist, then a polygamist, and now a misogamist: only protean Fela could have swung so publicly and so wildly in less than thirty years. The example of Fela is better understood not within polygamy but within the context of the gendered, modern, glitzy show business culture in which money, fame, women, sex, and a gigantic ego are the primary currencies of exchange.

Only when we disarticulate the seamlessness of the polygyny explanation in this way do the complexities of Fela's relations with the women begin to come fully into view. There is no law against promiscuity, but it would not be difficult to tally how much in money Fela's habit would have cost him with prostitutes on the street. Perhaps we could say it did cost him dearly in the end, given his AIDS-related death, but death as such does not necessarily disable the dominant-subordinate poles in a structured inequality; death only evacuates either pole for other sets of occupants. More important, what consolation is that death to the eight or so queens who remained with him to the end and whose futures become most uncertain with the king's death? Fela's mother, the nation's foremost feminist nationalist, stayed or visited often with Fela and all the women in the household. She never said much publicly about her son and his many women, but perhaps she did not need to. Her actions, in the eyes of the public, spoke louder in explicit affirmation of what was going on.

## "The Artist"

Perhaps in another life Fela would have been a visual artist, for inscribed in afrobeat is such a wealth of visual imagery that it demands of listeners a nimble visual imagination. Fela's acute sense of the dramatic was the source of much of the visuality of his music. He also lavishly drew from his Yoruba cultural tradition, with its very expressive sculpture, theatre, music, clothing, and so on, and its language. For instance, without a listener's ability to imagine and visually complete such tracks as "Let's Start" (to do what we have come into the room to do), its humorous and lewd suggestiveness would be missed. Part of the visual stimulation that "Lady" provides is its opposition of the "lady dance" to the African woman "fire dance," which the music, because it is music and not a visual art, cannot *show* but only lyrically state while demanding that we visualize the two kinds of dances to get the point. In "Shakara," the really sharp edge of Fela's satirical mimicry of the male braggart and the female pretender would be lost were one unable to visualize the whole range of body motions accompanying their speeches. When the braggart says "*Emi ke, ma kan na e pa!*" (Me, no-nonsense me, I will just pound you to death!) or when the pretender says with exaggerated snobbery "Me, no touch me-o" (Me, don't touch me, dearie), the real substance is not so much in what we *hear* but in what must *visualize*. Others elsewhere in the world say "traffic jam" or "traffic hold-up," which are clearly visually resonant in themselves, but Lagosians would say, as popularized by Fela, "Go Slow," which is much more visually imaginative than the alternatives, since in most cases what happens is actually neither a "jam" nor a "hold-up"—both implying complete standstill—for any length of time, but a crawl, a slow going or going slow. Fela had an uncanny ability to draw broad graphic strokes musically. In "Alagbon Close," he describes the tyrannical rudderlessness of the nation's premier police department this way: "Alagbon dey roll like one yeye ball wey one yeye wind dey blow from one yeye corner, ha ha ha!" (See Alagbon roll like a useless ball blown around by some aimless wind from some rubbishy corner). A decade later, he would deploy the same image of rudderlessness in his mockery of the postcolonial African state as a "perambulator" state. In both instances, the power of the rebuke lies in the unnerving visuality of aimless, directionless drift it evokes in a predominantly Yoruba cultural context, where such a walk is stereotyped as a visual marker of insanity. These are examples from afrobeat's lyrical discourse, but the visuality I am talking about is not found in that alone. Even in afrobeat's instrumental sound, there is no better way to conceive of the elaborate horn section, with its theatrical entrances, exits, underlinings, and extended solos, than as *graphic*. Fela's music is one that intensely calls attention to the relationship between the ears and eyes, between hearing and seeing.

We know there are usually all sorts of interests at work—from that of the hawkish financier or producer to that of the starry-eyed artist searching for money and fame—when a musical recording is publicized and marketed; it is therefore important not to impute special significance to what may actually be no more than marketing ploys. It is not that "marketing ploys" do not deserve serious attention; it is just that they must be recognized as such and not mistaken for something else. This cautionary note acknowledged, I would like to suggest that the graphic artists and designers of Fela's album covers over the years, who clearly responded to Fela's express wishes but also, and perhaps this is more significant, to the music itself, produced a body of work that played a significant role in shaping public perceptions and consciousness of afrobeat.

The design and cover art of Fela's albums dramatically changed over the years, and those changes closely mirror the musician's shifting ideological orientation. Two overlapping though distinct phases can be identified: the first phase, which lasted from 1970 to 1975; and the second, which began in 1974 but appeared more consistently from 1976. The two phases are marked by a dramatic contrast in both style and ideology; the style invented in the second phase lasted for the rest of the musician's career, though with a marked ideological change along the way.

With a new music full of attitude and a lifestyle that openly flouted established social norms Fela created a niche for himself as Nigeria's number-one and most popular maverick in the first half of the 1970s. The designs of the album covers during this phase follow the conventional practice in the recording industry. Functionally, they aspire to no higher purpose than promoting the egotistic bandleader and selling the music; conceptually, however, they visually—inadvertently, I suspect—embody an unmistakable theatricality that would become the enduring core of afrobeat sound whatever ideological shift Fela might make along the way. The background colors are usually tidy and contrast dramatically with the images they bear. The white background of the front cover of *Fela's London Scene* (1972)[56] bears the enlarged black-and-white picture of Fela's head, face animated and mouth open as if in midspeech. *Roforofo Fight* of the same year bears the exact opposite design: Fela's upper body appears in a white shirt against a pitch-dark background with lettering in red, yellow, and green. *Open and Close* (1971),[57] one of his more popular releases of the time, sports a solid rectangular block in which each of the four sides forms the base of a triangle, the apexes of which point inward to meet others at the center; opposite triangles are colored solid red and yellow. Upon this background are pasted cut-out pictures of scantily dressed young women demonstrating what the album presents as a new dance style called "open and close." The back cover, in addition to the formal list of tracks and Africa 70 personnel, has a picture of Fela in action at a performance, and this noteworthy dedication by him: "Dedicated to two important people: 1. My mother, Mrs. Funmilayo Ransome-Kuti. 2. His Excellency, Col. I. K. Acheampong, Ghana Head of State, the first head of state I ever entertained. It was beautiful." Fela was not yet a threat to political authorities; while his music differed markedly from that routinely patronized by those in power—highlife in Ghana, for instance—he was obviously not yet ideologically opposed to "entertaining" and "dedicating" his creative production to them. In light of Fela's later trajectory, he no doubt considered the dedication to Acheampong an embarrassment. Years later, the government of Acheampong would deport Fela from Ghana for his political art and general outspokenness.

By far the most notorious—which in this case means the same thing as the most famous—of the album covers of the early period is *Shakara* (1972), designed by the group itself, Africa 70 Organisation. Three groups of smiling, bare-breasted young women, some holding their breasts as if in offering or at least as if to self-consciously call attention to them, are arranged to draw a map of Africa and the numbers seven and zero, to make "Africa 70." Fela, himself in his signature underwear only, reclines in the middle of number zero, grinning naughtily. Apart from "Shakara," the only other track on the album is "Lady." Neither of them is about sex or sexuality; they are both about gender. The flaunting of breasts and skins here, and indeed as in *Noise for Vendor Mouth* with the pictures of four topless women, is gratuitous sensationalism, the kind that is execrable even within a context in which sensationalism comes a dozen a penny.

The same criticism of gratuitousness cannot be made of *Na Poi* (1972 but released 1975 and in a different version in 1976), which is clearly about sexual intercourse and features on the covers photographs of naked torsos of a woman and a man in sensual embrace. Fela may have been able to push the envelope a little further (into toplessness) in *Shakara* because of the absence or vagueness of rules about album covers, but overall, such sensationalism—the use of women, sex, voyeurism, and titillation—was (and remains) standard industry practice, especially in the larger Euro-American recording world of which Nigeria was (and remains) a mere appendage. The late 1960s and 1970s also happened to be the era of a widespread explosion of erotic album covers in Europe and America. Jimi Hendrix's *Electric Ladyland*, released in 1968, features a group of seated naked women on the cover.

Striking changes in the cover design and art of Fela's albums began to appear in 1974, with *Alagbon Close*. The neat, orderly arrangement, which calls attention to itself but never challenges the visual skills of the viewer, gave way to an extremely busy tapestry that commands attention to its details. The images, which before had been mostly photographs, were now more likely to be a drawing, a painting, or a collage. Between 1974 and 1976, for every photographic cover such as *Excuse O, He Miss Road, Noise for Vendor Mouth, Expensive Shit, Unnecessary Begging,* and *Everything Scatter,* there was a hand-illustrated one, and it was usually the more visually memorable and the one that quickly became a collector's item: *Alagbon Close, Yellow Fever, Confusion, Monkey Banana,* and *Kalakuta Show.* The conventional iconic realism of photography was becoming too restrictive and therefore inadequate to express whatever it was that Fela now wanted to convey as a visual preamble to encountering the evolving sound of afrobeat. We could see this most movingly in the cover photograph of *He Miss Road,* by AfroClick. A band of musicians foolishly expresses surprise as they arrive at a performance venue that turns out to be a "deaf and dumb settlement"; some of the residents on the doorway mock the stupid musicians. Although the actors and actresses in the picture tried to do all they could—in their gestures and facial expressions—to convey the biting irony of the situation, it is clear to the critical eye that a photograph cannot adequately capture the exaggerated slapstick incongruity that Fela appears to be aiming for.

Fela always aimed for the theatrical in the choice of the photographic images for the covers, but those appear staid in comparison to the infinitely more dynamic and animated paintings and drawings in the newly emerging trend. The latter is characterized by a distinctive graphic opulence, one that a cover often appears inadequate to contain as parts of images, in the apparent unstoppable sprawl of the tableau, disappear abruptly out of view at the edges. Even cover art that seems to be fairly straightforward is more than it appears to be. Take, for instance, the famous *Yellow Fever* cover art by Lemi Ghariokwu, with its mere three images of a busty topless woman from the breasts up, a side profile of probably the same woman from upper thigh to shoulders to show her bare ample buttocks, and a small tube of "skin bleacher" cream at the upper left corner. The images are striking enough, but numberless little visual details serve as both their background and adornment and therefore constitute them in a sense: the splotches on the breasts, chest, face and buttocks and even on some block letters; the differential coloration of the splotches in which the upper parts of the body are lighter than the lower ("Fanta face, Coca-Cola legs" was the popular verbal insult at the time to those who bleached their skins); the multicolored lettering, neck chain, and waist beads; and the seemingly perfect fall background of blue sky barely visible in the interstices of a network of color patches of yellow, brown, and fading green. The emerging brand of cover art, in short, offers not only an express visual excess but also much more complexity.

A new ideological orientation emerged along with the stylistic shift. The primary goals of the earlier covers were commercial advancement and the glorification of the purposeless eccentricities of the bandleader, Fela. He was a social rebel but one without an apparent principle; his critique of reigning norms was not only merely implicit but also often so far off course as to be counterproductive —his obsessive flaunting of sexuality is a case in point. In the second phase, however, the new covers—whether photographs or illustrations—began to formulate a different image of Fela as a socially conscious musician. There is, for instance, a more than subtle ideological difference between the covers of *Shakara* with the bare-breasted women and Fela, and that of *Expensive Shit* a mere three years later, with the same bare-breasted women and Fela, but now behind a barbed-wire fence cheerfully and energetically giving the Black Power salute. However, it is the painted or illustrated covers, not the photographic ones, that programmatically defined this new phase that established the image of Fela as an articulate social critic with a consummate sense of humor and satire. This evolution closely followed the development of Fela's ideology as reflected in the music itself: a reformist campaigning for individual moral rearmament—against skin bleaching in "Yellow Fever" or idiocy both in "He Miss Road" and "Monkey Banana," the latter with an exasperatingly lurid cartoonish tableau by Ghariokwu on the cover.

Beginning most consistently in 1976, the use of photographs fell out of favor and became a marginal practice, while hand-illustrated designs became the norm. Otherwise, there was very little stylistic change. However, there was yet another ideological shift: the content of the cover art changed significantly. From the focus on individual moral reform that the earlier covers embodied, Fela's album covers moved toward critical activist intervention in the sociopolitical arrangements of the nation. Although this ideological change did not become a major trend until 1976, its origins can be traced back to 1974. That was the year Fela released his first antistate composition, "Alagbon Close," the song that inaugurated the "political" phase of Fela's career and that would bring him both worldwide fame and unending brutal persecution by different Nigerian governments. If the song marked the emergence of "political afrobeat," it also marked the beginning of unambiguously political album cover art in Nigeria. The cover of *Alagbon Close,* by Lemi Ghariokwu, features a towering Fela in the center foreground, superhumanly breaking out of his chains anchored to Alagbon jail, which is on the extreme middle right tapering out of view. His Kalakuta Republic sits sturdily on the left, against a general rocky background, with a victory sign in unmistakable red imprinted on it. In the immediate lower foreground is a small drama in which a huge whale smashes into a police patrol boat, scattering the occupants, who are Lilliputian compared to the Brobdingnagian Fela, into the roaring sea. The off-white color of Fela's shirt and trousers and of Kalakuta Republic is tinged, like a halo, with a fiery yellow powerful enough to illuminate nearby rock surfaces. The same scorching yellow stretches to the gate and foundation of Alagbon jail, as if setting them on fire. This determined mix of potent, energetic colors contrasts spectacularly with the mournful, ghoulish blue that covers Alagbon police department. All the unmistakable symbols of power are on the side of Fela in this battle between him and the agents of law and order and, the cover clearly suggests, of evil. "Alagbon Close" the song was an instant hit; the cover art was, too. A new era in album sleeve design in Nigeria was born.

Although it is the hand-drawn covers that defined the second and final era of the evolution of Fela album covers, a few photographic ones stand out, such as the one for *Sorrow Tears and Blood,* with Fela on stage, his broken leg from a recent police invasion in heavy cast, and the photo montage on the cover of *Coffin for Head of State,* showing many of Fela's travails with the authorities and clippings of the newspaper headlines that publicly recorded them. Given the subject and the goal of these covers—state brutality against Fela and the need to show the world that what appears unbelievable actually happened—there is no doubt that they are best presented and represented by photography, with its lifelike reproduction of reality; pictures, we have been told countless times, do not tell lies. The classic covers of that lasting era belong, however, to the paintings and cartoonish illustrations for *Confusion, Upside Down, J.J.D., Ikoyi Blindness, Kalakuta Show, Mister Follow Follow, Fear Not for Man, Original Sufferhead, I.T.T., Shuffering and Shmiling, Underground System, Beast of No Nation,* and so on. The central figure in the new artistic revolution, the one who originated and transformed it into a tradition, is Lemi Ghariokwu. Henceforth, even when other talented artists—and they were many: Ajao Bello, Maxoh-Max-Amoh, Kenny Adamson, Boniface Okafor, Remi Olowookere, Tunde Orimogunje, Frances Kuboye, Okanlawon Banjoko, Dede Mabiaku—worked on Fela's albums, they were inevitably bound to follow the trail Ghariokwu blazed.

There is a way to conceptualize the evolution of the cover art of Fela's albums to really appreciate its significance in relation to afrobeat sound itself. At the beginning, the goal was the conventional, dominant one in the business: a cover designed solely to sell the music and promote the musician. It visually strove, directly or indirectly, to "complete" the music, as it were, and put the audience in harmony with it and the suggested image of the musician. Whether the covers were standard, such as those for *Fela's London Scene* or *Afrodisiac,* or controversial, such as those for *Shakara* or *Na Poi,* the goal was a cover that functioned primarily as an advertisement for the music and the musician; the covers were inextricably bound to those goals. However, beginning with the second phase, which was dominated mostly but not exclusively by illustrated designs, the cover art began to do much more than simply advertise the music or musician. It began to call attention to itself as art that was related to the music and the musician but not inextricably tied to them for legitimacy; it produced a visual discourse which neither "completed" nor duplicated the music but accompanied, extended, enhanced, and augmented it. Even when Fela changed ideologically, the style changed little. For instance, the difference between the covers of *Yellow Fever* and *Shuffering and Shmiling* is primarily ideological in terms of the represented thematic content of the images, not in the conceptual organization of the design or in representational style. The emergence of that style also marked the beginning of a significant shift in the perception of Fela's music by its audience: a recognition of afrobeat as a jumble of at least two major discourses, the musical and the visual. Henceforth, viewing another outrageous but thought-provoking cover became a big reason in itself for fans to visit a record store after another Fela release. I suggest then that we see the evolution in afrobeat album covers as a transformation of the design from being a *complement* to being a *supplement* to the music. A complement, because it presumes an inadequacy, performs primarily a completing, harmonizing, or balancing function. Its conserving, indeed conservative, goal is thus to blend in perfectly with other parts. In grammar, we remember, it is the complement that completes the meaning of the predicate. A supplement, on the other hand, is an extra, an excess, which, because it is not called forth primarily by any fundamental deficiency, does not dissolve into that to which it is added but retains its own character and therefore adds to and transforms the character of the whole; it turns a monodiscourse into a multidiscourse, a monophone into a polyphone.[58] Stated with adequate polemical pitch in the spirit of the musician himself, we could describe the evolution in afrobeat jacket design as one from "culinary" covers, after Bertolt Brecht's description of an art of trivial issues packaged to be consumed for mere mindless titillation, to "epic," an art that is a catalyst of questioning and critical thought, that is designed for the ultimate purpose of changing the world for the better for the laboring masses.[59] We can no longer postpone a more extended encounter with the figure whose imagination initiated the profound (r)evolution, Lemi Ghariokwu, whom Fela called, at a most poignant moment at the beginning of their relationship, "the artist."

Even before Lemi (also "Lemmi" or "Lemmy") Ghariokwu met Fela, he had been struck forcefully enough by the resonant visuality of Fela's recording "Roforofo Fight" (1972) to compose a graphical translation of it. He was a self-taught amateur artist in his late teens trying to make some money. He had done portraits for clients for small sums and a cover album for a group of musician friends; he also had in his portfolio images of popular culture icons such as local television stars and even of foreign-cinema ones such as Bruce Lee, painted from a poster for the film *Enter the Dragon*. A bar nearby proved a most opportune place to display his work. It was there that a patron saw the paintings and took interest. This was toward the end of 1974. The patron was a journalist from *The Punch,* the newspaper that would literally make its name with its extensive coverage of Fela over the coming decades. The journalist returned the second day with a picture of Fela for Ghariokwu to reproduce in painting. The excited young man completed the work in twenty-four hours. The journalist, Tunde Harris, took the painting and the painter to see Fela. No doubt because of the enormous psychological boost an affirmation from a person of Fela's stature and fame gave him at the time, Ghariokwu never forgot Fela's exclamation of pleasurable surprise and admiration, "Wow! Goddamn!"[60] Fela offered 120 naira for the portrait, five times the usual fee Ghariokwu charged. The latter turned it down and presented the work as a gift instead. But Fela insisted on recompense and gave Ghariokwu a free permanent pass to his concerts, something no one remembered Fela, as generous as he was, to have done before. The first assault by the Nigerian state on Fela happened shortly afterward. Tunde Harris took Ghariokwu to visit Fela at the hospital, where he was recuperating from the injuries he sustained in the attack. It is not difficult at all to imagine the effect on the young admirer of seeing his idol, the famous and indefatigable loud-mouth musician, in such a chastening, vulnerable circumstance. This made whatever Fela said all the more significant, beyond the obvious meanings. It was in this ambiance that Fela conferred the recognition that Ghariokwu would forever cherish: "When he saw me he said to me, 'But I recognise you, you . . . you are the artist.'" The struggling, unpolished amateur, who had demonstrated little else than the basic skills of reproducing images in a naturalistic manner, became an "artist," "the artist." A bonding between the two began. "I was moved that he recognised me like that," Ghariokwu confessed.[61] So began a long association that would be a dynamic, inchoate mix of relations of friendship, mentor-

mentee, and employer-employee; an alliance of ideological soul mates and politically activist artists.[62]

Ghariokwu's first sleeve design for Fela was for *Alagbon Close*. Fela had
announced at the hospital that he was going to write a song about the police assault. Ghariokwu set to work. He was not a witness to the attack, but he "listened
ardently to the numerous recounting[s] of the harrowing experience from the
man himself," and in attending all rehearsals and regular shows at the Shrine,
he became "privy to the various stages of composing the new tune."[63] This was
the greatest challenge he had faced so far as a budding artist. He was already
mastering portraiture—which begins with a model to reproduce—but was not
yet working wholly from an idea or set of ideas such as police brutality. It was
not that the idea was overly abstract; after all, he was operating within a context
of terrific political cartoonists who appeared regularly in newspapers to debunk
the tyrannical swagger of the uniformed forces.[64] But that was little comfort,
since he had not tried his hand at that genre before. He would have to depend
mostly on his own resources. The resulting artwork was far from the creation
of an amateur, especially one that had done mostly portraits; it was professional.
He created a visually arresting animated-action drama composed of several
scenes delineated by the adroit use of perspective. His capture and placement
of the Fela figure in motion between the huge whale in the foreground and his
residence in the left background is positively inspired, announcing boldly that
this artist would spare no visual technique he could muster in the execution of
the task at hand. Like the unmistakably fuming, strutting rhythm of "Alagbon
Close" the musical track, the album-cover art bore an unmistakably "bad" in-
solent attitude. Ghariokwu's reminiscence about the cover art decades later be-
trayed his hidden agenda of valorization of insolence against the authorities:

> *Alagbon Close* album cover was a poster colour painting of a scenario with a
> rocky background with Fela's "Kalakuta Republic" standing solidly on the left
> and a decrepit "Alagbon Close" jail house with a broken chain half of which is
> still attached to Fela's left wrist as he dances triumphantly over a capsizing Police
> patrol boat helped in effect by a prodigious whale![65]

And so the tradition of the afrobeat sleeve cover began a profound change; like
afrobeat music itself, the new jacket design was unprecedented in the country,
both stylistically and ideologically. We may not like obvious self-congratulation,
but given the significance of his invention, we have no choice but to accept
Ghariokwu's assessment in this case: "This cover sent signals to all quarters that
a new regime of album covers has begun."[66]

For an amateur without formal study of art, it was a remarkable achievement.
Fela in his polemical way advised Ghariokwu against higher education studies in art. "Don't bother yourself," Ghariokwu recalled Fela saying, "myself, I
went to a colonial university, I learnt colonial music. When I returned, people
were no longer functioning with what I had learnt and I was obliged to balance
everything. If I hadn't been strong, I would have become a loser just like many

others. You only need to buy some books and study about the Italian artists yourself."[67] It is vintage Fela to reduce university education in art to a study of no more than Italian artists. "The first book I bought in 1975 [was] 'A history of world art,'"[68] Ghariokwu reported. Apart from all he may have read in art books, one of his specific influences was the cover art of Osibisa, the Europe-based Ghanaian popular music band that emerged in the early 1970s. A few of the band's early album sleeves featured fantastic images of flying elephants, painted by the British artist Roger Dean. Dean, whose fame with Osibisa launched his sleeve-designing career and would ultimately make him a legend in that art, like Ghariokwu, had no formal training.[69] But Ghariokwu's greater attraction was to the cover art, mostly by Pedro Bell, of the albums of George Clinton and Funkadelic, with their gaudy, often-comic images of the urban scene. The bare-breasted female figure on *Yellow Fever* (1976) by Ghariokwu reminds one of a similar figure on Funkadelic's *Cosmic Slop* (1973), though the former has a more logical rationale than the latter in relationship to the music each purports to visually accompany. The focused, politically charged social criticism in Ghariokwu's work had no equivalent elsewhere until some of the punk bands of the late 1970s.[70] We only need to compare the cover art of *Alagbon Close* with that of Osibisa's *Osibirock* and Funkadelic's *Standing on the Verge of Getting It On*, all of which were released in 1974, to see the difference. Although of different and incomparable political significance, Ghariokwu-like illustrations began to appear by the 1980s on the album covers of reggae artists such as Yellowman (*Operation Radication;* 1982), Ranking Ann (*Something Fishy Going On;* 1984), and Steel Pulse (*Earth Crisis;* 1984).[71]

The relationship between Ghariokwu and Fela began on a high note with *Alagbon Close,* and Ghariokwu became a fixture at Fela's compound, literally every day for the next four years, from 1974 to 1978; he even went on tours with the band. Not only was he present at all rehearsals and performances, but he was with Fela as he composed songs, trying out various strategies that would work vocally and memorably without sacrificing ideological punch. He attended "ideological sessions" late into the night every day with Fela and a core group of committed followers, reading and discussing classics of African history, pan-Africanism, Afrocentrism, and African liberation.[72] He became a founding member of Young African Pioneers (YAP), the organization of young radicals Fela sponsored. Some of the propaganda leaflets and broadsheets they printed (*YAP Newss—The truths our newspapers can't print, we can pprinttt!*) featured Ghariokwu's satirical cartoons. Because of this general ideological education and political activism and because he was part of the thoroughly social process of producing afrobeat sound from the moment of composition to stage performance at the Shrine, Ghariokwu was able to closely approximate Fela's expectations for sleeve designs for the songs.[73] He also designed several of Fela's paid advertisements, "Chief Priest Say," published regularly in the papers in the mid-1970s.

The cover art of *Alagbon Close* is preoccupied with an unswerving veneration of Fela; subsequent designs shifted to a direct vilification of the agents of law and order and the class of the wealthy and powerful they defend, through lavish representations of their tyranny over the people or by means of garish, venomous satire. For instance, continuing the same theme of police brutality as *Alagbon Close,* the cover of *Kalakuta Show* is littered, against a background of Fela's Kalakuta Republic residence, with a squadron of police officers in their trademark blue shirts and black trousers pummeling scores of helpless residents—men, women, old, and young—to the ground with batons. The illustration is designed to be a visual news report of the police attack of November 23, 1974, just as the song was a verbal report of those events. "Look head dem break / Look blood him dey flow" (Look at the heads they cracked / See blood as it flows), Fela wailed in the track. On the upper left corner, above and facing away from the fray, is an idealized image of Fela from the shoulders up, gigantic in scale compared to the policemen, with an expression that combines imperturbable muscularity with mysterious, beatific calmness. When he illustrated *No Agreement* later on, Ghariokwu would draw from the conception of Fela here. The song "Kalakuta Show," unlike "Alagbon Close," is weighted down by its need to report; its rhythm rambles in a disjunctive relationship between sonic-musical and lyrical content. For this reason, the cover art is a major consolation and much more. In the war-zone tableau of utter devastation it set up, with scores of baton-wielding policemen running amok like rabid dogs, it prophetically hinted at the much bigger and more violent army invasion of Kalakuta Republic that would happen three years later.

Ghariokwu's popularity transformed him into an institution in his own right in the social production of afrobeat. In addition to his signature on the illustrations, he began to add his picture as well as ideological exhortations. "I have attempted capturing the reality of Fela's lyrics in my painting and designs. You will appreciate my effort in as much as you love this music—you sure will!" he explained and advertised on the cover of *Ikoyi Blindness,* which was about the implacable myopia and selfishness of the nation's middle class as they try to run away from the masses of the laboring poor. On the cover of the runaway hit *Zombie,* he harangued: "Africa my continent is the deepest sink in economic backwardness. She doesn't think for herself. She has the most appalling problems, because she follows and follows colonial methods in all her do's and don'ts. Africa is far from change and rapid progress—relevant progress because her colonial experience hangs a dead weight upon her. This can get us nowhere. We will always be at the bottom of the pit—the vanquished, the victims, and the . . . the FOOLED. We need a change—A CHANGE AFRICAN QUICK!!" His "Designer's Comment" on *Fear Not for Man* enthused about the master and the design: ."[I]n the face of it all, the man blows. . . . blows. . . . and outblows every damn mind—I mean FELA—the MAN! My cover design says this with the aid of brother Tunde's heavy photographs. I hope you like the design. I think it's a heavy combination. 'Practice without thought is blind, thought without practice is empty.' I have quoted the Osagyefo Kwame Nkrumah, Africa's greatest leader of our time!"[74]

Virtually every one of Ghariokwu's covers became instant classics. Nearly always in bold, bright, and highly contrasting colors, we see lurid caricatures of soldiers and policemen violently assaulting and shooting innocent citizens; local and foreign leaders with bloodied fangs for teeth and devil horns on their heads; Lagosians pushing their cars through waist-deep flood water on the streets as a sign of decrepit social infrastructure; culturally blind and, indeed, literally blindfolded Africans foolishly aping European ways; smiling heads of state while news reports announce extreme poverty, hunger, and disease for the people; endless stretches of slums and emaciated, obviously starving figures. It is a testament to the resilience of Ghariokwu's invention and its generally perceived appropriateness as a visual representation of afrobeat music that when Fela hired other artists, they found their creativity within the entrenched tradition. A few of the more famous illustrations and the artists who made them include the covers for *Shuffering and Shmiling* by the cartoonist Kenny Adamson; *I.T.T.*, *Original Sufferhead*, and *Perambulator* with its incorporation of ancient Egyptian and classical African art motifs, all by Ajao Bello; *Authority Stealing* by Frances Kuboye and Tunde Orimogunje; *Unknown Soldier* by Orimogunje; and *Underground System* by Dede Mabiaku.

But life with Fela was never a picnic for anyone within his circle for any length of time, no matter how high the operative degree of understanding between them. Ghariokwu was about the youngest of Fela's closest confidants and a fine example of a protégé thoroughly molded by the mentor. But Fela's egotism was such that it invited little other than subversive relativizing queries, except from the most servile bootlicker. To Fela, Fela was always right and every other person was wrong. Ghariokwu tried hard to put this diplomatically in an interview: "For example, he may be doing something wrong, and you show the other way to him; he may refuse to even look at it at all, not to talk of changing." Fela responded to persistent suggestions of other possible solutions to a problem or other directions of thought with taunts of ideological or political weakness and, specific to Ghariokwu, of being "Mummy's Pet," because he would rather return home daily than live in the compound. In the war-front mentality that pervaded the Fela circle because of persistent harassment by the authorities, passion became parochialism and the first casualty was calm strategic thinking, which was derided as feminine and inferior by a crass, often self-destructive masculinism. "That's why I had to relax my relationship with him—putting it philosophically," Ghariokwu reflected. The Nigerian army's destructive sacking of Kalakuta Republic was for him anticlimactic and utterly preventable, given his earlier conviction that Fela could use far more tact in dealing with people. This foreknowledge—that the mentor's often-uncalculated recklessness would bring him serious harm—which turned out to be useless because it did not lead to the prevention of tragedy when it came, made the experience particularly painful for the mentee. "With tact and diplomacy, he would have gotten away with it," Ghariokwu lamented. "One of his boys burnt an army motorcycle. That should have been settled amicably. And as a young person, I saw all those things, I felt bad. At home, I would sit and think about how to rectify things. We were then doing this YAP thing."[75]

"Why are these people running? What's chasing them?" The original cover art for
*Sorrow, Tears and Blood* that never made it. Disagreement over its details caused an
eight-year rift between Fela and his chief illustrator, Lemi Ghariokwu.
Courtesy of Lemi Ghariokwu.

Apart from personal and ideological collisions, there was also the familiar
issue of economic exploitation. Fela paid Ghariokwu the handsome amount of
120 naira for the design of *Alagbon Close*. In the hectic and prolific subsequent
years, however, there were always more designs made than were paid for. No
matter, since the designer was more or less part of the household and more than
just an employee in the organization. The major rift on money matters between
the two happened when Fela rebuffed Ghariokwu's request for a bulk payment
so that he can execute an important personal project. Echoing the damning
judgment of some of Fela's musicians at one point or the other, Ghariokwu concluded: "I felt it was a way of frustrating me. He is a person who doesn't like
someone around him to rise."[76]

However, it was misunderstandings over sleeve illustrations, not money, that would cause an extended separation between Ghariokwu and Fela. Throughout their professional relationship, Ghariokwu remembered Fela disagreeing only twice with his designs. The first, over the design for *J.J.D.*, was settled amicably. The second, over the cover for *Sorrow Tears and Blood*, proved far less amenable to cordial compromise and reveals a lot about the damaging pressures of state tyranny on the process of afrobeat production. Fela composed the song in late 1976, taking as inspiration the despotism of the apartheid regime in South Africa. Ghariokwu, as usual, took his hints from the contexts of composition and the lyrics. By the last stages of the production of the record in 1977, a seismic change had happened: the sacking of Kalakuta Republic. Apparently the song then took on a new—and more immediate and local—meaning for Fela. When Ghariokwu showed Fela his design, the harried musician exploded in disagreement spiced with condescending remarks, all in the presence of news reporters; the public occasion, more than anything else, seemed to make a painful difference to Ghariokwu, as we can deduce from his detailed account below:

> He recorded November–December 1976; his house was burnt February 1977. The theme that made him sing that song was South Africa's situation—Soweto. So, I illustrated with that concept. Unfortunately, when I took it to his place, he was having a full press conference. Everybody was around and some journalists booked interviews with me when they found out that I was Lemi. I was so happy. Then I placed the artwork and [Fela] said, "What's this? Why are these people running? What's chasing them?" I was stunned. It was Orhirhi Ejemba (the metaphysicist with Prime People) who was with us that answered him. He said, "Fela, it was in your song now that *My people dey fear for the thing wey dem no see*. That's what Lemi drew." I was too confused, but I knew where he was going. Then his son Femi put his foot on the artwork. He did that because he saw how his father was messing the artwork. In front of the whole press! Tears started coming from my eyes. I just stood up. Fela started saying "Check your mind; your mind is weak. Is it because they burnt my house? We are revolutionaries, the next day we may be living in gutters." I just left. I didn't warrant all that. He said I didn't put his house which was burnt in 1977.[77]

Ghariokwu was sick for a week. He produced a new cover afterward, "a bizarre jumble of burnt house, generator head and raped girls." Everybody was "ecstatic," but Decca, the recording company, rejected it outright. Phonogram too would have none of it, claiming bewilderment at "the sheer crudity of the illustration." Okanlawon Banjoko, an apprentice of Ghariokwu, finally "toned down"[78] the cover and used a black-and-white picture of Fela on stage in plastered leg, playing saxophone—conveying a message of irrepressibility of the master in spite of all the state violence visited upon him. Ghariokwu parted ways with Fela the next year, in 1978, and would not return until eight years later, 1986, when he was contracted to produce the cover for *Beasts of No Nation*.

But Ghariokwu would not hesitate to say that on the whole, his relationship with Fela was very positive. With that relationship—with Africa's most popular musician—as cultural capital, Ghariokwu went on to build a rewarding career in professional sleeve design and is today Nigeria's preeminent album designer.

He has won the coveted Sleeve Designer of the Year Award given by Nigerian Music Awards twice (1989/1990, 1990/1991) and was given similar recognition by Fame Music Awards in 1992. He has produced designs for musicians outside the country and is no doubt one of the leading homegrown album designers on the continent, and certainly the most prolific. Always one to remember to put things in perspective, he never ceased giving credit where credit is due. Fela, he has said in many interviews and in his own writings, "gave me advice that opened up the world. I'm happy that I followed the advice he gave me. He gave me the opportunity, a rare one, to express myself, which helped me to carve a niche for myself in my chosen profession."[79]

## The Photographer

It was Femi Bankole Osunla's first major concert assignment after meeting Fela in the mid-1970s and being accepted into the Africa 70 organization. Fela instructed the young, unseasoned photographer to "take very good action photographs with crowd effects." The photographer energetically set to work and expended rolls of film on the crowd, shooting from every imaginable angle, and then on Fela and the band. The pictures all came out well, and he was awash in a feeling of great accomplishment. He had passed with flying colors the real primary entrance examination into the most famous musical group in the nation, and his budding relationship with the most famous musician was all but secure. You can imagine then his precipitous fall from the heights of hope to the depths of disconsolation days later when he took the photographs to Fela and the musician "yelled, 'where is the crowd effect?'" Osunla explained in self-defense: "I thought what he meant was just to take pictures of the crowd." Now at a loss about what "crowd effect" meant, he uncertainly pointed to what were only too obvious in the photographs, the crowds. Fela, of course, never missed an opportunity to teach. "He said," Osunla remembered Fela lecturing him, "that is not how to take crowd effect pictures; you have to take the band or me singing and the crowd at the background." Osunla did not understand that the huge egos of pop stars require more than being liked by their audience; more important, they want to be clearly *seen* to be liked, and one way to continuously access that validation and the psychological gratification it brings is to photographically freeze such moments for life. Amid Osunla's dejection at failing his first test was an undertow of exhilaration at his newly acquired knowledge of an apparently significant photographic technique: "I was immediately excited and I told myself that I've learnt something new from Baba."[80] He was given more chances to prove himself, and he became a Fela convert for life.

Just like Ghariokwu, Osunla came into the orbit of Fela by chance. It was 1975 and the young man of twenty-one years had just successfully completed his apprenticeship in photography. A neighbor, who was a member of the Africa 70 band but was himself apparently starstruck, invited Osunla to a performance to take pictures of him on stage with Fela. It was while Osunla was doing that that Lemi Ghariokwu, who had been in the group himself for barely a year,

The photographer shoots for "crowd effect." Fela gives the double Black Power salute at a concert in the United States.
Courtesy of Femi Osunla.

encouraged Osunla to take some photographs of Fela too. Although the photographs were far from professional—"amateurish and raw,"[81] a profiler described them—Fela was not altogether unpleased when he saw them. For Osunla, that was enough encouragement. And so began a relationship that would last until the musician's death in 1997. Osunla, later popularly known as Femi Foto, became a regular fixture in the organization, an indefatigable photographic recorder of the tumultuous adventures of afrobeat musical practice both inside and outside the country. Of course, one needs more than skills to work and stay with Fela. Osunla was also part of the ideological education sessions at the Kalakuta Republic, and he liked to point to Fela and Afrocentric books such as *The Stolen Legacy* by George G. M. James and *The Black Man of the Nile* by Y. Ben-Jochannan as shapers of his consciousness. "We were exposed to serious ideological books that were meant for university students,"[82] he said. Today, Osunla holds an archive of nearly 5,000 pictures of aspects of Fela's life, lifestyle, and afrobeat production, making him, as a commentator rightly noted, "one of the most significant historical photographers of note in this country."[83]

Osunla was trained and operated within a class-structured context that prized photography more for its documentary than for its aesthetic function. Weddings, birthdays, funerals, child-naming and house-warming ceremonies, and the like were the prime occasions for picture-taking. Dynamic action shots, as at parties, were not unknown, but the most common were the meticulously posed still shots, to be kept in treasured albums or "glazed" and hung on sitting-room walls for generations. It was a practice that needed little technical affectation or experimentation and therefore encouraged little. When Osunla moved into the glitzier world of afrobeat production, he essentially held on to this technically rudimentary practice. Apart from the "crowd effect" episode, it was apparent that Fela, a stickler for musical form, never further engaged his protégé in discourse on photographic style. For these reasons, the greatest significance of Osunla's pictures of Fela will not be found in their style but in the images they show and their social, cultural, political, and historical value. This is the subtle regret evident in the apparent praise by Dapo Olorunyomi, distinguished journalist, of Osunla's "unpretentious affective style of practice."[84]

However, what we miss at the level of photographic style is often made up for in the dynamism of the images captured. Fela, we know, was a master of the theatrical pose. That in itself was bound to infuse the work of even a most conservative photographer with visual excitation. With his gaunt frame that belied the roaring, muscular voice it characteristically issued forth, Fela was always a joy to behold on stage as he twisted and contorted. Even while performing routines of supposedly "deep" African spirituality, his bodily movements and gestures rarely bore any recognizable African ethnic cultural anchor; instead, he exhibited a thoroughly urban African style with an ambiguous, dynamic mix of cultural streams. To go through Osunla's collection then is to be able to map the invention and evolution of embodied performative styles that afrobeat contributed to Nigerian urban popular cultural forms and meanings.

Most of Osunla's photographs are not publicly available yet. The first major exhibition of a selection was held in Lagos in 2002, sponsored by Independent News Communication Limited, one of Nigeria's leading media houses, and the French Cultural Center. But Osunla has been a major part of the construction and circulation of a particular kind of afrobeat image to the world over the years, mostly in the cover albums made, wholly or in part, of his photographs. His most famous covers are no doubt *Sorrow, Tears and Blood* and *Coffin for Head of State*. On the latter, he too, like Ghariokwu on many covers, posted his own swank: "No newspaper caught those front cover fotographs except brother Femi Osunla Afrika '70 fotographer." He is also represented on other covers such as *Yellow Fever, Stalemate* (Ghariokwu, in "Designer's Comment," wrote: "Brother Femi has made this design fantastic with important fotographs from his library. They carried all messages this album carried."), *Vagabonds in Power,* and *Original Sufferhead*.

Osunla remained one of the most fanatical defenders of Fela. To him, Fela's major fault was his blind generosity, allowing many hangers-on and layabouts into the compound with little question. He told me in an interview that all the talk of Fela dying of AIDS was a big ruse. Fela was killed, he theorized, by agents of the late tyrant General Sani Abacha, who arrested Fela on marijuana possession charges and kept him for days in a cell. The air-conditioning in the cell disoriented Fela—the agents knew Fela did not like air-conditioning—and gave the agents the opportunity to inject Fela with a slow-killing poison. "It's the same thing they did to Musa Yar'Adua,"[85] he said with the calm satisfaction of someone who has adduced incontrovertible evidence. There is no doubt that Osunla belonged to a group, among all those around Fela, of those most completely interpellated by Fela's charisma, ideas and lifestyle. With far less than the ingenuity and personal discipline of the master, many of these acolytes have turned out to be little more than wanderers after the death of their hero. Yes, there was a carefree drug culture at the Kalakuta, but it was always tamed by, and never hampered, the incredible hard work and creativity of Fela, the leader. However, that culture created in some followers a dependency that manifested itself in inconsistent job performance. This is, for instance, why Osunla has so far been unable, like Ghariokwu, to convert his relationship with Fela to a successful post-Fela career. The potential is still there, because there is hardly anywhere in the show business scene in Africa that such cultural and professional capital would not open doors. But the photographer remains as yet a casualty, locked within the charmed circle of a past countercultural social practice that he has so far been unable to prevent from being a liability, indeed a disability.

### "The Weed"

> A lot of people thought the only thing we did at Kalakuta was to smoke "igbo" marijuana. But that is not true.
>
> —Femi Osunla[86]

It is not an exaggeration at all to theorize that afrobeat would not have become "political" were it not for the role of marijuana, locally "igbo" or "weed," or "grass," in its factors and relations of production. And we can begin to imagine the significance of that role when we realize that it is the "political" Fela that subsequently became *the* Fela, the only one considered worthy of knowing and celebrating worldwide today. Fela had created successful afrobeat music before the chain of events that seemingly inexorably radicalized his consciousness and pushed him into antistate militancy. Without Fela's open marijuana smoking, he would still have had encounters with agents of the state; there were those many accusations of Fela's supposed abduction of young girls that the police could dust off and pursue any time they wished. However, the police knew how difficult those charges were to prove, especially with uncooperative "abducted" girls loudly expressing their wish to be with Fela and even escaping from juvenile welfare detention centers back to Kalakuta Republic to prove the point. Without marijuana in the mix, such cases would have faded eventually. The police no doubt rightly concluded that the marijuana issue was a far more substantive and promising way to get Fela for good; hence the frequent, unannounced, and often violent searches of his home at odd hours, and when all that failed, the resort to planting evidence. Once Fela finally responded to the harassments with the antistate recordings "Alagbon Close" and "Expensive Shit," a cyclic pat-

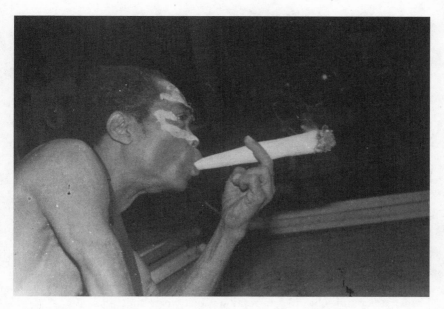

"The weed," a plantain-size wrap of Nigerian natural grass—not marijuana.
Courtesy of Femi Osunla.

tern of confrontational relationship with the state developed. "Political" afrobeat was born in this cauldron fueled originally by the catalytic firewood of
marijuana, "the weed."

The back cover of *Expensive Shit* features three black-and-white photographs
of bikini-clad Fela in a restful, reclining position, peacefully puffing away at his
marijuana roll and exhaling clouds of its smoke. It was a quietly defiant pose,
given the violent maelstrom the state had only recently swept him into to punish
him for marijuana use and from which he was, by his own account, lucky to
come out alive. Fela, of course, would not give up the weed but settled into a
pattern of often-dangerous cat-and-mouse games with the police; he was unyielding, but the police were also unrelenting. Fela was so frequently in the news
about marijuana use and run-ins with the law that Kalakuta was stereotyped in
public discussions as a drug haven. This is the stereotype Femi Osunla is referring to in the epigraph to this section. "But that is not true," he pled, and added,
"We were exposed to serious ideological books that were meant for university
students," as if reading scholarly books somehow attenuates or exculpates the
accusatory stereotype.

It is not necessary to be too particular about how Fela came in contact with
marijuana, since the weed has been a prominent part of international modern
popular culture since the early decades of the twentieth century.[87] Fela im-

mersed himself in the Nigerian highlife musical scene as early as the last years of his high school in the late 1950s; if he came across marijuana in that scene, there is no evidence that he tried it then. He remembered smoking the weed "once or twice" when he was in college and sampling the jazz scene in London and finding that he "liked" it, but he did not make it a habit until the mid-1960s, well after his return to Nigeria. As with other significant milestones in Fela's life and musical practice, the occasion of his substantive introduction to marijuana is soaked in gender significance:

> How did I get into grass? You may not believe me, man. But it was a girl who started me "smoking" in Nigeria. Her name is Eunice. I'd always see her eyes red and a friend said she "smoked" a bit. So one day I asked: "Do you smoke?" She said: "Tell me, man; tell me, make him some try some too." So I tried it.[88]

At first, Fela used the weed only recreationally and was particularly ecstatic at its effect on his sexual performance. "[W]hen this girl gave me the smoke and I had sex with it," he enthused, "Ohhhhhhhhh, it was fantastic! I'd never had sex with it before."[89] Marijuana is not exactly an aphrodisiac, and scientific evidence is inconclusive on its effects on sex hormones.[90] But no matter; in these issues, rumor and subjective perception usually reign supreme.

Fela, who confessed that he remembered being warned long ago by his brother, a professor of medicine, that "if I 'smoked' I would go crazy,"[91] now began to boldly experiment with the weed in other directions apart from sexual. Needless to say, whatever remaining fear the warning instilled in him was drowned by the rapture that marked the weed's entrance into Fela's musical-professional life. It was first as an infrequent means of relaxation, then it became a regular means of stimulation: "I used it a couple of times to relax. Then one night, I went on stage stoned. Man, I used to just stand there stiff as [a] stick. My feet were glued to the floor. This night I started jumping, dancing, flying. The music poured out. From now on, I said, we all turn on!"[92] This narrative is familiar in the world of popular music. For early jazz players, marijuana was a revelation. "While high," writes Saul Rubin, "they learned to add slurs, melodic phrases, and syncopation that created an overall 'hot' sound."[93] A *Time* magazine report on the drug's presence in the early 1940s jazz scene in the United States of America noted: "The drug's power to slow the sense of time gives the improviser the illusion that he has all the time in the world in which to conceive the next phrase. And the drug also seems to heighten the hearing—so that, for instance, strange chord formations seem easier to analyze under marijuana."[94] Louis Armstrong's arrest for the drug in 1931 is common knowledge, but as a critic noted, "a list of jazz players who dabbled in marijuana would run as long as a Charlie Parker bebop phrase."[95] But the musical genre that became most commonly linked with marijuana at the beginning of the afrobeat phenomenon in the 1970s was reggae. The dreadlocked Rastafarian, reggae, and marijuana constituted a venerable holy trinity, embodied most popularly by Bob Marley and Peter Tosh, that was broadcast everywhere and worshipped by many; Tosh's 1976 classic "Legalize It" was the accompanying liturgical hymn.

Marijuana subsequently became part of the counterculture of the Kalakuta. Ghariokwu remembered trying it, "to 'elevate' my talent," as Fela prodded, and confessed that "the resultant effect was superb."[96] It is clear then that Fela conceived the weed, against the enduring popular Nigerian stereotype of it as a straight road to insanity, as an energizing tonic, a stimulant of natural abilities. He would henceforth endlessly ridicule the stereotype during *yabis* sessions at the Shrine, linking it to the general racist miseducation initiated by colonial rule and continued by the postcolonial state. With a plantain-size wrap that he puffed theatrically now and then, he would, to the raucous delight of the audience, lampoon the state bureaucratic name for the weed, Indian hemp. Why, this thing grows right here in our country, so how can it be "Indian" hemp, he would ask? He subsequently rechristened the weed "Nigerian Natural Grass" (NNG), and composed an unreleased song of same name. In the song, according to Mabinuori K. Idowu, "Fela tries to make people see why grass (hemp) is not a drug as people characterize it. Nigerian natural grass is not a drug like LSD, Red Devil, Cocaine, etc. It is natural herb, a product of Africa's nature. . . . As a fact, anything the whiteman has no ability to control, he discredits, that is why African's [*sic*] natural grass is classified as [a] drug."[97] This is typical Kalakuta Republic polemic, a muddle of grain and chaff so complex that perhaps only the weed can induce it. And at the level of musical sound, too, it is no exaggeration to read the weed's effect in afrobeat's roaring, aggressive horns, and their resolute though ever-unhurried mesmerizing tessellation.

To the very end, Fela risked life, limb, and career for the weed. There was the most scandalous though less violent episode of his arrest in Italy in September 1980. The Italian Communist Party had invited him. Arriving in Milan, Italian customs officials found some quantity of marijuana sealed into the bottom of some of the suitcases of the 74-member traveling party. It was later discovered that an expatriate woman who was loosely affiliated with the band and who had bought the new suitcases for Fela's women, kept the marijuana there. Communist Party lawyers succeeded in getting Fela out of jail and the tour was completed, but it had been soured irretrievably, and the episode badly affected relationships in the band.[98]

To the different regimes that pursued him for nearly three decades, Fela remained a bad example to the very end: he neither became mad as the reigning propaganda said nor died of any marijuana-connected cause. On the contrary, his prodigious creativity seemed to send a message to all of the salutary effects of the weed on the creative imagination. We need not disabuse the narrow and hypocritical minds of the police about the weed. More modestly, we can read the marijuana drama, sensationalized as it is by Fela, as a reflection of part of "the universal human need for liberation from the restrictions of mundane existence," a liberation "[which] is satisfied by experiencing altered states of consciousness."[99] The excessive, irrational rationalism of the state has no language or space of accommodation for altered states of consciousness outside the well-policed, sanitized medical clinic, a development Richard Rudgley in his well-known history of cultural intoxicants, *Essential Substances,* attributes to the aggressive march of secularity in modern society.[100] The absence of such a language or space can only postpone "a better understanding of the importance of altered states of consciousness in both our collective and personal lives"; it will neither reduce the human disposition to, or predilection for, such states nor diminish the role those states have always played in the shaping of culture.[101] It is for this much larger reason that we could say that for Fela, following Rudgley, marijuana was no more and no less than a part of society's "essential substances," to the extent that society as such is perpetually constituted by, and constitutive of, part reality and part vision or dream, and cultural intoxicants are some of the prime generators of visions and dreams. But there is the fact that physiologically and psychologically, bodies respond differently to cultural intoxicants. Fela was never addicted to marijuana to the point of incapacitation, but this cannot be said of all of those around him who began the habit either through the master's urging or by his example. Society may need cultural intoxicants as essential substances, but that does not mean that they are without costs, human and social.

I am far from suggesting that what I have done here exhausts the vast and tangled web of relations that went into the social production of afrobeat. There are, for instance, Fela's shifting, volatile relations with recording companies over decades. A careful study of such also promises useful insights about the imbrication of both local and global economics and the politics of musical recording, distribution, and marketing and how these specifically shaped the production of afrobeat. I do not have the space to go into that here, but I do hope that what I have done suggests a clear outline of what is to be gained from such investigations.

# 7 Pedagogue, Pedagogy, and the Pedagogic Form

## "I.T.T.": The ABC of How Euro-American Multinational Corporations Underdeveloped Africa

Fela designed the sprawling composition "I.T.T." (International Thief Thief) as a detailed expose of the insidious manner in which Africa is cheated of its immense wealth by Euro-American multinational corporations. Against a background chorus of "International Thief Thief!" and a chaotic din of complaints of lack of social services by the people, Fela's voice, beefy and authoritative, rises to address the crowd. "Make I yab dem?" (Should I roast them?), he asks, in the manner of a union leader holding a rally with fellow workers against the management. "Yab dem! Yab dem!!" (Yes! Roast them!) the crowd roars its assent, which sounds very much like an excited appeal by eager students for gems of wisdom from a revered sage-professor. While the precise meaning of "yab" in urban southwest Nigerian pidgin English is to roast, criticize, or abuse, its connotations are much wider—to expose one's wrongdoing in public, to discomfit, humiliate, deconstruct. Indeed, one of the most beloved features of a Fela concert was "*yabis* time" during which, to intermittent interventions from the audience, he would range widely round the world critically picking apart and ironizing news items and events: the minister of culture in an African country who always dresses in three-piece suits imported from West End London; the escape, for the umpteenth time, of yet another group of armed robbers from police custody while, as usual, police "investigation continues"; the sick African vice president who had to be jetted to a hospital in Europe because of the dilapidated state of the hospitals in his own country; the latest ploy by Thatcher and Reagan to prolong the reign of apartheid in South Africa; the UN and its announcement of one more program to save Africa while African presidents cheer like a pack of beggars; and more. *Yabis* time was a consummate scene of educational instruction in which, led by Fela, the audience came to know a lot about itself and its place in the contexts of the nation, the continent, and the world and the dominant relations, historical and contemporary, among those entities.

A chief cynic himself, Fela never expected to convince the audience without a struggle. So he kept in stock an array of rhetorical strategies to aid his task. He resorted to an extreme one early in "I.T.T.," apparently to demonstrate the gravity of the matter at stake. "Na true I wan talk again o" (I want to tell the truth again), he cleverly announces both the immediate occasion and, more important, the fact that the occasion is just another one of his usual—"again o"—truth-telling sessions. But this one is graver, so its truthfulness needs unusual underscoring. "If I dey lie o, make Osiri punish me o" (If I am lying, may Osiri punish me), he commences an extended swearing which invokes the wrath of African deities and mythological figures on himself if what he is about to say is not the truth. The swearing works well musically; he heavily accents the enchanting repetitive phrase, "punish me o" to the thrashing chorus of "well well!" Beyond musical rhetoric, however, the oath has a substantive content. In a cultural context where people generally steer clear of this kind of self-directed oath-taking and not simply out of civility, the musician here puts something more than his reputation on the line to guarantee the truth of what he is about to tell.

The much-expected truth, when Fela finally tells it, appears to be lightweight. At first, that is. He has, he says, researched the culture of shit-carrying that is rampant in many poor neighborhoods in 1970s Lagos[1] and has discovered that it is not African at all. A "long, long time ago," Africans "no dey carry shit" (didn't carry shit). They shit in big holes dug in the ground. To prove it, he rifles through several African cultures to give the various indigenous names of the shit hole. For a large part of his audience: students, dropouts, clerks, messengers, the unemployed and underemployed, the lumpen proletariat, he provides a handy cultural nationalist education. "Na European man dey carry shit / Na for dem culture to carry shit" (It is Europeans who carry shit / It is their culture to carry shit), he declares authoritatively, adding that it is Europeans who forced Africans to learn shit-carrying during colonial rule.

If "I.T.T." had ended there, it would still have been an interesting song and very much in line with Fela's vociferous nativism. But it turns out that Fela is aiming for something weightier. Without the usual brief instrumental interludes or bridges that both connect and separate different scenarios or sections, Fela launches into what he apparently designs as a lesson note, an ABC of how "many foreign companies dey Africa carry all our money go" (many foreign companies in Africa steal all our wealth). The chorus excitedly urges the teacher on: "Say am, say am!" (Reveal it, tell all!). The companies, he begins, "write big English for newspapers dabaru we Africans" (The companies bamboozle us with their big English in newspapers). They begin to cause "Confusion! Corruption! Oppression! Inflation!" But this is pronouncing judgment without trial. Trying hard to be very meticulous as a teacher, he backtracks to systematically explain the companies' modus operandi:

| | |
|---|---|
| Dem get one style wey dem dey use | They have a particular style |
| Dem go pick one African man | They will pick one African man |
| A man with low mentality | |
| Dem go give am million naira bread | They will give him millions of naira |
| To become up high position here | To become a notable figure here |
| Im go bribe some thousand naira bread | He too will bribe some thousands of naira |
| To become one useless chief | To buy a useless chieftaincy title |

| Like rats dey do dem go dey do for corner corner | Like rats, they will begin hiding in corners doing shading deals, deeds |
| Pass pass, under under, side side, in in, out out, etc. | |
| Den gradually, gradually, gradually | After a while of influence peddling |
| Dem go be friend friend to journalist | They become friends to journalists |
| to commissioner | |
| to permanent secretary | |
| to minister | |
| to head of state | |
| Den start start to steal money | Then they begin to steal money |
| start start dem corruption | They begin their corruption |
|     inflation | |
|     oppression | |
|     confusion | |
|     oppression | |
|     to steal money | |
| Like Obasanjo and Abiola!— | |
|     International thief thief! | |
| I.T.T.! | |
| International rogue— | |
|     thief— | |
| We go fight dem—well well | We will fight them |
| We don tire to carry any more dem shit | We are tired of carrying their shit |

Apart from the anticolonial nationalism of the 1950s and 1960s, the 1970s, the decade in which "I.T.T." was composed, was the most radical in Africa in the last century. Many dictators were swept out of office, and for once, ideological distinctions among politicians sharpened dramatically, a situation many military regimes used to oust the politicians and reimpose dictatorships in some countries. Intellectually, radical scholarship won the propaganda war for commitment to egalitarianism and ethical probity, even though only a tiny minority of intellectuals produced it. The latter wrote accomplished tomes, pamphlets, even newspaper articles on "neocolonialism," "the domination of African economies by international finance monopoly capital" with the help of "local comprador 'agbero' bourgeoisie," and the like, but none of these could explain the whole process in the most accessible form better than Fela in the few minutes of "I.T.T." Even as a written text and not a song accompanied by an irresistibly riveting music, it is still difficult not to be impressed with the teacherly and student-friendly qualities of the excerpt. The song's immediate context was Fela's dispute over recording contracts with the late M. K. O. Abiola, multimillionaire local director of Decca, and Africa and Middle East representative of International Telephone and Telegraph, the global arm of American Telephone and Telegraph (AT&T). The song skillfully and aptly read the urgent personal into the larger political. The other name Fela mentions as a local "rat" representing international thieves is Olusegun Obasanjo, the military head of state.

This last half of the song about global political economy, with its direct references to real live institutions and personalities, is so engrossing in its own right that we have almost forgotten the exotic first part about shit-carrying and shit holes. But the last line of the song above returns us forcefully to the earlier smelly scene. Africans did not carry shit until the colonizers introduced them to it, both literally, as in the infamous case of Lagos human waste carriers, and metaphorically, as in contemporary African businessmen and leaders who are no more than mere local agents, shit carriers, of Euro-American multinational corporations. The powerful local people who rule the country are really lowly and powerless in the global scene, like the lowly, powerless shit carriers in the local scene. The strongest intellectual support for Fela's idea of the African bourgeoisie as shit carriers of foreign capital is provided by Frantz Fanon in his merciless excoriation of that class in *The Wretched of the Earth*. The African bourgeoisie, Fanon wrote during the apogee of anticolonial nationalism, is characterized by "intellectual laziness," "spiritual penury," the "absence of all ambition," and a gross "incapacity" to "fulfill its historic role of the bourgeoisie." In this class, "the dynamic, pioneer aspect, the characteristics of the inventor and of the discoverer of new worlds" that are found in any bourgeoisie worth that name, are "lamentably absent." It is an unoriginal class that is "not engaged in production, nor in invention, nor building, nor labor; [but] is completely canalized into activities of the intermediary type." It is a class afflicted with a signal lack of initiative; its "mission has nothing to do with transforming the nation" but rather seeks to be "content with the role of the Western bourgeoisie's business agent."[2]

The political phase of Fela's musical practice is anchored by a predilection for teaching, explaining, and sermonizing about local and global social relations and the myriad inequalities that often underpin them. In tracks such as "Teacher Don't Teach Me Nonsense," he foregrounds the pedagogical process and the politics of its content and form. I have given extended attention here to "I.T.T.," one of the classics of that phase, as an example of Fela at his most pedagogically resourceful. The contemporary world music scene is not lacking in musicians with talent, but it has few in whom talent and clear social vision have found productive cohabitation. It is not that there are no local exceptions here and there, but the era of the musician-activist pedagogues of world stature such as the canonical figures of Bob Marley and Fela Anikulapo-Kuti appears, sadly, to be over. Rare is the musician of standing today who would claim as his or her goal anything loftier than the "entertainment" of the audience. We know, of course, that pleasure is never innocent or innocuous and that there is no entertainment without pedagogical content, irrespective of whatever goal is proclaimed. All the more reason then to make a critical return in this chapter to the pedagogical art of one of that atypical breed of accomplished popular musicians who were never shy about publicly defining their art in terms of a cause; musicians for whom, in words and in deeds, art and a "heavy" cause are never strange bedfellows.

We know Fela would never have won a prize for being subtle in anything, so

Musician as pedagogue. Fela in concert at the Amphitheatre, University of Ife (now Obafemi Awolowo University).
Courtesy of Femi Osunla.

it is not surprising that not only did he employ an array of devices deeply embedded in his music to advance his pedagogical agenda, as one would normally expect, but he also went on to explicitly thematize scenes of instruction and teacher-student relationships in his lyrics. He never wanted to be regarded as just a musician, even a political musician. He wanted above all to be regarded as a teacher, an educator, the one who lifts the veil of ignorance from the faces of oppressed black people worldwide and thereby empowers them to fight their oppressors; the Promethean with the fiery searchlight of knowledge to root out inequities and injustices wherever they exist. There is little doubt: Fela was about the only popular musician in the world who dedicatedly made the university campus lecture circuit round his country, organized regular educational press conferences, and bought space in the newspapers—all to discuss such matters as African precolonial and colonial history, Euro-American imperialism in Africa, the tyranny of postcolonial African leaders, why the indigenous chewing stick cleans better than imported toothpaste, why bearing European and Arabic names is part of the reason for Nigerian underdevelopment, and the like.[3] He held "ideological sessions" far into the night with band members, which included even the band photographer and jacket illustrator, to read and discuss books on African history and political economy. Apparently convinced that oppression could persist in the world only because the mind of the oppressed had been colonized by the oppressors, Fela orchestrated a gargantuan ritual, with his far-less-than-subtle-and-humble self as chief priest, of critical consciousness-raising, of conscientization, as Paulo Freire described it in his famous book *Pedagogy of the Oppressed*. I have invoked in the title of this section a similarly engaged scholar, Walter Rodney, and the title of his famous book *How Europe Underdeveloped Africa* primarily because there is hardly a better way to conceive of "I.T.T." than as a creative musical application of Rodney's central ideas in the book.

Although Fela generally never missed a potential teaching moment, his best showings are no doubt those I have labeled as political classics. The reverse is equally true: the political classics would hardly be political classics without their pedagogical dimension.

## The Pedagogic Musical Aesthetics

Fela is not a singer as such but a storyteller, a narrative singer. He tells stories, narratives complete with charged scenarios, vivid characters, and dramatic conflicts. We know that storytelling is humanity's first and still most complex pedagogical tool in fashioning an imaginative culture. It places us in space and time in imaginary situations from which we learn both corporeally and mentally, directly and indirectly, modalities of interaction with reality.[4] While human beings learn from all imaginative creations, narratives perform this function far better than, say, painting. Fela and Bob Marley are both accomplished political musicians who composed pieces of great artistry and intellectual depth. But Marley is the lesser pedagogue, and one of the reasons for that is his comparatively more conventional and less "narrative" or storytelling compositions.

A narrative can only take place in time and space, and the more capacious the two the better for narrative to perform its pedagogical function. Not even the profoundest proverb can challenge the shortest story to a pedagogical competition. It is Fela's defining narrative bent that is responsible for his uniquely lengthy compositions. Fela is probably the only pop musician in the world who successfully damned the global music industry's dictate of three- or four-minute songs to fit radio broadcast programming. After 1971, the shortest Fela composition was never less than seven minutes long; the majority were between fifteen and thirty, while quite a few were close to forty. "I.T.T." is 24:02 minutes, while "Army Arrangement" and "M.O.P. (Movement of the People) Political Statement Number 1" are 29:59 and 37:04 minutes, respectively. Fela literalized the meaning of "long-playing."

Anyone who ever saw Fela perform live knew that he was notorious as an extremely strict conductor. He might have been a radical many ways but he was very traditional when it came to structuring his narrative: he was a stickler for logical, orderly, linear structure. Linear narrative structure is generally considered as ideologically conservative, but the fact is that it remains a pedagogically effective tool. This is why, in spite of all our sophistication, we still treasure ABC simplicity when we open those manuals to install that latest software or to program the TV/VCR to record next Wednesday's episode of our favorite program. Listen to Fela in "Perambulator" break down the lives of African workers, who are superexploited and then discarded like torn, overused rags:

My father, your father
African fathers must start to work at the
   age of twenty
Comfort, success, riches are all his targets
Perambulator!
Then
*Chorus:* Perambulator
every morning
6 in the morning
going to work
6 in the evening
coming back home
every month
small salary
for 55 years

| | |
|---|---|
| him go tire | he will be tired (worn out) |
| if he no tire | if he is not tired |
| dem go tire am | he will be retired |
| dem go dash am | they will award him |
| one gold wristwatch | |
| for 55 years service | |
| All him property: one old bicycle | All his property: one old bicycle |

I have seen individuals stealthily wipe their eyes when they hear this section of Fela's song; I have no doubt at all that that response is induced in large part by the unembellished linear simplicity of the presentation. In just a few lines and minutes, Fela systematically disassembles the entire seventy-five years of an individual African worker's life, demonstrating how there is nothing more to show for all of that in the end than an old, decrepit bicycle. The excerpt from "I.T.T." quoted earlier about the making of local comprador elites who collude with international thieves is another example.

Fela wrote hundreds of songs, but I can count on the fingers of one hand those that could be considered slow in tempo. Most of his compositions range from mid-tempo to fast, and all the wildly popular hits such as "Alagbon Close," "Zombie," "Original Sufferhead," "I.T.T.," and "Perambulator" are fast-paced. There is a grand irony here. In performances all over Nigeria, Fela often told the audience to just sit down and listen. It seems he was often torn between his vocation as an accomplished musician and his social commitment as a frequently overenthusiastic pedagogue. It is not as if the two cannot go together, but how could the audience just sit down and listen to a music that, while undeniably containing much food for thought, does not expressly present itself as an aid for calm reflection? No one with any ear for music would mistake a deep, swift-paced infectious rhythm with heaving saxophones, tweeting key-boards, and throbbing percussion for anything other than dance music. Fela was thunderous and passionate in both his music and lifestyle, and the ruling spirit of his musical practice is the wild Ogun, not the serene Obatala. His presiding deity inevitably calls up the predominance of up-tempo tunes in Fela's music. Both slow and fast tempos can be deployed effectively to pedagogic ends, but a fast tempo articulates that core of music, repetition, in particularly gripping—corporeally and mentally—ways. It teaches and socializes the body and mind in ways the two often cannot resist; for the musical pedagogue fixated on captur-ing the mind of the listener, a carefully modulated mid to fast tempo becomes an invaluable musical and ideological ally. The military is an institution that everywhere prides itself on the way it consummately indoctrinates its recruits; we need wonder no more why most martial music is up-tempo.

Fela's music is perceived as largely message-driven. He sometimes attempted to temper this perception both by singing on only one track of an album and devoting the other track or tracks to instrumentals exclusively and by prefacing the song track with an extended instrumental introduction. In a typical LP of thirty-six minutes, the total song section may account for no more than nine minutes. But invariably it is the politically charged and sensational lyrics that win out in the end with the audience. This reception of Fela is not altogether unfair, for the main currency of exchange in the terrain of politics that he chose to musically intervene in was not music but words, words, and more words. Since there is no effective pedagogy without a facilitating language, part of Fela's main challenge earlier on was to invent such a language. His wholesale adoption of pidgin in the 1970s followed his political radicalization and ex-pressed commitment to the lowly urban masses who speak that language. With pidgin, Fela's pedagogy found a most appropriate mass language.

But language in Fela's musical practice is not just verbal and sonic as with most musicians; it is also decisively visual. The unusually high graphical quo-tient of the imagery of Fela's lyrics is part of it, but there is also visuality in the more literal sense. The pedagogical process of Fela's musical practice does not begin or end musically, which is a strange thing to say of a musician. On the contrary, it begins and ends visually. On the cover of every Fela LP is usually a sumptuous visual representation of the lyrical theme of the songs. The cover art became so famous that it was a reason in itself to purchase a new Fela release. Even more than the music, which needs expensive electronic gadgets to access, this visual medium is a much more easily accessible mass language. For Fela, the album cover was not only decorative; it was another significant terrain of op-portunity to advance his message, an intimate component of his pedagogical aesthetics. Since the age of compact discs with their truncated space for cover art, Fela's LPs have become collectors' items mostly because of their remarkably atypical cover art.

I have often been struck by Fela's deft handling of what audio technologists call aural perspective.[5] Aural perspective is the manipulation of sound to situate the listener in certain ways in relation to the music and the subject the music represents. The use of perspective in visual culture studies—the ways the artist manipulates angles of vision and image-to-viewer distance in order to suggest certain meanings—is very well known. Although sound is not an image one can view but an enveloping medium one hears, musicians nevertheless manipulate sound-to-listener distance in order to create certain kinds of impressions or symbolic meanings with the aural perspective such manipulation intimates. By sound-to-listener distance, I mean the relative loudness or softness of the recorded sound or music, not our ability to turn the volume knobs on our stereo sets up or down. For instance, no matter how much we turn up the volume on Barry White, what we are going to get is still soft music, and heavy metal remains earsplitting and abrasive no matter how low we turn the volume. Because Fela's voice is central to the entire sonic organization of afrobeat as well as to his pedagogical agenda, it is particularly important to examine its apparent relationships with listeners.

Through a careful variation of aural perspective with his voice, Fela creates various calibrated degrees of familiarity or otherwise—imaginary social distance—between the music and what it represents and the listener. The distance the voice conveys on particular issues and/or at particular moments profoundly impacts the authority of the singing pedagogic voice, its trustworthiness, and its persuasive potential in the court of the listener. The degree of social distance a music conveys could range from intimate distance, in which the voice constructs an imaginary intimacy with the listeners by "whispering" or generally deploying "maximally soft voices," to public distance, which deploys a "maximally loud" voice to stretch the limits of formality between sound and listener.[6] Fela, as we all know, was a highly opinionated musician. It is not surprising, therefore, that the predominant form of social distance in his works is the formal public distance, in which the relationship between sound and listener is imagined to be a serious official business: the voice is frequently very loud, decidedly not conversational but projected as if at a rally for all to hear. This is the voice he deploys to hammer into our heads his overt sociopolitical messages. He saw foolishness and suffering all around him, and he earnestly wanted to teach his audience—that variegated middle group between the non–western-educated peasant below and the western-educated elite above—to fight for better lives. In his thinking, it seems, only the loud, formal voice is appropriate for the grave issues at hand. He is the guru who is knowledgeable about these things, ready to bestow on us the audience his rare gems of wisdom. This is protest music, and the clamorous voice is the paradigmatic protest voice. In fact, Fela's notoriety—and therefore, fame—along the West African coast is due in large part to the uncompromisingly loud and harsh bellows of most of his famous songs. Culturally speaking, this roughly approximates the voice of *akede*, the town crier, an indigenous institution with which Yorubas are all too familiar.[7] Appropriately, the town crier's task is to disseminate significant messages to the community.

But we come to a conundrum here. I have argued that the paradigmatic voice in Fela is the officiously formal one that keeps listeners at formal distance, the kind of voice seasoned pedagogues will theorize as tyrannical and ineffective as a pedagogical tool. Yet judging by Fela's popularity, it would be hard to doubt his potency. I suggest two propositions for unraveling the conundrum. First, the shrillness of Fela's voice is often tempered by other sound elements such as humor, the use of common slang, tone shifts, and the highly infectious rhythm of the music. In other words, a sense of play is rarely completely missing even at the height of his formality. Second, in the real world outside the music, Fela's reputation as a committed radical willing to risk his life on behalf of the common people by speaking truth to power is very well known and secure. This makes it difficult to read his vocal officiousness as tyranny or as unduly formalizing his relations with the listener. These two points in some ways blunt the apparent formality of Fela's voice and keep the unsubtle pedagogic project on course.

More infrequently, Fela makes creative use of the relaxed, casual voice, signifying an informal social distance between sound and listener. Well-known examples include the opening of "I.T.T.," parts of "Lady," "Roforofo Fight," and "Go Slow." Through this, he suggests a genial familiarity and alliance with his audience. The relaxed, casual, and friendly voice with which he addresses his audience enhances the authority of that voice and the foregrounded content of what it has to say. But it is significant that we are far less likely to find Fela using this mode of aural perspective in his explicitly political songs.

I am not in the least suggesting that an instance or two of that extremely close social distance and informality known as intimacy is entirely absent in Fela. But if it were absent, it would be very much in line, for Fela was an artist who devoted his creativity entirely to mass politics, a realm that allows little room for intimacy between the addresser and the addressee, the political figure and his/her constituency. A political pedagogy must be a civic, public one. Having affirmed this, we can point to that famous brief moment in "Shuffering and Shmiling" when the otherwise roaring voice of Fela softens to a whisper in order to tell us some "confidential matter." "Don't tell anybody outside," the intimate, conspiratorial voice urges, "it is between me and you." It is a delectable moment, attention-grabbing and effective, but it does not last; the supposed confidential matter pours out in a near-roar. But the juxtaposition and dramatic shift in aural perspective serves its purpose; that moment remains one of the most memorable in the track. Woe betide the pedagogue who does not know how to verbally create memorable moments.

I do not have the space to more exhaustively detail Fela's pedagogical strategies. For instance, I have not considered repetition mainly because its centrality in musical composition and pedagogy is common knowledge, though Fela's particular use may yield uncommon insights. Then there is his remarkable skill at inventing catchy terms, names, phrases, and acronyms or borrowing existing forms and subverting them; all of these serve both as mnemonics and as a means of transmitting his pedagogy: "Zombie," "Lady," "Yellow Fever," "I.T.T.," "B.B.C.: Big Blind Country, "V.I.P. (Vagabonds in Power)," "Shuffering and Shmiling," "N.N.G. (Nigerian Natural Grass)," and more.

Rehearsal time; musical reflections.
Courtesy of Femi Osunla.

A "pedagogical anxiety" hangs spectrally over Fela's musical practice. There is nothing new or unique about an artist making advocacy a goal and articulating an appropriate pedagogical form to carry out that agenda. What is unique about Fela is an obsessive double anxiety to teach and to make sure that we get the message of the teaching completely. This is a tall order indeed. I know of no other popular musician in the world who is so explicitly, even sometimes tastelessly, didactic or "preacherly" in his or her musical practice. Add to this Fela's predilection for satire, with its omniscient perspective and Olympian height from which it self-righteously dishes out derision left, right, and center, and the full import of my argument is clearer. Given the consensus in critical taste that sermonizing in content and unsubtlety in form are the enemies of aesthetic delight, that other major goal of art, it is a testament to Fela's genius that he was able to turn out one record after the other that have become classics in the pleasures they give us, in spite of, or perhaps actually because of their uncompromising and open advocacy. But of course, this statement demands that we overlook the missed opportunities, the releases that failed woefully either to teach or to delight, primarily because of their pedagogical anxiety; I mean releases such as "Stalemate," "Fear Not for Man," or "Look and Laugh."

There is a preponderance of the imagery and thematic of blindness and insight in Fela's corpus. "Na we open dem eye," he sings in "Perambulator." "Open your eye everywhere," he counsels in "Shuffering and Shmiling." Or I could just point to tracks such as "Ikoyi Blindness" and "Follow Follow." For the Yoruba, the meaning of being civilized and knowledgeable is implicated with having "open" eyes. To "la oju," which literally means "to open eyes," is to be discerning, civilized, cultured, enlightened. Fela appropriates this cultural worldview and makes it the organizing principle of his pedagogical aesthetics in which the task of the pedagogue is to "open" the eyes of the people; that is, to teach them, raise their consciousness, and lift the veil that cloaks their oppression so they can resist it. I have therefore given Fela the last word here: "I have opened the eyes of the people to oppression in our continent. The people know I did it. I'm honest and consistent. That's enough."[8]

# 8 The Cosmopolitan Nativist: Fela and the Antinomies of Postcolonial Modernity

The frank admission needs to be made right away that an even-tempered critique of such a multisided, spectacular popular artist as Fela who excites little but untethered passions is indeed a challenge. Popular encyclopedias and "world beat" pamphlets have had a field day with their one-dimensional, cash-and-carry profiles. These pretend to no higher purpose than advertisement, that plainly motivated and unashamedly biased genre of persuasion, and so they succumb to the pressures of "watered-down" labeling demanded by mass-culture marketing, not to say marketers. But even otherwise useful studies have been understandably awed by this or that particular side of Fela, sacrificing a more robust assessment as a result.[1] Yet as the preceding chapters make clear, Fela's musical practice is too multitextured to gloss and discipline into a univocal narrative, no matter how alluring that option is. I suggest that a chastening, and therefore potentially more rewarding, study of that musical practice is best pursued by examining what I identify as its conceptual hallmark: its antinomies.

## The Antinomies of Postcolonial Cultural Production

Musically, Fela was an accomplished musician, but his extrasonic or extramusical reputation dominated and still dominates that of the musical. He thoroughly enjoyed this extramusical reputation and repeatedly stoked its fire in pronouncements and lifestyle, but he nevertheless struggled laboriously in each of his canonical songs to subvert and redirect that attention to the musical. He did this by emphasizing instrumental sound and drastically scaling down the time allotted to the rhetorically ostentatious and politically inflaming lyrics. At the level of personal lifestyle, he was an indefatigable campaigner against tyranny but he ran a strictly hierarchical household, much like a palace, though with hardly the structural checks and balances of model indigenous Yoruba monarchies. He was the son of Nigeria's foremost nationalist and campaigner for women's rights, but he was also the one who gave many boys of my generation a popular language of sexism and made that sexist language extremely musically pleasurable. In terms of political ideology, he was fundamentally a cultural nationalist, but he was also acutely class conscious and some of his main intellectual props are categorically left-leaning and anti–cultural nationalist intellectuals. We could go on and on with the apparent paradoxes. The critic and

Fela's friend John Howe hints at these antinomies when he notes that Fela "had no interest in perfect philosophic correctness" and that "contradictions of a sometimes painful sort were apparent in Fela's own life and household."[2]

Antinomy describes a contradiction between conclusions or inferences drawn from equally warranted or necessary principles. It marks the radically dispersed heterogeneity of desire and a reaffirmation of the irrepressible bursting seams of the social in the face of the usually disciplining aspirations of thought, of the knowing subject. A "fundamental aporia,"[3] antinomy is the condition of incommensurability between judgments that each seem to be just as valid, coherent, or essential as the other. The antinomies of Fela's art, because they are persistently and publicly given full play at the levels of thought as well as praxis, underscore their immediate sociality in a dependent postcolony's unequal social relations within itself and with the outside world. A close study of the antinomies promises larger insights about cultural production in postcoloniality, that condition of an unresponsive but nevertheless enticing modernity.[4]

The especially interesting antinomy I will explore at some length here is the one that is central to the ideological matrix that subtends Fela's musical practice: his unyielding nativism—his insistence on privileging "authentic" African paradigms and institutions in search of solutions to many African problems today—from corrupt leadership to a health care system in collapse—as well as his simultaneous, equally relentless cosmopolitanism—a deliberate anchor of his practice and passions in the transnational and the global. For him, "authentic" postcolonial music, especially a committed political music, could speak only with the voice of a "cosmopolitan nativist," borrowing tools from wherever in defense of African ways of knowing conceived as embattled by Euro-American cultural imperialism.[5] In this conception, postcolonial musical modernity—indeed, postcolonial modernity—is best theorized as an aporia pulling together two or more apparently contradictory paradigms. In a condition of aporia, social and political action can only be contingent and continuously subject to revision; only a full affirmation of this in both thought and praxis can make aporia enabling.

Tyrannical leadership, political instability, flagrant disregard for rules and entrenched nepotism as the currency of official transactions, economic malformation, epochal inequalities between the few and the many, impossible cities, recurrent devastating interethnic wars, antistate rebellions and the attendant heart-breaking dispersal of populations: these are a few of the components of postcolonial African history that catalyze Fela's nativist exertions. He seems to be exasperated not so much with the crises as with their seeming permanence, their normalization. Because he reads this contemporary "crisis-as-norm" as without precedent in the entire preslavery history of Africa,[6] he invests that period and the "African past" and "traditions" more vaguely with great polemical power as potential ameliorative capital. Perhaps it is understandable then that Fela strategically locates the origin of the African crisis in slavery and colonialism. The question he asks is the simple interrogative, "Why Black Man Dey Suffer" (1971), but he also means it to be explorative by the absence of the required question mark. In either case, his answer sets the stage for his obsession with reclamation and reinstatement of authentic African subjectivity:

| | |
|---|---|
| We dey sit down for our land jeje | We were living peacefully in our land |
| We dey mind our business jeje | Minding our own business peacefully |
| Some people come from far away land | |
| Dem fight us and take away our land | They fought us and stole our land |
| Dem take our people and spoil all our towns | They enslaved our people and destroyed our towns |
| Na since then trouble start | That's when our troubles started |
| . . . . | |
| Dem take our culture away from us | They suppressed our culture |
| Dem give us dem culture we no understand | They imposed on us their culture which we don't understand |
| Black people we no know ourselves | Black people we don't know ourselves |
| We no know our ancestral heritage | We don't know our ancestral heritage |

Fela would repeatedly return to this "original scene of the crime" to draw from it the justified anger at European despoliation of an innocent Africa. In the scenarios, Africa is often presented as in the death grip of cultural deracination by westernization, with Fela the Afrocentric[7] liberator wielding the heavy cudgel of venomous satire against the agents of Euro-American cultural imperialism, whether those agents be native or foreign.

Much more popular exemplars of Fela's nativism are "Lady," a satire against westernized African women, and "Gentleman," a companion piece about overly westernized African men. The phenomenon of skin bleaching that was rampant among urban Nigerian youths of the 1970s and early 1980s—a practice Fela read as self-hatred and a craving for Caucasian standards of beauty—is savaged in "Yellow Fever." He articulates the yellowness that results from bleaching as a disease by adroitly playing upon words and linking it to malaria, the local name of which is "yellow fever." In Fela's larger scheme of things, Africa as a whole is infected with the fever of westernization, of which this craze for skin lightness is just one instance. In "African Message," the indigenous "chewing stick" cleans the teeth much better than toothpaste and the local habit of using water is much more hygienic than the foreign-introduced toilet paper threatening to supplant it.[8] "Shuffering and Shmiling" ridicules Africans held in the thrall of foreign religions such as Christianity and Islam. As Fela sees it, abandoned African deities are not deceived, hence contemporary African prayers remain unanswered as Africans bow sheepishly to this and that alien divinity. On the album cover art, suffering Africans, against pleas by their own beckoning deities, cart all their resources to the altars of Islam and Christianity, while the priests of those religions, the bishops and imams, grin broadly. What poor Africans get in return are cheap illusions that, as the lyrics say, tell them to accept their sufferings in this world so they can "enjoy for heaven." "Why not African religion," the cover art asks, in Fela's characteristic omission of the question mark, and reminds us, in case we have forgotten, that the arranger, composer, and producer of the record is Fela, "The Undisputed Black Mind." And as we remember

To our ancestors mythological and historical, a white cock in sacrifice.
Courtesy of Femi Osunla.

in the wild hit "Perambulator," the solution to the sorry state of modern health care delivery in Africa lies unequivocally in "African medicine." Even if enthralling lyricism alone was our yardstick, it would still be extremely difficult not to qualify and complicate Fela's nativism. Take, for instance, the very language of the lyrics, pidgin English, which I have analyzed as a potent denativizing and transethnic mass language. Even at the moment of articulation, Fela's nativism raises subversive queries about itself.

If the saying is true that how one talks says volumes about who one is, then Fela's well-known and particular mode of enunciation is worthy of consideration. His speech during performances or in interviews is often liberally sprinkled with such decidedly North American idiomatic expressions as "shit," "gonna," "fucking," "motherfucking," "ain't," "hell," "outta," "bullshit," and the like that were originally made global by the cultural imperialism of the Hollywood film industry. Were it not Fela himself who so publicly displays his deep subjection to such an "un-African" idiom, he would have been one of those repeatedly savaged by the musician in many albums as afflicted with the colonialism-induced inferiority complex he called, in a famous 1978 release, "colomentality" ("Colonial Mentality").

Even the musician's music is anything but nativist. Fela originally began playing the hybrid form of highlife jazz. Even when Fela's mother famously admonished him to "start playing music your people know, not jazz," Fela did not shift to any of the more indigenous forms such as *juju, apala, fuji,* or *sakara.* And when he finally invented "afrobeat," it was only by the seductive power of his great will and rhetoric that we all—crazy fans—agreed to accept his description of the form as "authentically" African. Others were more measured in their attitude to afrobeat. In the early 1970s, the late *apala* king Haruna Ishola was no doubt referring to Fela's music then conquering Lagos, and foreign disco music generally, to which the older musicians were wont to consign afrobeat, when he sang the noted rebuke:

| | |
|---|---|
| Ta wa ya to si t'awon ajo foniloju | You won't blind anyone [with your wild wigwaggings] dancing to our fare |
| I am very sorry kii se pe a bu won | We can't say this of the music of some musicians we know |
| Ero gbede ni'jo oni gbendeke | I am sorry, but we are really not abusing them |
| Bata nsuru lani ki amu wa | Just distinguishing our subtle, mannered style.[9] |

Haruna here hinted at one of the more obvious perceived differences between afrobeat and the existing dominant indigenous forms: its aesthetic relationship, as dance music, to established Yoruba body language. Afrobeat is faster in tempo and generally calls on much physicality in dancing.

Before afrobeat, existing musics such as highlife, but more decisively *juju* and *apala,* had fashioned for the Yoruba body a tempo that idealized royalty in bearing, a stately elegance, and a majestic gravity; its articulating principle is the *middle*—not too hot and not too cold—culturally valorized for its supposed philosophical poise, wisdom, and openness. This is consummated by the musics' panegyric form, in which only the superlative praise, and then some more, is due the aristocracy, the elite, and the wealthy. *Juju* music is virtually impotent outside of a context that glorifies and mythologizes wealth and status and, in the final analysis, considers poverty a kind of curse. *Juju* suggests to its listeners dreams and visions of infinite affluence and everlasting grandeur. Afrobeat subverts this constructed native ideal with its much faster and therefore ruder tempo. The Yoruba royal body is the richly clothed body, and here too, afrobeat spits on the culturally dominant sartorial etiquette. The flowing, capacious *agbada* or the elaborately woven meter-high *gele*[10] that is supposed to "sway *gently* to the beat" in *juju*—"*e sa ma miliki o*" (just keep swaying gently) as leading *juju* musician, Chief Commander Ebenezer Obey, puts it in a famous release, *E Sa Ma Miliki* (1970)—find no regard here. Just imagine dancing afrobeat in *agbada* or *iro, buba,* and *gele*! The sartorially decorous class of the rich that is showered with praises in *juju* is the same that is relentlessly abused and lampooned in the more agile and frenetic afrobeat. Even the afrobeat inventor's body frame rebels against the valorized cultural norms. Embodied in *juju* is an aesthetics of corpulence in which the more flesh on the bones the better and ampleness is the privileged marker of both opulence and wellness. From the point of view of *juju* and indeed other Yoruba panegyric musics, Fela, with his gaunt frame (made more noticeable by his usual bare clothing or his signature skin-tight shirts and trousers), cuts the image of a hungry and sick man indeed. King Sunny Ade, leading *juju* musician, is gaunt too, but he is ever resplendent in capacious agbada, and that makes the whole difference. *Juju* trains your vision on the end goal of all aspiration, defined as the acquisition of limitless wealth, many children, high status, and a magical triumph over all enemies real and imagined; its implied horizon does not extend beyond the immediate culture where those elements carry great cultural capital. On the other hand, afrobeat hails you as a member of the oppressed lower classes; its harried, rabble-rousing tempo insistently reminds you of the harshness of your life and now and then shows you in a very bad light those who profit from the harsh system so that you can confront them; its horizon is simultaneously transcultural, transnational, and transcontinental. It is the most cosmopolitan of Nigerian popular musics. Fela nativized his surname Ransome-Kuti to Anikulapo-Kuti, and Koola Lobitos became Africa 70, and Egypt 80, but the apparently westernized orchestra,[11] complete with the trumpets, saxophones, and keyboards all remained. *Dundun* or *bata,* those most culturally distinctive Yoruba percussive musical instruments, never made it to his orchestra.

## Taming Enchanting Modernity

But how do we read the antinomies that constitute and structure Fela's musical practice? I have been using "antinomy" to avoid the two pitfalls the more familiar term "contradiction" commonly produces: the "contradictions" in Fela as caused by his personal failings at the level of thought or ideology or by the chaos of postcolonial history that created him.[12] The first invests Fela with an absolutely autonomous individual subjectivity, which no human being really has, and the second completely divests him of it. The best way to read the antinomies, it seems to me, is at the interface of these two; that is, to see the "contradictions" as located at the juncture of Fela's individual subjectivity and the structural conditions that produce it. I have borrowed "antinomy" to tap into that sense in which, given the historically determinate choices confronting a subject, a "contradiction" between two necessary choices may be inevitable.

Fela's colossal exertion, I suggest, is willfully aimed at taming the modernity that is dominant today, that historical aggressive western imposition on other lands, which he felt had dealt Africa an unfair blow. To tame at all, much less do so successfully, demands that what is to be tamed is readable within the hermeneutic horizon of the tamer. What is to be tamed must be known and digestible within that most elementary but fundamental forms of understanding—friend or enemy, good or evil, and similar oppositions by which we categorize our world. The significance of these oppositions in ordering relationships, knowledge, and action is underscored by the distinguished sociologist Zygmunt Bauman when he writes that "we may say that friendship and enmity, and only they, are forms of sociation; indeed the archetypal forms of all sociation" and that between them, "they make the frame within which sociation is possible, they make for the possibility of 'being with others.'"[13]

The distance between friend and enemy is not as important as their mutual self-recognition. This is not to say that there is always a symmetry of power relations between them but to emphasize the mutual self-(re)production. And the poles are so expansive as to be capable of disciplining in either direction all the messy surplus of variations within their spectrum. Without friends, there would be no enemies, and the reverse is true. "Being a friend, and being an enemy," Bauman writes, "are the two forms in which the other may be recognized as another subject, construed as a subject 'like the self', admitted into the self's life world, be counted, become and stay relevant."[14] The basic condition of coherence of Fela's project of taming is that modernity is readable within this opposition, as friend or enemy, to make it fully compliant—by yielding its secrets—before Africa's hermeneutical gaze. But the historical circumstances of that modernity's encounter with Africa firmly preclude any such certainty of readability, though the urge to forcefully impose a reading is often irresistible. Friends and enemies are on the terrain of the known and decidable, but the modernity imposed on Africa is outside this orbit and defines and occupies an undecidable entity. I have elsewhere characterized this multifaced, undecidable nature as enchanting, an aporetic situation in which modernity is simultaneously railed at as an alien, oppressive, and bewitching illusion (a *dis*-enchantment), and as a catalyst for further striving (a *re*-enchantment).[15] It is as yet untamable, but it is also inescapable. Bauman's term for this enchanter is the "stranger," a figure that short-circuits the (discord-ridden, tension-soaked, yes, yes, but also fundamentally psychically comforting) friend-enemy economy and disperses the protocols of recognition that sustain their opposition and therefore capacity to generate coherent meaning. I quote Bauman in some detail:

> Against this cosy antagonism, this conflict-torn collusion of friends and enemies, the stranger rebels. The threat he carries is more awesome than that which one can fear from the enemy. The stranger threatens the sociation itself—the very possibility of sociation. He calls the bluff of the opposition between friends and enemies as the compleate mappa mundi, as the difference which consumes all differences and hence leaves nothing outside itself. As that opposition is the foundation on which all social life and all differences which patch and hold it together rest, the stranger saps social life itself. And all this because the stranger is neither friend nor enemy; and because he may be both. And because we do not know, and have no way of knowing, which is the case.[16]

The stranger thus poses the greatest challenge to taming. Most attempts to tame the stranger will have to be prepared to accommodate the inadequacies, wobbly edges, and bursting seams that will inevitably result. There may be no want of heroic effort to rise up to the challenge, and the productivity may even be gargantuan, as in Fela's case. But victory is never guaranteed, and even many of the successes will appear to be condemned to something like a perpetual self-suspicion.[17] And since the purpose of taming is control, the decisive imposition of one's own will and imprint on the borrowed or imposed, the inability to fully tame has meant the inability to exercise critical control over the stranger—that is, modernity—in Africa.

Taming a stranger, a stranger that may be friend or foe, is thus bound to leave a trail of paradoxes, contradictions, and, to be more precise, antinomies. Fela rhetorically foregrounds his nativism more than his cosmopolitanism, but given the circumstances of his socialization and then self-resocialization, he *cannot not* be cosmopolitan, a citizen of the world. But the same factors of resocialization demand that he anchor his cosmopolitanism, unlike the conservative free-floating version that is celebrated as paradigmatic today, in a collectivity embattled precisely by the same historical forces of that cosmopolitanism. It is for this reason that Fela also *cannot not* be nativist, exposing the repressions and inequities that underwrite the reign of the cosmopolitan.[18] In this regard, Fela seems well aware of that perspicacious critique of the new cosmopolitanism launched by Timothy Brennan:

> The new cosmopolitanism drifts into view as an act of avoidance if not hostility and disarticulation toward states in formation. The dichotomy and the binary almost universally deplored—as much in official policy statements and editorials as in literary theory—continues to make sense (indeed, is demanded) dialectically, not in the name of authentic, non-European culture or any other useful fiction but in the name of what this conflict over colonialism and postcolonialism has largely been about: collectivity, community, self-sufficiency.[19]

Unlike Brennan, I am not anxious at all about the word "authentic" and therefore am willing to say that Fela's nativism is a quest for authentic subjectivity. "Authentic subjectivity" is, after all, an oxymoron, and this should begin to lead us to an appreciation of a peculiar contribution that studying Fela specifically and postcolonial cultural production generally makes to critical social theory. "Authentic subjectivity" is an oxymoron because subjectivity as such can never be authentic, meaning completely self-fashioned. After all, we achieve subjectivity only in language, a fully formed symbolic economy—with all its tendentious structuring predispositions—to which we are born without choice. Our subjection to—or, if we prefer the soothing euphemism, immersion in—the given language is the condition for our speaking, our subjectivity. Because our subjection here is so foundational and enabling, we rarely lament it as inauthentic or as oppression but mostly speak our language and bear our names proudly about, as if we chose them ourselves. At this fundamental level, our subjection enables our agency—that is, our capacity to act on the world—in a "natural," unobtrusive way. But this is a narrative of subjectivity in the foundational, normative sense, which is far less complicated—because it is more "natural"—than the production of the (post)colonial subject. Unique in the latter is the second layering, a second subjection, this time to an alien symbolic economy, western, that is neither fundamental nor escapable. What is neither fundamental nor escapable cannot but constantly call attention to itself, which is why our subjection to the second layer is often experienced as a corruption, a circumscription of our agency, and therefore inauthentic. It is in the context of the double layering that it is possible to speak of "authentic subjectivity": as a gesture against the visibly oppressive second layer of subjection and toward the (illusion of) autonomy or self-control that constitutes subjection at the first, fundamental level.

Nativism in postcolonial cultural production is not a rejection of the encounter with Europe or of modernity as such; it does not fear openness, and hybridity is not alien to it. What it laments is the "forced necessity"[20] of the native to capitulate, appropriate, or borrow: a characteristic condition of capitalist modernity that rules out equality in advance. Fela's nativism is not an atavistic return to roots but a reclaiming of "authentic subjectivity": a subjectivity that expresses—that is, subjects—itself "freely" without the element of a crudely obvious compulsion; the power and autonomy of Africa to direct itself and its place in the world. In other words, Fela's nativism is not against the foreign as such but against the seemingly unappeasable—that is, untamable—power of the foreign and the seeming inevitability of its dominance in the lives of the natives. Inevitability precludes choice, and subjectivity without (the illusion of) choice will forever have the taint of the inauthentic. We can keep "authenticity" as a powerful energizer and rallying cry once we keep in constant focus that "inauthenticity" is and remains a catachresis, a misapplication of terminology, since what it means to say is not really "not original" but "dominated." Antinomy, given such an unparalleled expansive play by Fela's musical practice, promises to be a useful figure for cutting through the dense perplexities of our postcolonial modernity.

# 9 The Political, the Libidinal

## The Social Activism, the Outrageous Sensationalism

Fela's artistic practice, the composite of all the musical and extramusical exertions that go into the production of afrobeat as a musical genre and social stance, is constituted by two broad streams of thought and action that are often perceived as antithetical. On the one hand is Fela's deep commitment, although it is admittedly shot through with inconsistencies, to oppositional anti-establishment action toward more egalitarian social and political relations. The commitment is evident in afrobeat's incendiary verbal attacks against the unresponsive postcolonial state and its retainers and foreign backers; it is also palpable in the music's embodiment of a whole range of sounds that dramatically disconcerts the existing sonic landscape in its mass broadcast of truant, insubordinate modes of hearing, listening, and even body rhythm. "Outside" the music are the musician's interventions in the nation's sphere of politics: his sponsorship or formation of activist groups and a political party, his many polemical public lectures, and his newspaper interviews and advertisements that discuss the state of the nation. This is the compound side of Fela that everyone recognizes as the "political." Most of the available scholarship on Fela is preoccupied with this "political" aspect, no doubt for reasons of its obviousness or for its uniqueness in the Nigerian, and African, popular music scene.

But on the other hand is Fela's equally deep absorption in a terrain that is not immediately considered "political" and is in fact often regarded to be subversive of his politics: his pervasive and enduring narcissism composed of gross sexual exhibitionism, a huge egotistical striving for effect, and a broad outrageous sensationalism. We can see all these in the musician's countercultural lifestyle: the nature of the household he ran, the valorization of sexual excess and permissiveness, the culture of marijuana use, and the general flagrant flouting of conventional morality. Sonically, we can point to Fela's famous extended instrumental compositions—a hankering after "pure" sound that is unusual in a popular form in a musical-cultural context in which verbal dexterity is the primary currency of exchange, indeed a major marker of musical greatness. In other words, while the emphasis in dominant Nigerian popular musics is the *sound of sense*, afrobeat foregrounds the *sense of sound*. The sound of sense is perceived primarily—though not exclusively—through lyrics and reaches out to the social, where verbal representations are commonly shared and the meanings of lyrics are easily deciphered. The sense of sound, on the contrary, is primarily sonic and gestures in to the structure of the sound itself and the virtuosity of the creator; the sound is commonly shared but its meaning cannot be easily assumed or deciphered or can be done so only ambiguously; in a context ruled by lyrics, Fela's extended wordless instrumentation is often read as conceit, self-absorption. I am borrowing from the language of psychoanalysis to label this other part of Fela's practice the "libidinal."[1] Libido and the libidinal are located in the imaginary, the realm of the imagination, where mental images, "unreal" and illusory as they are, are nevertheless capable of exacting great power on an individual and catalyzing action in society.[2] In much of the current scholarship on Fela, little useful insight is available on this aspect of the musician's pursuit of the satiation of sensations, pleasures without boundaries, and extremities of intensities. And needless to say, there has been virtually no attempt to think about how the two aspects, the "political" and the "libidinal," might be conceptually or practically linked other than the simplistic valorization of one—the political—and the equally simplistic condemnation of the other—the libidinal.

In Lacanian psychoanalysis, the two dimensions, the political and the imaginary with its libidinal content, have specific figurations that I find very suggestive in reading Fela, and I will soon return to the point. Ordinarily, the two dimensions ought not to be opposed[3]; after all, there is no imaginary without a political-sociological context. The political is not devoid of imaginary investments, while libidinal productions do have their own politics.[4] If the two parts appear to be incompatible in Fela's musical practice, it is because he makes them seem so by garishly playing out their difference in apparently opposed directions. It is for this reason that many have read the two parts as constituting a sort of predicament, a quandary, in Fela's musical practice.[5] It is important to closely examine the perception.

We can read the "predicament" from two points of view: first, from the point of view of public perception, which sees Fela's absorption in a rational politics of mass empowerment and his equal absorption in various forms of arational amorality as antithetical. And second, from the point of view of political theorizing, in which Fela's progressive politics and crass hedonism, his simultaneous quest for egalitarian orderliness in political economy, and his espousal and exhibition of mental dispositions that are seen as constitutive of disorder appear to be little more than lawlessness and mayhem. The realm of the "political" need no further exemplification in Fela; it is the imaginary and its libidinal productions that we need to sketch out in detail.

The imaginary is the first of Jacques Lacan's three-part narrative of the formation of subjectivity—the imaginary, the symbolic, and the real. The imaginary is that fantasy-laden phase and component of mental development which is characterized by misrecognitions of self and the other and the energetic dreaming up of substitute scenarios that are difficult to realize or are unrealizable within the society's hegemony of culturally sanctioned norms. The symbolic is the realm of society: of culture and language, where the main weapons of our transactions in defense of our interests are symbols, representations.[6] The real is not "reality" but that which cannot be made palpable in the symbolic—

that which cannot be symbolized, "that which resists symbolization absolutely."[7] I am more immediately concerned with the imaginary. It is

> the realm of image and imagination, deception and lure. The principal illusions are those of wholeness, synthesis, autonomy, duality and, above all, similarity. The imaginary is thus the order of surface appearances which are deceptive, observable phenomena which hide underlying structure; the affects are such phenomena.[8]

The imaginary is a domain of an extreme volatility of emotions that are capable of shifting in moments from blissful contentment to excruciating discontentment, undue narcissism, and a preoccupation with the signified and signification rather than with the signifier. In short, the imaginary is that phase of comparative psychic comfort and luxury in which we, corporeal bodies, imagine ourselves not only as the center of the universe but as the universe itself, free from the dictates and taboos of culture. Classically exemplified by the "mirror stage,"[9] with its various sexual and other libidinal transactions, the imaginary is a field of illusions, but those illusions are often so powerfully (emotionally) cathected as to lead the subject to concrete action in the realm of the symbolic, the realm of culture.

I describe the imaginary above as a phase and component of mental development. Let me clarify. The mirror stage has two kinds of value in Lacan's theory of the subject: historical and structural. As a historical value, the mirror stage describes that stage of a child's development, from about six to eighteen months, characterized by the child's jubilant identification with its image in a mirror and its consequent assumption of self-recognition and mastery, which is actually a misrecognition since it is illusory. As a structural value, it represents a permanent aspect of the composition of subjectivity as such, irrespective of age. In Lacan's words, the mirror stage is "a phenomenon to which I assign a twofold value. In the first place, it has a historical value as it marks a decisive turning-point in the mental development of the child. In the second place, it typifies an essential libidinal relationship with the body-image."[10]

My suggestion is that Fela's contextually transgressive morality be read as a loaded symptom of his overinvestment in that less culturally policed order of subjectivity known as the imaginary. That he reveled so voluptuously in a discourse and practice of sexuality that always scandalously breached the hegemonic norms in his cultural context should tell us how intensely he was invested in the imaginary, where desires run rampant and relatively unchecked by social taboos and canons of civility. Take, for instance, the unusually high volume of things implicitly or explicitly sexual associated with his public image, of which these are just a few: his public XXX-rated claims about his own generous sexual appetite and escapades and the universally pervasive exaggerations and circulations of same in the public arena by his audience; his unhidden objectification of women solely as sexual; his many songs about sex, most of them quite gratuitous; his many women in the household and his "wedding" of twenty-seven women in one fell swoop; his train of scantily clad female dancers; his own frequent minimalist dressing even for stage performances, and more. It

"Ayakataa!" Fela dances at the Africa Shrine.
Courtesy of Femi Osunla.

is as if because Fela felt the restrictions[11] of the symbolic realm—the society—so profoundly, he frequently needed to resort to imaginary dreams and exertions as a counterpoint. But the "law" of society is that we may imagine but not actualize the dreams; Fela's transgression is his nearly routine aggressive attempts to actualize the imaginary in the realm of the symbolic. There is just no conceptually rewarding way to read this garish dramatization of the pursuit of libidinal intensities other than as a sign of Fela's overabsorption in the imaginary.

Although for Lacan the sexual is a principal component of the imaginary,[12] all narcissisms and illusions of wholeness as such are sponsored by the imaginary. And in Fela can be found a bagful too of narcissisms. Fela's enclosed residence, which he styled a "republic" independent of the Nigerian republic, and his role in that republic as president and absolute lawgiver are only small monuments to his untethered egotism. He meticulously cultivated the sign "Africa" and invested it with an essential content that is supposedly immediately obvious to all and therefore not necessary to prove. Henceforth, that sign became a touchstone of everything good—a weapon of resistance against the recalcitrant contradictions of a dependent postcolony. Toward the end of his life, he was wont to distance himself from the label he invented, "afrobeat," as too commercial, with the rider that the true name of his music is really "African" music. If we concede to Fela that afrobeat is really authentically "African" music, and if we know that our combative Fela would never have classed his music among others, then what of all those musics that are not afrobeat but were invented and are played by Africans?[13] Yes, Fela is that absolutist in quest of wholeness. He was a great musical stylist, yet we could also say that in other matters, he cared very little for style; it didn't seem to matter to him whether a style matched a purpose or not, and often the style was the purpose and the meaning. His stock in trade as an artist was producing and broadcasting significations, representations, yet he had a cultivated disdain for any self-reflexive critical exploration of the primary tools of that task, the signifiers, as if only representations and their meanings matter. In fact, the disdain was so acute that one cannot but suspect that he was forcefully willing representation into becoming presentation, a typical imaginary act that aims for the supposedly immediately accessible, that aims to overcome symbolization and its restrictive and unpredictable rules and processes.

I could go on, but I will give only one more example. This is what I call the pedagogic anxiety that saturates Fela's musical practice. Since the beginning of his socially conscious afrobeat phase in 1970, Fela's music has been defined by a goal, advocacy, and by a form designed to achieve that goal, the pedagogic. I have argued that there is nothing new or unique about an artist making advocacy a goal and articulating an appropriate pedagogical form to carry out that agenda and that what is unique about Fela was his obsessive double anxiety to teach and to make sure that we get the message of the teaching completely. This is a great challenge indeed. Fela obviously saw the task of liberation as urgent, and he could not bear that the oppressed would misread his self-labeled revolutionary messages by the time those messages reached the people. This is why he distrusted the gap between signification and meaning and constantly tried to close it. In addition, he perceived the gap as already fully occupied by the ruling oppressive norms with which the system indoctrinates the people, as he sang about so eloquently in such popular tracks as "Lady," "Gentleman," and "Shuffering and Shmiling." So he rams the messages repeatedly into our heads. In addition, Fela's penchant for satire and the satiric form, with its omniscient perspective and Olympian height from which it self-righteously dishes out sanctions left and right, assumes that the satirist is the sole possessor of truth. The great urge to sermonize repeatedly and the anxiety that the listener get the message completely without any error are part and parcel of Fela's imaginary exertion to disregard the signifier and close the inevitable gap and time lag between representation and meaning, address and addressee, ideology and effect, desire and fulfillment, between "event" and "eventuality," as Homi Bhabha would say.[14] Fela refused to seriously countenance any theory of interest or ideology, resorting instead to the idea of miseducation—"colomentality"—to explain conceptions and performances of Africa that diverged from his. Because he believed that human beings could be educated "correctly"—never mind his disregard of the issue of who decides what is "correct"—he was obsessed with the pedagogical task of changing consciousness, as if "correct" consciousness signals the end of ideology, as if it is not itself an(other) ideology. Even a revolutionary discourse must acknowledge its own contingency to prevent its transformation to merely another tyranny.

It is important not to rush to judgment; Fela's "imaginaryphilia," if we could say that, is neither a liability nor an asset in absolute terms. By his stalwart refusal to abide by the regime of the cultural norm in his context, a norm with its partisan exclusions and inclusions, he helped immensely in deconstructing the ideological normality of that norm and expanding the horizons of possibility within the culture. It is not an exaggeration to say that without Fela, the entrance of sexuality into Nigerian public discourse would have been at least one decade behind the level it is today. And when we realize that the ease with which a polity is able to publicly confront its sexuality is related to the ease with which it is ready to play open politics, then we can begin to realize the constructive political dimensions of Fela's public hankering after libidinal gratifications. His narcissism, his attempt to close the unpredictable gap between ideology and effect, to transform the pedagogical into the performative without any risk or effort—in short, his attempt to make representations transparent without the labor of interpretation because interpretation cannot always be trusted to yield the correct meaning—could even be read as an inspiring glimpse of utopia that puts in gaudy relief the inadequacies of the symbolic realm of culture where we always have to do the real hard work of interpretation and persuasion with no guarantee of success.

But there is another side to this, for there is a sense in which Fela's willful fixation on the imaginary could be seen as an escape from the realm of the symbolic, where matters of inequality and justice are ultimately decided. The symbolic is a messy realm of unpredictability, but the subject has no choice but to affirm it and its compromises, for that is essentially what culture or society is. The tyrannical dimension of Fela's pedagogical anxiety is that to want to close the gap between representation and meaning is really to deny the dominated one of the few structures of possibility they have in exerting agency over ideologies directed at them by those with the might and means to do so. For the gap between signification and meaning is a potential zone of instability in which intended meanings could be scrutinized and turned on their heads. Of course, Fela was right to be suspicious of, even cynical about, the vaunted possibilities of the gap, since the presence of so many oppressed people in the world who are completely sold to the ruling norms is evidence enough for him that oppressive ideologies are passing through that zone unsubverted and are catching the people. But he was wrong to assume that the task of a liberating pedagogy is to evacuate the people of a "false" consciousness deposited in them by oppressive ideologies and instead deposit in them a "true" radical consciousness crafted by the all-knowing avant-garde musician-intellectual. Either way, the people's agency is discounted, even subverted.

Because the symbolic is structured by a lack, by a disjunction between the signifier and the signified, the struggle at this level is not between compromise and no compromise, between correct and incorrect readings; instead, the struggle is frequently between enabling and disabling compromises based on a set of declared goals, between readings that impede or advance a declared set of interests.[15] The precondition for subjecthood is an affirmation of the cultural symbolic order, with all its partisan arrangements and inequities, and an affirmation of its overall disciplining power over the imaginary. Anything else is, well, merely imaginary. This is the point where we can locate a critique of Fela's imaginaryphilia. To be sure, we must acknowledge that he was working with a form, music, which is capable of whipping up human emotions with an irresistible immediacy that makes it particularly prone to activating exertions of the imaginary. In particular, afrobeat's swift tempo and signature hypnotic repetitions and looping rhythms can only accelerate and amplify that generic affect. Music wraps us in an acoustic envelope and heightens our emotional response, whatever color that response takes, even before we are conscious of it. In fact, it could be argued that the power and our love of music reside precisely in the fact that it is capable of transporting us momentarily to fantasyland, where we are relieved of all the tensions of quotidian life in society. Otherwise, music would not be the preeminent language worldwide of the means of human mastery over reality—ritual, whether sacred or secular. But the problem, the predicament, in Fela's musical practice is that the ritual often subverts the declared goal of mastery.

## "What Predicament?"

Fela never cared about any supposed predicament in his musical practice. He was quite satisfied playing both the political and the imaginary dimensions in all their flamboyance and sensationalism. Now and then, he would veer precipitously toward folding the political into the imaginary, as one would expect of an unrepentant sybarite, rather than toward disciplining the imaginary with the whip of political symbolism, as one would normally expect of a political artist and activist. When he formed the political party Movement of the People and campaigned for the presidency of Nigeria, one of the many things he said he would do if elected was to play music for the country every day so that everyone could dance and be happy. "Imagine the president playing music to announce budgets and policies," he enthused.[16] The famous song "Army Arrangement" is an attack on the Nigerian military for its corruption and nepotism, but Fela still has time in the track to compose an eloquent homage to the shapely "wonderful material property" that is the buttocks. It is very brief and obviously used as a filler, but we know that what seems marginal at the level of conscious content is often central at the level of the unconscious. In 1997, the year of his death, Fela complained to a journalist about the local effects of global political-economic policies and threw in the sex without missing a beat: "Dem don devalue crude oil and cocoa. What I made them realize is that when you don devalue the naira, you make African toto [vagina] cheap. May be in the U.S., you will require 500 dollars to fuck. But here, ten dollars is enough. You see what I mean?"[17] In the song "Chop and Clean Mouth: New Name for Stealing," we are treated to the usual "Felaisms": the oppression and exploitation of Nigerians and Africans by both locals and foreigners; the musical-chairs leadership since independence in which one leader appears, embezzles, cleans up his acts as if he did nothing, and then vanishes for another one to take his place; the killing IMF–World Bank–sponsored Structural Adjustment Program (SAP), which he says actually means "Suck African People" until they die; and more of the same. Then halfway through the song, as it is building toward one of its many climaxes with the deafening roar of the live audience coming more into the foreground, Fela bursts into a refrain of "You see a woman you see a vagina. The penis is hard, the vagina is wet. Vagina! Penis! Balls! Give me vagina!! Where is vagina!! I want vagina!!" and so forth, in both Yoruba and Hausa. Absolutely gratuitously; nothing in the song so far prepares us for the sexual drama. He returns again to the refrain after another stretch of political harangues and laments. Needless to say, those refrains are what his core male audience remembers most in the track, the stretch you are most likely to catch them humming, not the sprawling tirades about political and economic injustice. If Fela, our very own bold, daring, and courageous Fela, can be seen as squeamish and cowardly, it would be on this score, this self-subversive sacrifice of the political on the altar of imaginary libidinal intensities and thereby a retreat from the realm of the symbolic where the messy struggle of inequality is more substantively fought. But I have argued that this cannot be the last word on Fela's indulgence in the imaginary. After all, it is not as if the imaginary could be done away with in the operation of the symbolic where the political is constructed. In fact, without the fantasies constantly generated by the imaginary, it would be impossible to constitute the symbolic as such. I earlier described society as a compromise; fantasy is what holds the compromise together. When Yannis Stavrakakis wrote perceptively that "[i]f political reality is a symbolic construction produced through metaphoric and metonymic processes and articulated around *points de capiton* and empty signifiers, it nevertheless depends on fantasy to constitute itself,"[18] he should have made clear that political reality also needs fantasy not just to constitute but to ever and perpetually *reconstitute* itself. If the imaginary is this significant to the ordering and reordering of the political, then ultimately what is at stake in Fela's practice is not so much his opposition of the political with the imaginary but the kind of imaginary exertions he is suggesting to us. And those exertions, while ideologically disagreeable in many instances, are on the whole salutary in their unyielding breaching of the frontiers of our hegemonic norms.

# 10 Conclusion: Afrobeat after Fela

## Unity into Multiplicity

Ancient lore has it that the Yoruba pantheon was originally composed of one entity, the primogenitor or original one, and its servant, Atunda, literally, recreation. As the deity was hoeing its farm on the slopes one day, Atunda rolled a huge boulder that smashed the original deity into a thousand and one fragments.[1] Several of the scattered shards metamorphosed into the many different deities, each taking its unique temperament from the character of its constituting splinter. Unity became multiplicity, and contingency replaced essence. Thus, the Yoruba pantheon emerged from and as an act of revolution. Fela was the "original one" of afrobeat till a few years before his death. Now there is a flowering of re-creations of afrobeat, each taking its character from this or that fragment of the essence-afrobeat. Given the uniqueness of Fela's music and his noted reluctance, indeed outright failure, to cultivate new entrants to the genre, the current flowering is nothing short of a revolution.[2]

There are several reasons why young aspiring Nigerian musicians did not take to playing afrobeat much earlier, apart from Fela's own apparent disinterest in encouraging a dispersal of the genre. Although Fela had been playing afrobeat for over three years before he became "political," the genre quickly took on a binding identity as "political music" by the time promising musicians could have studied it enough to be confident in expressing themselves in it. Given that Fela himself did not set out to be "political" but was imposed upon by historical circumstances to be so—and so he grew into the mode organically—it would have been a great challenge indeed for a musician to set up shop in the same way as Fela. This is especially so when we remember that Fela was not just "political" in this or that track in one album out of five but made "politicalness" the very fabric of his musical practice. Retroactively, afrobeat became a "quintessentially political" genre. This is already a prohibitive implicit demand from would-be afrobeat musicians; it becomes even more so when such a musician figures into the calculation Fela's sacrifices that made afrobeat so political: endless persecution by the state. It is a testament to the enduring image of afrobeat as essentially a "political" music that most of those who play that genre today feel bound, in one way or another, to take on the political themes of Fela. A related reason is that afrobeat, of all Nigerian popular music genres, is the one most identified with a particular inventor-figure who was the only exemplar of the genre for a long time. Fela's brand of antiestablishment politics and the unique counterculture he built from which afrobeat derived sustenance further solidified the popular impression of afrobeat as another name for charismatic

Fela. To play afrobeat music was literally to be trespassing in Fela's territory. Veteran drummer Tony Allen left Fela with rancor in the late 1970s and went solo. In spite of the fact that he was generally regarded as the one who put the beat in afrobeat, he never thrived as an afrobeat musician. Afrobeat was apparently more than the drums, and only Fela held the key to the other components of its identity.[3]

In addition, to choose afrobeat as a budding musician is to decide both musically and ideologically against the panegyric form. In a cultural context where all the richest and most famous musicians play nothing but panegyric music, the great economic risk of that decision is truly chastening. Most Nigerian popular musicians are from humble origins, and in addition to their talent and the love of music they may have, the dream of affluence is hardly a hidden inspiration for going into the profession. Indeed, this was for a long time a subterranean source of conflict between Fela and the original Africa 70 musicians. They took a risk with Fela's antipanegyric music and were lucky and wildly successful. The unspoken rule and practice among the panegyric musicians such as the *juju* stars was to spread the wealth somewhat among band members—thinly, but at least enough to ideologically temper the egregious and unequal gulf between bandleader and musicians; a pervasive discourse of kinship—borrowing from the Yoruba regard for kinship relations—now transferred into business relations helps cement the ideological work. But afrobeat was a "political" music and Fela was deep into politics, so he poured all the returns into politics, *his* passion, shared by his band members but certainly not to the same self-impoverishing degree. And he was not very interested in any ideological covering of relations—whether between bandleader and musician or not—other than the self-righteous assumption, made clear in the track "No Agreement," that everyone could see his transparent commitment to mass empowerment and egalitarian politics; the unjustified implication here was that that thereby put him above suspicion of domination in his many relations.

Finally, and by no means least important, are the factors of production of afrobeat. Of all Nigerian popular musics, an afrobeat orchestra, which depends heavily on horns, is the most expensive to set up. Even before the latter stage is reached, the difficulty of access to instruments because of their cost, as well as the cost of training where available, impact the consistency and intensity of training, the depth of skills a musician acquires, and therefore the available pool of skilled musicians. Add to this point the fact of afrobeat's intellectually dense and cosmopolitan lyrical content—it is as if it comes labeled with "college education required," Fela's belittling of college education notwithstanding—and we can see the elitism of afrobeat in its production even if not in its consumption.

By the 1990s, afrobeat had lost its newness, though not its uniqueness. It had become an old, established genre on the African popular music scene. In addition, due to ill health, Fela was much less in the news; he was not broken by the system but he had calmed down considerably, both musically and in terms of his contentious interventions in the social and political events and issues of the day. The result of these two circumstances was that afrobeat became much more available as a musical model; its previously felt attachment to the "political" had loosened considerably and the immediate and heavy shadow of the towering inventor-owner had lifted a great deal. And so opened the window of opportunity for aspiring afrobeat musicians who could scale the other hurdles of putting such a band together.

While bands playing afrobeat have begun to appear only recently, afrobeat instrumental patterns have over the years been amply sampled by leading Nigerian musicians such as Sunny Ade, Dele Abiodun, Segun Adewale, Sonny Okosun, and Ephraim Nzeka. Nzeka produced an album of Fela's recordings titled *Ephraim Sings Fela* in the 1980s. Across Africa, musicians such as Hugh Masekela of South Africa, Brice Wassy of Cameroon, and the group Hedzolleh Soundz of Ghana have acknowledged Fela's influence.[4] For many, the spirit behind Masekela's homage is typical: "Fela introduced me to his afrobeat, which I found magical. I had to be pulled away from the microphone; I literally could not stop playing with the patterns his wonderful rhythm section wove behind me. From this experience, I found the gateway to West African culture. . . . For this I remain ever grateful to Fela."[5] Masekela contributed to the tribute compilation *Afrobeat . . . No Go Die: Trans-Global African Funk Grooves* (2000) with other artists and groups such as Daktaris, Antibalas, Lagbaja, Tony Allen, Kiala, and Femi Kuti. Outside Africa, Fela learned a lot from African-American music, but the exchange has not been one way. Fela's influence is evident in certain compositions of James Brown after his 1970 trip to Nigeria; George Clinton, Alfred "Pee Wee" Ellis, Branford Marsalis, and Steve Turre have all incorporated aspects of Fela's afrobeat in their music. Trumpeter Lester Bowie of the Art Ensemble of Chicago stayed with Fela in Lagos for months in the late 1970s and was featured as guest artist on Fela's song "Perambulator." He would subsequently incorporate afrobeat into his compositions. Roy Ayers toured Nigeria with Fela in 1980, and they recorded *Music of Many Colours* together. Other leading musicians who have acknowledged and eulogized Fela include Stevie Wonder, David Bryne, Brian Eno, Paul McCartney, Robbie Shakespeare, Afrika Bambaataa, and Miles Davis.[6] Distinguished Trinidadian calypsonian David Rudder devoted two tracks to Fela in his *International Chantuelle* (1999). In 2002, the Red Hot Organization, a company based in the United States that produces a variety of projects to raise funds and awareness to fight AIDS worldwide, released *Red Hot + Riot*, a CD compilation of selected songs by Fela; the wide array of artists who performed the songs is itself a testimony to Fela's wide and still-growing influence: Mixmaster Mike, Dead Prez, D'Angelo, MeShell Ndegeocello, Cheikh Lo, Manu Dibango, Sade Adu, Yerba Buena, Ray Lema, Baaba Maal, Archie Shepp, and more.[7] Afrobeat, apparently, cannot be arrested. In July 2003, a huge multimedia exhibition on Fela's influence globally, *Black President: The Art and Legacy of Fela Anikulapo-Kuti*, was staged in New York by renowned curator Trevor Schoonmaker, who also edited the exhibition's companion collection of essays, *Fela: From West Africa to West Broadway*.

The future of afrobeat as a distinct kind of music will, however, depend on musicians who are committed to playing it as a genre, and there are several already. Tony Allen has released a number of LPs such as *No Discrimination* (1980), *N.E.P.A.* (1985), and *Afrobeat Express* (1989); his contribution to the genre is immense, even if he is not widely recognized yet. The irony is that his profile remains low even as afrobeat thrives in realization of his cherished dreams: "The only thing I want is to make sure this afrobeat spreads, like what reggae has done, like what funk has done, what jazz has done. Now is the time for this music."[8] One of the youngest of the new afrobeat bands is the New York–based Antibalas Afrobeat Orchestra, headed by Martin Perna. Formed in 1998 by a panethnic group composed of Latinos, Africans, African Americans, Asian Americans, and Euro-Americans, Antibalas ("bulletproof" or "anti-bullets" in Spanish) has released two compilations to some acclaim: the debut *Liberation Afrobeat Vol. 1* (2000) and *Talkatif* (2002), whose album cover was designed by Lemi Ghariokwu, Fela's artist. Unabashedly treading the lines grooved deep by Fela, Antibalas describes itself as "the next generation of afrobeat in the tradition of the Black President, Fela Anikulapo-Kuti. This fourteen-plus piece band hits hard with the left and the right—monstrous horns and bass layered over funky polyrhythmic beats and breaks coupled with furious lyrics challenging and attacking the dehumanizing capitalist system and inciting insurrection in English, Yoruba, and Spanish."[9] Quite a mouthful. The band's approximation of Fela in their debut release was so literal that a critic accused them of "sounding like a tribute band."[10] The group's second release shows that it is certainly a band to watch; it is gradually carving its own unique voice within afrobeat, as shown especially in the title track, "Talkatif," with the terrific Nigerian vocalist/percussionist, Duke Amayo. In the second album, it toned down its lyrics and generally cut back on them; after all, it does seem odd to sing against international monopoly capital right in the center of New York and be dependent on the patronage of a well-heeled middle-class clientele simply looking for a mindless night out. But in adjusting to its context, Antibalas runs a grave risk in the other direction: the aestheticization of afrobeat, its transformation to no more than dance music. That risk is already evident in *Talkatif,* which emphasizes afrobeat instrumentation for dancing. Antibalas has successfully toured North America and Europe and is already building a good following. Part of their success as a young band with a socially conscious agenda is evident in the fact that the U.S. National Public Radio network featured it on its popular program *Weekend All Things Considered* as the group that provides "America's only live Afrobeat party."[11] But by far the leading contenders for the afrobeat crown are two talented Nigerians, Femi Kuti, Fela's son, and Lagbaja (Bisade Ologunde).

## Femi Kuti

Perhaps it is only appropriate that the veteran of the new generation of afrobeat musicians is the eldest son of Fela himself, Femi Kuti. Femi was in his father's band for several years as a vocalist and saxophonist before striking out on his own in 1986 with the Positive Force band he formed. While he has no doubt been immensely helped by the name recognition conferred on him by his father's fame, the beginnings were far from rosy. Fela had little confidence in the young lad's skills, and he never hid his feelings about that. He once derided the son publicly as mediocre and the son nearly gave up. "That day, I felt like committing suicide but I kept trying," Femi recalled.[12] For a while, it appeared that father was right after all, as Femi played to empty houses after going solo. But his years of hard work and persistence ultimately paid off and won the dad over: Fela, never one to miss an opportunity for drama and exaggeration, swung to the other extreme and proclaimed Femi as the only other person who could play afrobeat like himself.[13] But those challenges, serious as they were, turned out to be preliminary battles. Femi would later find much more challenging the task of carving a distinct voice and space for himself, within yet outside the colossal shadow of Fela. He has had to bear the burden of popular expectations, both real and imagined, that he ought to replace Fela in all respects. He has been fervent in rejecting such expectations:

Nobody wanted to give me a chance, because I was Fela's son. They said I must do exactly what my father is doing. They thought that if I was going to take over playing afrobeat, I must smoke grass, have a lot of women around me, and if I'm not going to do all that, I can't be Fela's replacement. I said "Look, I don't intend to be Fela's replacement. I'm going completely different from where he's going. I must find my own way."[14]

Both in lifestyle and in music, Femi is carefully and determinedly finding his own way. He is by no means the dapper-suited musician, but he is not one to be caught in provocative bikinis either. He has tried assiduously to project a clean-cut image and to redefine seriousness and responsibility more conventionally and conservatively than his father did. Indeed, part of his reason for leaving his father's band was his dissatisfaction with Fela's implicit condoning of some of the objectionable behaviors and activities that were going on around the Shrine.[15] But this is not to say that Femi has gone puritan in an extremist revolt against the image of his father; much of the old block is still in this chip. Indeed, one of Femi's best-known songs, which was banned by some radio stations in Nigeria, is "Beng, beng, beng," which is about, in popular parlance, fucking.

Musically, Femi is much less invested in any supposed authenticity of afrobeat as African music, and in a move that would no doubt have earned Fela's disapprobation, he interfaced afrobeat with hip-hop and even had tracks electronically remixed to expand his audience base. His songs are shorter, and he has been very pragmatic in thinking about this in relationship to potential earnings, a thought that his father would have considered crass:

My music is more direct, more to the point. My father plays a number for about an hour now, his music is very relaxed. His music is more spiritual, I think. . . . Because I want to play music as well as make money, I will not play a number for that amount of time. I can understand the European mind, or the Western mind. They don't want to spend an hour trying to decide whether they like this number or not.

*Conclusion: Afrobeat after Fela* 179

Whereas the African man, he's ready to digest it for an hour, listen to the same rhythm. They believe the longer it is, the better it is for them.[16]

The overt racialization of musical taste should tell us that in terms of ideas and outlook, Femi is very much his father's son. As is typical with Fela, he turns a product of the pressures of the historical production and consumption of particular forms of art and leisure in different societies into a racial feature. The subtending ideology of Femi's afrobeat is a racialist cultural nationalism, with all its insights and contradictions. His class politics, unlike those of his father, are rudimentary, in spite of the many tracks he has devoted to attacking bad leadership and social inequality.

Femi has been releasing records at steady intervals of two to three years since the late 1980s: *No Cause for Alarm* (1989), *M.Y.O.B. (Mind Your Own Business)* (1991), *Femi Kuti* (1995), *Shoki Shoki* (2000), and *Fight to Win* (2001). Apart from the regard he has won in Nigeria, he has toured Europe and North America to enthusiastic receptions, and in terms of connections, he is pretty much plugged into the contemporary African-American popular music scene. He has won notable accolades both in Africa and beyond. In 1999, he won the Kora All Africa Music Award for Best Male Artist as well as for Best Artist/Group in West Africa. His other crowning achievement is the nomination of *Fight to Win* as Best World Music Album by the U.S.–based Grammy Award Nominations Committee in 2003.

Politically, Femi has taken on the father's agenda of attacking corruption and injustice in Nigeria in particular and in Africa generally but minus some of the father's extramusical political activities, especially his antagonistic confrontation with the authorities. In other words, the means of Femi's interventions in politics are primarily the music. He engages in other activities, though the operative principle now is "diplomacy":

We have a weekly radio broadcast, criticizing or praising the government. We have a paper now that comes out at the end of the month. We come out with statements, and things like that. We're very diplomatic because I don't think we should ever be too antagonistic, because we do not want any more wars in Africa, so we have to be very careful and we have to think about how to win the battle without blood.[17]

And then there is that very unique kind of politics imposed on the son by the manner of the father's death: AIDS awareness activism. In 2002, he agreed to be a special representative of UNICEF (United Nations Children's Fund) in the global struggle for AIDS awareness. "It is a natural partnership between one of the world's most prominent activist entertainers and the most influential organization working on behalf of the world's children," enthused UNICEF's executive director Carol Bellamy. "Femi Kuti is more than a talented and inspiring musician, he is a model for anyone who wants to make a difference in the world today. UNICEF is honoured that he is joining us and together we will not only make a difference for children, we will be able to save lives."[18] Two years earlier, Femi had published "Commentary: Speaking Out against AIDS" on UNICEF's

Femi Kuti.
Courtesy of *The News*.

Web site, an article about Fela's illness and death, the tragedy of AIDS in Africa, and a call for concerted action to fight the disease as well as poverty.[19]

There is no doubt that Femi has achieved a lot so far in his musical career; it is also true that in spite of that achievement, he is still very much an afrobeat musician in the making, with plenty room for improvement, especially in three areas of his music. First, his sonic arrangements are often cluttered, monotonous, and deficient in memorable sonic moments; the instruments frequently appear to be competing with themselves at the same decibel level. Second, his lyrics are often insipid even while conveying heavy sentiments. They are sometimes overly direct and lacking in developed imagery, as if snatched from the day's headlines; but the artistry of journalism is hardly the artistry of composition of lyrics. Third, and finally, Femi is nearly completely humorless, which is a serious impairment for an artist—a musician—who wants to make it a business to attack unjust and unequal political arrangements as well as entertain the audience.

The album *Femi Kuti* is a compendium of these limitations. The mid-tempo first track, "Wonder Wonder," starts the album on a promising note. Its brief instrumental introduction, which has a striking annunciatory quality to it, soon settles into a rhythmic pattern that wants to aid calm reflection if not that it is a little bit too lively. But it works well with Femi's lamentation, which nicely overlaps with the chorus and is underlined by the horns, of the many "wonders" in this world that will "surprise you, confuse you, depress you," such as the lack of "African unity"—decades after Kwame Nkrumah—and religious charlatanism and fanaticism. The track is thematically related to the up-tempo "Nawa," an expression of wonder in pidgin English about official corruption. Most of the other tracks try futilely to measure up. "Survival," with its staccato rhythm, sounds like a mere accompaniment to the lyrics which, like "Plenty Nonsense," are embarrassing in the obviousness of their observations and ordinariness of their sentiments. The same is true of "Frustrations," which crudely assumes that only "our young men," because they cannot "build house and buy car, marry wife and enjoy life," are frustrated by the contemporary Nigerian condition.

*Shoki Shoki,* the next album, is a significant advancement. "Truth Don Die O," the opening track, jettisons the newspaper headlines for a thoughtful allegory of the death of truth, crushed by a tractor-trailer while evangelizing for the dominance of truth; now, lies reign everywhere. The wildest hit in the album and perhaps the most famous of all Femi's songs is "Beng, Beng, Beng," about a sexual encounter with a girl. The great significance of the song is what it reveals about Femi's musical practice. The track's delightful storytelling, the suppleness and commanding authoritativeness of Femi's voice as he narrates the story, and the inspiring, flawless response of the ensemble and chorus have no parallel in any other song by Femi. But the "problem" is that the song is not "political"; it only titillates. The song reveals the extent to which Femi can enjoy singing and brilliantly communicate that enjoyment to the listener; by the same token, it also reveals in hindsight how little Femi really enjoys singing his "political" songs, whether he realizes that or not. Freed from the anxieties of being "political" and doing that satisfactorily, in "Beng, beng, beng" Femi literally stumbles into a deeper creative pool within himself that he has yet to fully tap. All programmatic conscious agendas also have programmatic limitations; because Femi was born into politics, he hardly had any space to explore directions outside the close supervision—or surveillance, shall we say—of the dictates of that program. This is unlike Fela, whose "politics" came much later when he had cut his musical teeth. In any case, in its very eloquent conjunction of form and content, "Beng, beng, beng" ought to be a model for Femi's "political" compositions to aspire to. This is particularly significant because Femi's acclaimed album *Fight to Win* is nearly all serious politicking with very little of that extra ingredient of sheer pleasure, lyrically or in sonic organization, that makes a "political" music memorable. The sentiments are glowing, uplifting, and unimpeachable; the titles themselves reveal as much: "Do Your Best," "Walk on the Right Side," "Traitors of Africa," "Fight to Win," "Stop AIDS," "One Day Someday," and "The Choice is Yours." The uplifting sentiments of the album no doubt account for the way it has been lauded and promoted. It is difficult to quarrel with motivational sentiment, especially when it is expressed well, but there is a problem when the sentiment calls attention more to itself than the sound of its expression. Sometimes even the would-be inspirational sentiment is damned by the commonness of its articulation. This album confirms Femi's weakness as a lyricist. This is dramatically clear in the title track in which the juxtaposition of two verses of lyrics by African-American Jaguar Wright puts the less-polished nature of Femi's lyrics into sharp relief. Or, for another instance, the utter and unrelieved predictability of "Stop AIDS":

> There is something going on
> The matter serious now
> This one no be joke oh
> This disease dey kill now
> AIDS my brothers!
> This disease dey for real
> Now if you love yourself
>
> You better protect yourself
> Come! Come! My brothers listen to me
> Come! Come! My sisters do you hear me
>
> Stop AIDS!
> Fight AIDS!

But perhaps we could say that the issue at hand, AIDS, is such a serious one that it might be counterproductive to needlessly adorn it. Very well, but this point of view would have to confront the fact that adornment, far from being the enemy of message, is in fact its handmaiden. Femi himself knows this well, as we can see in the comparatively better-wrought tracks such as "Traitors of Africa," "Eko Lagos," and "Alkebu-Lan"; their deep grooves alternate between sinuous and bum-shaking choppiness. There is no doubt that Femi is on to great things with afrobeat. His laments about the burden of bearing people's Fela-induced expectations are well justified; if he has achieved as much as he has with that extra weight on him, we can only imagine the heights he can reach as he finally leaves the burden and its anxieties by the wayside.

## Lagbaja

Given the fact that the Nigerian masked musician Lagbaja could be much more popular than he currently is outside Nigeria, it is no exaggeration to say that he is the as-yet-undiscovered revelation in the ongoing afrobeat revolution. Lagbaja, whose real name is Bisade Ologunde, developed his interest in music from informal and inauspicious circumstances: "Musically, I've been playing in bands from school. First of all, it was Government College, Ibadan. Later, Obafemi Awolowo University, Ile Ife. I was lucky to have friends that were active in music too. So, together we kind of taught ourselves through reading books and discussing and arguing, sometimes ignorantly, until over time our interests grew and our skills too on some instruments."[20] He acquired a bachelor's degree in biology education and a master of business administration degree, but the pull of music was stronger. Musically, he recognized all the forms such as *juju, apala,* and *fuji* that he was culturally socialized into, but the local influence on his music, he says, is "mainly Fela." His foreign influences are revealing: "I will say the very first artiste that I got into was Carlos Santana. And rock. But you see, there were some instrumental rock pieces like Samba Patti. And as a matter of fact, it was from that style, that instrumental rock thing, that I got to recognise that there were other pieces called jazz. So, it was from Carlos Santana I got into Bob James and Earl Klugh. And it was my surprise about a year later I found out that there were even more exciting forms—swing, big band, bebop."[21]

Lagbaja is without doubt a most innovative afrobeat musician, both in self-presentation and in the music. Take his famous mask, for instance. It looks very much like a stunt Fela would have performed. Theatrically, the mask arrests attention and makes an encounter with Lagbaja an unforgettable event. The oddness of it all also whets the excitement of his followers and the active curiosities of the unconverted, all of whom are wondering whether he will keep the mask, indeed the masquerade, forever. Imagine Lagbaja making the concert rounds in tropical Nigeria—and he is a much-sought-after favorite on the concert circuit—locked up in that mask on stage for hours, night after night. As an indicator of his popularity, he and his mask have become the subjects of outlandish urban legends, and more than a few Yoruba comedians are having a field day with rib-cracking routines built around similarly masked figures. Ideologically, the mask creates a bond of sympathy with the teeming masses of Nigeria and Africa who are anonymous and voiceless in the important transactions of

Lagbaja.
Courtesy of *The News*.

society; the mask makes them visible in their anonymity, and the voice behind the mask speaks for their interests. The verbal accompaniment to the ideological function of the visual mask is the name itself, Lagbaja, a verbal mask signifying anyone, everyone, and no one in particular.[22] But as in all things Lagbaja, there are more layers of meaning:

> It has to do with wanting to be private. Because initially I was going to perform as Lagbaja myself before I came up with the idea of steering my original band, Colours, as a party band and have somebody perform Lagbaja as a different person. So, I wanted to be a private person. I wanted to be successful at my work and yet be devoid of the so-called glamour attached to show business. Like on Sunday, I just walk from my house, I stroll to the Shrine to go and watch Femi (Anikulapo-Kuti) or walk down Allen Avenue (in Ikeja area of Lagos), nobody knows me. Last week, I was at Tejuoso Market to buy some things. Last Saturday I was at Wasiu Ayinde's show at Yaba Tech. Things like that you couldn't do if your face were known all over by everybody. They would harass you, I mean, in a friendly manner. But you don't have the freedom.[23]

Thus, the mask also serves a pragmatic function for the bandleader; but given the craze for fame by music stars, such a rejection of recognition is also meaningful ideologically.

Lagbaja's afrobeat is shallower in horns and deeper in percussion than any other. It is for this reason that it is the most distinctive version of the genre now available. Along with the saxophone, keyboards, wireless guitars, and bass, classical Yoruba instruments such as the *dundun, bata,* and *sekere* are arrayed. The latter group never made it to Fela's ensemble, and to listen to Lagbaja is to imagine the difference their presence would have made. It appears that what Lagbaja is doing is giving afrobeat the deep Yoruba instrumental anchor that it never had with Fela. Femi also uses *dundun* drums, but they play a very minor role in his music. In a sense, we could say that while Femi is opening up afrobeat to contemporary North American popular musical forms, Lagbaja is securing for afrobeat a deep cultural mooring. The latter is the more challenging task, since what it promises is no less than a reconfiguration of the relationship of afrobeat to forms from which it has stood apart such as *juju, fuji, apala,* and *sakara.* Two points can be made about the possible consequences of the reconfiguration. First, the much-needed consequence: at the sonic level, Lagbaja has made afrobeat available to older generations of Yoruba who never cared much for it. For those listeners, the Yoruba instruments serve the function of defamiliarizing an afrobeat long perceived as too westernized in instrumentation. But also, fanatical Yoruba listeners of afrobeat who had given up on *juju, apala,* and *fuji* as the musics of the obscenely rich can end their alienation and dance to *dundun* and *bata* in Lagbaja's music without feeling guilty. Second, the risky and undesirable consequence: if Lagbaja is reconfiguring the sonic relations between afrobeat and those other Yoruba popular forms, then we must worry about what will happen to the glaring ideological distinction between them. It would be regrettable if afrobeat were to lose its basic oppositional identity in the reconfiguration. Of course, the risk is very low, and Lagbaja is far from going panegyric even while foregrounding those instruments that have become primary signifiers of the panegyric genres. In this sense, he is also reclaiming those instruments from any libelous thought that they were usable only for singing in praise of the rich.

The latter issue of ideology is worth raising at all only because of the very low-key oppositional political content of Lagbaja's afrobeat. Indeed, he seems to be stuck in what we may analogize as the early phase of Fela's development of afrobeat before he radicalized it—the musically exhilarating years of "Lady," "Shakara," "Who Are You," "Jeun Ko Ku," "Je'Nwi Temi," and so on. A majority of Lagbaja's own songs such as "Oyin Momo," "Coolu Temper," "Please Try Later," "Konko Below," "A O M'erin J'oba," and "Put Am Well Well" most powerfully recall Fela's 1970–1974 years in their limber sonic arrangements, lyrical inventiveness, unbeatable humor, and—most important for my point—easily domesticated cultural nationalist politics. Fela did not totally give up the cultural nationalism but later on revamped and infused it with potent oppositional content. It is not likely that Lagbaja will move in this direction, and, unlike Femi, his "political" songs are few and far between. But he never fails to be engaging whenever he composes one. "Bad Leadership" is conceptually provocative in its juxtaposition of AIDS and bad leadership as just two of Africa's many "diseases" and its assessment that the latter is in fact the worse affliction. The track is rhythmically fragmentary, like the ruling policies of many an African polity, and so it cannot be danced to—but then, it is doubtful if it is meant for dancing, for it is presented more as performed poetry or speech with musical accompaniment, in the manner of the Jamaican Mutabaruka, than as a conventional song. Equally thoughtful and by turns funny and poignant is "Suuru Lere," his musical video cartoon of Nigerian political history from colonial rule to independence and the musical-chairs leadership since then to General Abacha's annulment of the June 12, 1993, elections and his later death—the video affirms the sensational rumor on the street—in the arms of an Indian prostitute. In Lagbaja's musical practice, it is as if the trade-off for mainstreaming afrobeat within Yoruba culture is the very modest volume of oppositional political content in his work.

Lagbaja has been very prolific since he began recording in 1993: *Colours: The Color of Rhythm* (1993), *C'est Un African Thing* (1996), *We* (2000), *Me* (2000), and *Abami* (2000). He conceives *We* and *Me,* as the titles suggest, as reflections on the relations between the community and the individual. "We have been moving away from the traditional institutions that put community at the front of society," he lamented to *Afropop Worldwide.*

> We grew up knowing that you were part of a bigger community and that you were supposed to contribute to its growth. But over time, especially when we started having dictatorships and corruption started to grow, individuals in power started

looting the treasury and corruption became a very big thing, and then everything turned into a very selfish individualistic thing. Far from what things used to be. I believe that [these albums] say that we should go back to the way that things used to be, where I was my brother's keeper and we were all part of a society, and we placed the interests of the group above the individual personal interests.[24]

These sentiments are impeccable even if nostalgic, but only few of the tracks actually express them. Such sentiments are no doubt part of his formula for his wide popularity and the expansion of the audience base of afrobeat in Nigeria. In February 2001, he won six Nigerian Music Awards, including Producer of the Year, Artist of the Year, Album of the Year, Best Afrobeat Artiste, and most important for a strand of my argument so far, Crossover Music of the Year. In 1996, he was chosen by the International Red Cross to be part of its campaign called to draw world attention to the predicament of child soldiers in African war zones.

All Lagbaja's albums were published in Nigeria by Motherlan' Music and were not distributed much outside that nation; this is one reason why he has not become more widely known in Europe and America. His first international album, *We before Me* (selections from both *We* and *Me*), was released in 2001 by IndigeDisc Records, based in the United States of America. He toured the United States successfully that year and also in 2003; he has also toured Europe. In the summer of 2002, he performed on the Africa stage at the BBC Music Live Festival during the Queen's Golden Jubilee Celebrations at London's Hyde Park. Even so, I would submit that the recognition Lagbaja has been accorded abroad is not at all commensurate with his achievements. He is without question the most imaginative lyricist of all practicing afrobeat musicians today, and the philosophical depth he brings to the music has no parallel except in Fela himself. For instance, among the handful of recordings of tributes to Fela by artists young and old and within and outside the genre of afrobeat, it is impossible to find any that are as conceptually original, deeply moving, riotously celebratory, and richly satisfying as any of the four tracks Lagbaja collected in his tribute album, *Abami*.

Two of *Abami*'s tracks, "Vernacular" and "Put Am Well Well," stage relaxed humorous conversations between Lagbaja and Fela, dramatizing the cultural nationalism that they both share. "Vernacular" takes up the issue of linguistic colonialism and the resulting denigration of African languages, especially by the African afflicted with, yes, a "colonial mentality." Both Lagbaja and Fela chide us to care less about speaking English correctly—after all, "English no be your mother tongue" (English is not your mother tongue)—and then argued: "If I fire and you laugh, I don't care" (If I speak imperfectly and you laugh, I don't care). To those who know Fela, part of the thrill of the track is that intellectually, its subject is one of Fela's undying pet themes, and technically, making effective use of available technology, it "reproduced" Fela's voice flawlessly and in great hilarious detail, such as Fela's very ripe coughs.[25] The interaction between master and protégé is even more animated in the sizzling party favorite "Put Am

Well Well," an infectious paean to Yoruba dishes. Lagbaja sings to the established rhythm, while Fela talks directly. They argue, agree, disagree, bump into one another verbally, apologize, and begin again—a veritable drama:

Lagbaja: Ijebu omo ala're, dem no dey joke with ikokore
    The Ijebu are avid consumers of ikokore

Fela: And garri, morning, afternoon and night

L: Kwara, dem no dey joke with wara
    Kwara people can't do without wara

F: And eko

L: Ekiti, early morning iyan

F: Ah, you no know, nyam! Twenty-four hours ni!
    You don't know? They eat it all day!

L: Early morning iyan, count me out

F: What are you talking about?

L: Count me out. It's too early.

F (*Combatively*): Try!
    

L: Try wetin?
    Try what?

F: Try!!

L: Make I come dey sleep for work?
    So that I can be dozing off at work?

F (*Feigns disappointment*): Nooo, no be that!
    Nooo, not that!

L: Wey bread and butter dey
    When there is bread and butter

F: (*Animatedly*) Nooooooo! Excuse me. You see, colonialism makes you think bread and butter is better than garri.

L: Me I no be colo; bread and butter get in own advantage
    I am not colonial-minded, but there is a case to be made for bread and butter

F (*Contentiously interrupts*): Lai lai!
    Never!

L: E get.
    There is.

F: Lai lai!!
    Never!!

L: I say e get.
    I say there is.

F: Lai lai!!!
    Never!!!

L: Oh baba, you no go wan hear . . .
    Oh baba, you've not allowed me to make the point . . .

F (*Contrived apology*): Okay, tell me.

L: Bread and butter no go weigh you down
    Bread and butter won't make you feel bloated

F (*Determinedly interrupts again*): Dat one no concern me.
    I don't care about that.

L: Ah ahaa?

F: E no concern me. You see now, educated men will eat sausage and egg every morning; they forget that ewa and moinmoin taste better.

L (*Theatrically swoons in concession*): Aaaha, to ba je ti moinmoin emi wa fun yen o. Abi you sef like am?
    Aaaha, if its moinmoin, I am all for it. You like it too?

F: Me?

| | |
|---|---|
| L: Hen. | Yes |
| F: Me, Fela? | |
| L: Hen; you like am? | Yes, you; you love it? |
| F: Hmm, you no know? Just cut am sham, shenshere; (L breaks into laughter) put am, pam, pam! Hmmm, straight, nyam! | Hmm, you don't know? Just cut it like this, sham, in small bits, and to the mouth it goes, straight! |
| L: (*Still laughing*): You go finish am? | You will finish it? |
| F: Patapata!! (*Chuckles*) | Completely!! |
| L: (*Chuckles too*) Baba! | |
| F: (*Boastfully*): Ah, you no know? My name is Fela. | Ah, you don't know? My name is Fela. |

The music then ratchets up in pace and intensity as Lagbaja, rhetorically varying his own humor-laden lines about his favorite dishes as an "African man," transitions into a mesmerizing call and response with the chorus:

> Lagbaja: Gimme gimme better food chop!
> Chorus: Put am well well!

I said earlier that Lagbaja appears "stuck" in Fela's mainly cultural nationalist years. I should now add that that "stuckness" has all the stamp of deliberateness. He has taken only selectively from the master, and that selection he has ingeniously transformed into his own. The protégé has indeed won the right to sit in leisurely conversations with the master.

## "Do I want to leave an imprint on the world? No. Not at all."

Fela was asked in the early 1980s whether he cared about leaving any imprint on the world; here is his—very much in character, I should emphasize—reply:

> Do I want to leave an imprint on the world? No. Not at all. You know what I want? *I want the world to change.* I don't want to be remembered. I just want to do my part and leave. If remembering is part of the world's thing, that's their problem.[26]

Afrobeat as a kind of music is here to stay. In creating a whole musical genre with a worldwide following, Fela has obviously left an indelible imprint on the world *and* has changed the world. Given the demands of modesty—especially his own special brand of it, polemical modesty—we really do not expect Fela to say that he would like to be remembered or leave an imprint on the world. But his people and primary constituency, the laboring masses of Africa and the world and their allies, well understand him, this lifelong advocate of historical consciousness and critical memory as tools of liberation. They accept that remembering is part of their "thing," and they embrace it; they understand that remembering Fela and his many legacies is an indispensable part of changing *their* world, which is also *the* world, for the better.

# Notes

## 1. Introduction

1. See Antonio Gramsci, *Selections from the Prison Notebooks,* edited and translated by Q. Hoare and G. N. Smith (New York: International Publishers, 1987), 276. The quoted phrase in my title is borrowed from Nadine Gordimer, "Living in the Interregnum," in *The Essential Gesture,* edited by S. Clingman (London: Penguin, 1989), 261–284. For trenchant explorations of the "morbid symptoms" of the postcolonial incredible, see, in a different context, Achille Mbembe, "The Banality of Power and the Aesthetics of Vulgarity in the Postcolony," *Public Culture* 4, no. 2 (1992): 1–30, and *On the Postcolony* (Berkeley: University of California Press, 2001); and Mbembe and Janet Roitman, "Figures of the Subject in Times of Crisis," *Public Culture* 7, no. 2 (1995): 323–352.

2. I am borrowing from Walter Benjamin in the context of fascism: "A historical materialist cannot do without the notion of a present which is not a transition, but in which time stands still and has come to a stop." *Illuminations: Essays and Reflections,* translated by Harry Zohn (New York: Schocken Books, 1969), 262.

3. Bertolt Brecht, *Brecht on Theatre: The Development of an Aesthetic,* translated by John Willett (New York: Hill and Wang, 1964), 181. See also Richard Middleton's chapter "'Lost in Music'? Pleasure, Value and Ideology in Popular Music," in his book *Studying Popular Music* (Milton Keynes: Open University Press, 1990), 247–294.

4. See Kofi Agawu's perceptive comments on this state of the field: "[A]mong the things I missed in Africanist ethnomusicology were competing transcriptions of publicly available compositions that could form the basis of informed, vigorous contestation of appropriate modes of representation. The fact that the analyst of Beethoven's Fifth Symphony could take its familiarity for granted, whereas that of Akan funeral dirges or Igbo *atilogwu* music could not, was a source of frustration." *Representing African Music: Postcolonial Notes, Queries, Positions* (New York: Routledge, 2003), 176.

5. See track 1, "Abami."

## 2. The "Apolitical" Avant-Pop Hustler

1. See John Collins, *West African Pop Roots* (Philadelphia: Temple University Press, 1992), chapters 2, 6, and 16. We can concede Frank Tenaille's weighty description of European instruments as "musical instruments of colonization" but go on to underscore the more significant fact that the history of cultural practice by the colonized African consists of little else but colossal efforts to fashion voice out of imposed silence, subjectivity out of subjection, even if the results are, as with most cultural negotiations, not always un-

equivocal. Such is the case with highlife. See Tenaille, *Music Is the Weapon of the Future: Fifty Years of African Popular Music* (Chicago: Lawrence Hill, 2002), 13.

2. See Agawu's useful overview and critical analysis of highlife and especially E. T. Mensah in *Representing African Music*, 125–145.

3. Ronnie Graham, *The Da Capo Guide to Contemporary African Music* (New York: Da Capo Press, 1988), 52–69, 76–104; Michael E. Veal, *Fela: The Life and Times of an African Musical Icon* (Philadelphia: Temple University Press, 2000), 35–36; "Highlife on the 'Net."

4. Yebuah Mensah, the older brother of the Ghanaian E. T. Mensah, had this to say: "During the early twenties . . . the term 'highlife' was created by people who gathered around dancing clubs . . . to watch and listen to the couples enjoying themselves. Highlife started as a catch-name for the indigenous songs played at these clubs. . . . The people outside called it 'highlife' as they did not reach the class of the couples going inside, who not only had to pay a, then, relatively high entrance fee of 7s. 6d., but also had to wear full evening dress including top hats." See Collins, *West African Pop Roots*, 21.

5. For a useful social history of *juju*, see Christopher Alan Waterman, *Juju: A Social History and Ethnography of an African Popular Music* (Chicago: University of Chicago Press, 1990). See also T. Ajayi Thomas, *History of Juju Music: A History of African Popular Music from Nigeria* (Jamaica, N.Y.: Thomas Organization, 1992).

6. Olaiya would recall in 1997 that the young Fela was "very restless and a very big rascal" but that he had "traces of greatness" and musical talent in him. Quoted in Veal, *Fela*, 36.

7. Collins, *West African Pop Roots*, 78.

8. See Carlos Moore, *Fela, Fela: This Bitch of a Life* (London: Alison & Busby, 1982), 55–59.

9. Veal, *Fela*, 42–43. See also his "Jazz Music Influences on the Work of Fela," *Glendora Review: African Quarterly on the Arts* 1, no. 1 (1995): 8–13. For an introduction to jazz styles, see the useful outline by Mark C. Gridley in *Jazz Styles: History and Analysis* (Englewood Cliffs, N.J.: Prentice Hall, 1994).

10. Benson Idonije, "Koola Lobitos . . . The Beauty of Melody," *The Guardian* (Lagos), October 13, 1999, 52. See also Idonije, "The Legendary Highlifer," in *Scenes from the Underground: Exhibition of Fela Anikulapo-Kuti's Photographs* (Lagos: The News and Femi Osunla, 2001), 6–9.

11. Quoted in Veal, *Fela*, 41. On bebop and modal jazz, see Gridley, *Jazz Styles*, 139–173 and 383–384, respectively.

12. For a brief introduction to the politics of this period, see Eghosa E. Osaghae, *Crippled Giant: Nigeria since Independence* (Bloomington: Indiana University Press, 1998), 31–55.

13. See Bode Omojola, *Nigerian Art Music, With an Introductory Study of Ghanaian Art Music* (Ibadan: Institut Français de Recherche en Afrique, 1995).

14. Moore, *Fela*, 73.

15. Idonije, "Koola Lobitos . . . The Beauty of Melody," 52.

16. Idonije, "Koola Lobitos . . . The Beauty of Melody," 52.

17. Quoted in Veal, *Fela*, 54.

18. Gary Stewart, *Breakout: Profiles in African Rhythm* (Chicago: University of Chicago Press, 1992), 118.

19. Idonije, "Koola Lobitos . . . The Beauty of Melody," 52.

20. Idonije, "Koola Lobitos . . . The Beauty of Melody," 52.

21. Idonije, "Koola Lobitos . . . The Beauty of Melody," 52.

22. Idonije, "Koola Lobitos . . . The Beauty of Melody," 52.

23. The classic study of the instrument is Akin Euba, *Yoruba Drumming: The Dundun Tradition* (Bayreuth: E. Breitinger, Bayreuth University, 1990).

24. See Isaac O. Delano, *The Singing Minister: The Life of the Rev. Canon J. J. Ransome-Kuti* (London: United Society for Christian Literature, 1942), and *Josaiah Ransome-Kuti: The Drummer Boy Who Became a Canon* (Ibadan: Oxford University Press, 1968); and on Funmilayo Ransome-Kuti, see Cheryl Johnson-Odim and Nina Emma Mba, *For Women and the Nation: Funmilayo Ransome-Kuti of Nigeria* (Urbana: University of Illinois Press, 1997).

25. Fela quoted in Moore, *Fela*, 42.

26. Moore, *Fela*, 64.

27. Quoted in Veal, *Fela*, 45.

28. Wole Soyinka, *Art, Dialogue and Outrage: Essays on Literature and Culture* (Ibadan: New Horn Press, 1988), 260.

29. Moore, *Fela*, 63–64.

30. Quoted in Veal, *Fela*, 44.

31. Fela quoted in Moore, *Fela*, 64.

32. Idonije, "Koola Lobitos," 52.

33. African writers have had a field day deploying this social figure in their writings. See William Lawson, *The Western Scar: The Theme of the Been-to in West African Fiction* (Athens, Ohio: Ohio University Press, 1982).

34. Veal, *Fela*, 54–44. See Moore, *Fela*, 73.

35. Unlike most common usage of "counterculture" that automatically conceives it as the road to dystopia or utopia, an indication of degeneracy, or a way out of the crippling weight of dead traditions, my goal is a more "objective" apprehension of the phenomenon in its social context before the rush to evaluative ideological judgment. After all, countercultures do not bear a single relation to their subtending context or do so at all times, and they often exhibit diverse ideological orientations. In this regard, I have benefited from J. M. Yinger's modest empirical observation that "countercultures combine three forms of protest: direct opposition to the dominant values, but opposition also to the power structures and opposition to patterned exchanges that are entangled with those values" and his tempered definition that we can appropriately invoke the term "whenever the normative system of a group contains, as a primary element, a theme of conflict with the dominant values of society,

where the tendencies, needs, and perceptions of the members of that group are directly involved in the development and maintenance of its values, and wherever its norms can be understood only by reference to the relationship of the group to the surrounding dominant society and its culture." *Counter-cultures: The Promise and Peril of a World Turned Upside Down* (New York: The Free Press, 1982), 5 and 22–23, respectively. I have emphasized in this study not just the ideological but also the structural reading of counter-cultures, where their role in history's dynamism comes fully to the foreground. Situated as other in the margins, they have the capacity to deconstruct the reigning regime of normality as mere ideological construction and thereby re-lativize its authority, make it vulnerable—and make it admit its vulnerability—to rethinking.

### 3. The Afrobeat Moralist

1. Fela did try to gingerly incorporate elements of soul into his music, but that did not work or change his fortunes. For a discussion of such minor record-ings, see Veal, *Fela*, 63–65.

2. First in Lagos and then in Accra, Pino came to town and conquered: "I was playing highlife jazz when Geraldo Pino came to town in '66 or a bit earlier with soul. That's what upset everything, man. He came to town with James Brown's music, singing, "Hey, hey, I feel all right, ta, ta, ta, ta." And with such equipment you've never seen, man. This man was tearing Lagos to pieces. Woooooooh, man! He had all Nigeria in his pocket. Made me fall right on my ass, man. Ahhhhhh, this Sierra Leonean guy was too much. . . . I'll never for-get him. . . . After that motherfucking Pino tore up the scene, there wasn't shit I could do in Lagos. So I went to Ghana in '67." But by the time Fela ar-rived in Ghana, Pino had been there and, again, won the battle hands down: "[O]ne day in Accra we entered this club, Ringway Hotel. The place was packed, man! Geraldo Pino was playing there. . . . In Lagos, I was using this old equipment . . . museum antiques, man. I had only one microphone for the whole band. One microphone! This motherfucking Pino had six! The whole place was jumping. The music carried me away completely. . . . Can you understand my situation that night? Needing to find a job myself, but enjoying the music so much that I even forgot I myself was a fucking musi-cian." Moore, *Fela*, 74–75.

3. Moore, *Fela*, 75.

4. Moore, *Fela*, 75.

5. Fela quoted in Veal, *Fela*, 62.

6. Fela quoted in Moore, *Fela*, 75.

7. Fela quoted in Veal, *Fela*, 66.

8. Idonije, "Koola Lobitos," 52.

9. Fela quoted in Moore, *Fela*, 81.

10. Fela quoted in Veal, *Fela*, 67. Even Britain fared badly, in Fela's estimation: "'Great' Britain? *Little* Britain beside America!" See Moore, *Fela*, 81.

11. Moore, *Fela*, 81.

12. See Veal, *Fela*, 66–69; Moore, *Fela*, 81–82; Mabinuori Kayode Idowu, *Fela: Why Blackman Carry Shit* (Ikeja, Nigeria: Opinion Media Limited, 1986), 32–38.

13. On the Nigerian civil war, see Osaghae, *Crippled Giant*, 56–67; I. Nzimiro, *The Nigerian Civil War: A Study in Class Conflict* (Enugu: Fourth Dimension, 1979); and T. N. Tamuno and S. C. Ukpabi, eds., *Nigeria since Independence: The First 25 Years*, vol. 6, *The Civil War Years* (Ibadan: Heinemann Educational Books, 1989).

14. Fela quoted in Moore, *Fela*, 81–83.

15. Fela quoted in Moore, *Fela*, 77. In another interview in 1988, he explained: "Tribalism was used at the time to oppress the Igbos all over Nigeria. I was a witness to that. Igbos were being slaughtered all over Nigeria. Even in Lagos, everywhere. . . . Gowon was saying 'To keep Nigeria one, is a task that must be done.' What one? To keep Nigeria one, does it mean that innocent Nigerian women, children and other innocent people must die? Do we have one Nigeria today?" Quoted in Veal, *Fela*, 69.

16. Fela quoted in Moore, *Fela*, 83.

17. On the party itself and its larger political, cultural, and intellectual contexts, see Charles E. Jones, ed., *The Black Panther Party Reconsidered* (Baltimore: Black Classic Press, 1998); Essien Udosen Essien-Udom, *Black Nationalism: A Search for an Identity in America* (New York: Dell, 1964); and John T. McCartney, *Black Power Ideologies: An Essay in African American Political Thought* (Philadelphia: Temple University Press, 1992).

18. Fela quoted in Moore, *Fela*, 85.

19. Fela quoted in Moore, *Fela*, 85.

20. Roland Barthes, "Whose Theater? Whose *Avant-Garde*?" In *Critical Essays*, translated by R. Howard (Evanston, Ill.: Northwestern University Press, 1972), 68.

21. Fela quoted in Moore, *Fela*, 85.

22. There are two classic articulations of the mental subjection of African Americans. One is Carter G. Woodson's *The Miseducation of the Negro*, where he argues forbiddingly that "taught the same economics, history, philosophy, literature and religion which have established the present code of morals, the Negro's mind has been brought under the control of his oppressor. The problem of holding the Negro down, therefore, is easily solved. When you control a man's thinking you do not have to worry about his actions. You do not have to tell him not to stand here or go yonder. He will find his 'proper place' and will stay in it. You do not need to send him to the back door. He will go without being told. In fact, if there is no back door, he will cut one for his special benefit. His education makes it necessary"; (1933; reprint, Trenton, N.J.: Africa World Press, 1990), xii, xiii, 192. This was also the argument of W. E. B. DuBois thirty years earlier in the equally popular *Souls of Black Folk*, that the African American is smitten with a lesion that will not heal by "a world which yields him no true self-consciousness, but only lets him see himself through the revelation of the other world. It is a peculiar sensation, this double-consciousness, *this sense of always looking at one's self through the eyes*

*of others, of measuring one's soul by the tape of a world that looks on in amused contempt and pity"*; (1903, reprint, New York: Vintage, 1990), 18; emphasis added. The controlled mind Woodson describes is what DuBois means by seeing "one's self through the eyes of others."

23. Malcolm X, *The Autobiography of Malcolm X* (New York: Ballantine Books, 1965), 165–171. (For the benefit of those with other editions, this is from the chapter titled "Satan.")

24. Frantz Fanon, *Black Skin, White Masks,* translated by C. L. Markmann (New York: Grove Press, 1967), 176.

25. Malcolm X, April 1964. Speech on audio. Microsoft® Encarta® Reference Library 2003. © 1993–2002 Microsoft Corporation.

26. Here is Ossie Davis, leading actor and cultural figure, on the psychological revolution in blacks, especially men, the story and example of Malcolm produced: "White folks do not need anybody to remind them that they are men. We do! This was his one incontrovertible benefit to his people. Protocol and common sense require that Negroes stand back and let the white man speak for us, defend us, and lead us from behind the scene in our fight. This is the essence of Negro politics. But Malcolm said to hell with that! Get up off your knees and fight your own battles. That's the only way to win back your self-respect. . . . Malcolm, as you can see, was refreshing excitement; he scared the hell out of the rest of us, bred as we are to caution, to hypocrisy in the presence of white folks, to the smile that never fades." "On Malcolm X," appended to Malcolm's *Autobiography,* 464–465.

27. See Veal, *Fela,* 70–71; Idonije, "Koola Lobitos," 52; and John Kofsky, *John Coltrane and the Jazz Revolution of the 1960s,* rev. and expanded ed. (New York: Pathfinder, 1998).

28. On soul and the civil rights struggle, see Ward's illuminating book, *Just My Soul Responding: Rhythm and Blues, Black Consciousness, and Race Relations* (Berkeley: University of California Press, 1998). See also Veal, *Fela,* 58.

29. Fela quoted in Moore, *Fela,* 85. Emphasis in original.

30. Fela quoted in Moore, *Fela,* 88. Emphasis in original.

31. Perhaps this is what Fela meant when he explained his new insight to John Collins in an interview: "I had been using jazz to play African music, when I really should be using African music to play jazz. So it was America that brought me back to myself." Collins, *West African Pop Roots* (Philadelphia: Temple University Press, 1992), 78.

32. See Peter van der Merwe's excellent discussion, *Origins of the Popular Style: Antecedents of Twentieth-Century Popular Music* (New York: Oxford University Press, 1989), 33–39.

33. Fela quoted in Moore, *Fela,* 88–89.

34. Fela quoted in Moore, *Fela,* 89.

35. So when Fela described Sandra as the "saviour" (quoted in Moore, *Fela,* 84) of his American trip, we are permitted to be as generous to her in gratitude as our imagination can offer.

36. Fela quoted in Moore, *Fela,* 89.

37. Idowu, *Fela*, 39. Fela would subsequently latch on to instances such as this and the conservatism of the Nigerian ruling class to generalize on the comparative political consciousness of Africans and African Americans in which, in his typical Manichean way, African Americans are more radical than Africans. "It's crazy," he would famously theorize in 1977, "in the States people think the black power movement drew inspiration from Africa. All these Americans come over here looking for awareness. They don't realize they're the ones who've got it over there. Why, we were even ashamed to go around in national dress until we saw pictures of blacks wearing dashikis on 125th Street" (quoted in Veal, *Fela*, 71). Of course, this is true only of himself and the small, ideologically vapid, and most Europhile section of the 1960s and early 1970s Nigerian middle class to which he belonged then. His observation cannot even be said to be exactly true of his own parents, who were both notable cultural nationalists. Fela's sensationalism is useful polemically but limited in insight.

    We cannot ignore the fact that there is a major disparity in the understanding and performance of race and race relations by Africans and African Americans. This is caused by their differential subjection, as "blacks," to Euro-American racial hegemony. The subjection of African Americans to this hegemony is deeper, and there are several interactive reasons for this: the fact of being of a racial minority in a majority white society; the peculiar composition of the history of that minority status—racial slavery, systemic economic exploitation, political domination, and social and cultural inferiorization and their innumerable rituals, such as, to cite merely one iniquitous example, that uniquely American cannibalism known as lynching—and finally, the *continuing* overwhelming character of whiteness, damagingly coupled with a liberal racial climate with a phony, impoverished language for articulating the specificity and depth of post–civil rights movement black racial hurt.

    On the other hand, most Africans live in largely racially homogenous, majority-black societies. Racism and racial inferiority/superiority complexes are not unknown to them, but because they do not live those experiences daily, Africans tend to grasp them more as political and intellectual matters than as deeply ingrained psychological and embodied ones. They are largely oblivious to the many subtle, unspoken but thoroughly embodied rituals of daily racial transactions in the societies of Europe and America. For these reasons, their degree of subjection on the altar of "race" is very low compared to that of African Americans. This differential subjection very often puts Africans and African Americans on different pages and leads to misunderstandings when matters of blackness and strategies of racial negotiation are at stake. For more on this issue, see Tejumola Olaniyan, "Economies of the Interstice," in *Problematizing Blackness: Self Ethnographies by Black Immigrants to the United States*, edited by Percy C. Hintzen and Jean Muteba Rahier (New York: Routledge, 2003).

38. James Brown and Bruce Tucker, *James Brown: The Godfather of Soul* (New York: Macmillan, 1986), 221.

39. See Idowu, *Fela*, 39–41.

40. Michael Veal quotes a fan who says it is through Fela that he "learned a lot of traditional rhythms. . . . And where in the case of traditional music, you have

a talking drum which people can decode, he has his horns. If one of them goes off into a solo, suddenly some kind of traditional Yoruba adage or proverb or folk song will come out of the horn. There are people in the crowd who will decode it just like a drum, and you will see these people going wild at this point." *Fela*, 93.

41. See P. O. Sada and J. S. Oguntoyinbo, *Urbanization Processes and Problems in Nigeria* (Ibadan: Ibadan University Press, 1978); and Hyacinth I. Ajaegbu, *Urban and Rural Development in Nigeria* (London: Heinemann, 1976).

42. On popular creative responses to the boom, especially in theatre, see Karin Barber, "Popular Reactions to the Petro-Naira," *The Journal of Modern African Studies* 20, no. 3 (1982): 431–450.

43. Fela acknowledged his indebtedness to the common people in a 1988 interview: "Like 'Yellow Fever,' it was the people at Mushin [a neighborhood in Lagos] who first called traffic wardens Yellow Fever. So I decided to call the [skin] bleaching people 'Yellow Fever.' It was not my original idea. Even 'Shakara,' it was from the Mushin people. I don't work in isolation from the society. Shakara was a Mushin word but it was not popular. . . . I made it popular through my record. . . . When I want to write lyrics, I think about my environment, I think about catchy words, words that can easily be identified with society. . . . [T]hat is why they are very successful." Quoted in Veal, *Fela*, 91.

44. See Moore, *Fela*, 29, 89.

45. Conveniently, Nkrumah was left out. A fuller and just passable entry is available in Encarta Africana, part of the same package, Microsoft Encarta Reference Library 2003. Microsoft® Encarta® Reference Library 2003. © 1993–2002 Microsoft Corporation.

46. Only apparently, said Fela; those instruments were "invented here in Africa," he argued much later. Fela quoted in Idowu, *Fela*, 158. And, most perplexingly for a Yoruba, no talking drums!

47. See Tejumola Olaniyan, "Africa: Varied Colonial Legacies," in *A Companion to Postcolonial Studies*, edited by Sangeeta Ray and Henry Schwarz (Oxford: Blackwell, 2000), 269–281.

## 4. Dissident Tunes

1. Fela quoted in Moore, *Fela*, 89.

2. See Veal, *Fela*, 100–102.

3. See Veal, *Fela*, 140.

4. Fela quoted in Moore, *Fela*, 122.

5. See Moore, *Fela*, 122–127 for Fela's extremely hilarious account of the whole episode.

6. For a perspicacious critique of the general "climate of indiscipline" fostered by the Nigerian leadership, see Achebe, *The Trouble with Nigeria* (Oxford: Heinemann, 1983), 27–36. Achebe was writing in 1983, but one of his exem-

plifications of the "siren mentality" and tyranny of the uniform remains unquestionably medieval: "Early in 1983 I was traveling from Nsukka to Ogidi with my wife and daughter and driver. As we were driving through Awka we heard a siren and performed the appropriate motions of mild panic and pulled up. Three police vehicles—a jeep, a car and a lorry sped by in the opposite direction. From the side of the lorry a policeman was pissing on to the road and the halted traffic. You may not believe it; and I can't say I blame you. Although I clearly saw the fly of his trousers, his sprinkler and the jet of urine, I still would not have believed it if I had not had confirmation in the horrified reaction of other travelers around us, and if my wife and driver had not recoiled instinctively from the impact of that police piss on their side of the car. Fortunately for them the glass was wound up. It was almost humorous" (35–36). For a general introduction to the Nigerian military, see Jimi Peters, *The Nigerian Military and the State* (London: Tauris Academic Studies, 1997); Nwabueze, *Military Rule and Social Justice in Nigeria* (Ibadan: Spectrum Books, 1993); and the insider account by M. Chris Alli, *The Federal Republic of Nigerian Army: The Siege of a Nation* (Lagos: Malthouse, 2002).

7.   Fela quoted in Moore, *Fela,* 129. Compare Fela's details to the restrained report by the government-owned *Daily Times* of November 25, 1974, which, however, also joined the chorus of public outrage and called for an official probe of the incident: "Afrobeat king, Fela Ransome-Kuti, has been admitted into Lagos University Teaching Hospital for injuries he received when anti-riot policemen were called into his home at 14A Agege Motor Road on Saturday morning. Fela was reported to have refused entry into his barbed-wire fenced home to plainclothes policemen who had come for a 'routine search.' Saturday's search was the third to be conducted at Fela's house by the police during the last six months." Quoted in Veal, *Fela,* 143–144.

8.   Fela quoted in Collins, *West African Pop Roots,* 72.

9.   It was as if Fela was answering Fanon's famous challenge: "The future will have no pity for those men who, possessing the exceptional privilege of being able to speak words of truth to their oppressors, have taken refuge in an attitude of passivity, of mute indifference, and sometimes of cold complicity." Frantz Fanon, *Toward the African Revolution,* translated by Haakon Chevalier (New York: Grove Press, 1969), 117.

10.   By "political classics," I mean those tested songs of the political afrobeat phase in which there is a most opportune convergence of exacting sonic organization, profound lyrics, aptness of rhetorical weapon in relationship to target, and, above all, a cutting-edge mixture of exuberant rhapsody and poignancy. I mean songs such as, in addition to the two already cited, "Alagbon Close," "Zombie," "Upside Down," "Sorrow Tears and Blood," "Coffin for Head of State," "I.T.T.," "Perambulator," "M.O.P. (Movement of the People) Political Statement Number 1," "Army Arrangement," and "Confusion Break Bones."

11.   Fela in Moore, *Fela,* 259–260.

12.   Robert C. Tucker, ed., *The Marx-Engels Reader* (New York: W. W. Norton, 1972), 11–12; emphasis in original.

13. In the case of "Who're You," the alhaji reportedly wanted to get into a Fela performance but without buying a ticket: "Fela asked the man why he did not want to pay to enter his show—after all he was an Alhaji who could afford to waste our foreign exchange just to travel to Mecca to kiss a Black Stone. The Alhaji's reply to Fela was 'Who are you?' pushing Fela on the chest. Before the Alhaji knew what was happening, Fela slapped him on the face; seeing stars, the Alhaji took to his heels." Idowu, *Fela*, 41.

14. "Afrika Shrine," *The Punch* (Lagos), August 25, 1979, 12.

15. Fela Anikulapo-Kuti, "Chief Priest Say: For Pope Country . . . ," *The Punch* (Lagos), February 26, 1982, 19.

16. Fela Anikulapo-Kuti, "Chief Priest Say: If Expenses of 80,000 Pilgrims . . . ," *Daily Times* (Lagos), January 1, 1976, 24.

17. Fela quoted in Veal, *Fela*, 217–218.

18. Frantz Fanon, *The Wretched of the Earth*, translated by Constance Farrington (1961; reprint, New York: Grove Press, 1963), 167.

19. See Soyinka, *Art, Dialogue and Outrage*, 247–261.

20. On the prophetic insight of Fanon, see Olufemi Taiwo, "On the Misadventures of National Consciousness: A Retrospect on Frantz Fanon's Gift of Prophecy." In *Frantz Fanon: A Critical Reader*, edited by Lewis Gordon, Tracy Sharpley-Whiting, and Renee T. White (Oxford: Blackwell, 1996), 255–270.

21. Jacques Attali, *Noise: The Political Economy of Music*, translated by Brian Massumi (Minneapolis: University of Minnesota Press, 1985).

22. We will not be distracted by the now-clichéd critique made famous by Theodor W. Adorno that popular music is characterized by standardization, pseudo-individualization, political quietism, and a comparatively higher degree of repetition in relation to other musics that is a sign of infantilism and psychosis. See Adorno, "On Popular Music," *Studies in Philosophy and Social Sciences* 9 (1941): 17–48, and "Perennial Fashion: Jazz" (1955), in *Prisms* (Cambridge, Mass.: MIT Press, 1981), 119–132. Many scholars have persuasively demonstrated the crudity of these observations, and there is no need to further flog a dead horse. And more to our purposes here, the idea of a popular political music that simultaneously embraces the standardization offered by technology and broadcasts sonic and emotional attitudes not wholly recuperable by industrial capitalism never crossed Adorno's mind. For a useful and comprehensive assessment of Adorno's positions, see Middleton, *Studying Popular Music*, 34–63.

23. To some extent, we can borrow Richard Middleton's terms to label these two types of repetition as "musematic" and "discursive." The former is repetition at the level of musemes, the minimal unit of musical meaning, and the latter is repetition of "longer units, at the level of the phrase, the sentence or even the complete section." Middleton, *Studying Popular Music*, 169, 247–294.

24. I have had not a few North American students confess that they feel guilty "enjoying" Fela's music. "The music is irresistible but the content of the lyrics is so depressing," they complain.

25. Compare these lyrics with Soyinka's in the satirical song "I Love My Country," released a year after "Original Sufferhead":

One time we stack groundnuts so high
Like pyramids nearly reach the sky
Palm oil dey flow from here to London
Cassava, plantains, our fruits be champion
Our cocoa compete with that of Ghana
Mouth dey water to look the banana
Yam wey big like wrestler's thighs
Which rice get fame like Tapa rice
But now to eat na half my budget
Food dey cost like golden nuggets
The rain wey fall from open skies
E only float Presidential Rice.

From the LP *Unlimited Liability Company* (Ewuro Productions, 1983).

26. In a game of musical chairs that would further justify Fela's cynicism about the Nigerian ruling class, retired General Olusegun Obasanjo was elected civilian president in 1999 after the national trauma of the General Sani Abacha years (1993–1998). Obasanjo won a second and final term in the widely disputed elections of April 2003.

27. A notable political scientist assesses the program: "OFN was well received, but it was too superficial to address the deep-rooted agricultural and food crisis. For one thing, its main target seemed to be the urban elites and working classes rather than the rural producers, and for another, the program never really progressed much beyond the impressive launching ceremonies in state capitals. Thus it is not surprising that in 1976–78, when OFN was active, the total estimated area under active cultivation fell from 18.8 million to 11.05 million hectares, while food imports rose from N353.7 million to an astronomical N1 billion." Osaghae, *Crippled Giant*, 93–94.

28. The Non-Aligned Movement (NAM) is an association of countries that refused to ideologically declare formally to be on either the side of the United States or the Union of Soviet Socialist Republics during the Cold War. Originally composed of twenty-five countries when it was founded in 1961, its membership grew to over 100. For a while, the NAM was the main transregional global voice of the formerly colonized countries from Africa, Asia, and Latin America. Its significance has declined rapidly since the end of the Cold War. For a history, see Peter Willetts, *The Non-Aligned Movement: The Origins of a Third World Alliance* (New York: Nichols Pub. Co., 1978); and in relation to Africa, see Bala Mohammed, *Africa and Nonalignment: A Study in the Foreign Relations of New Nations* (Kano: Triumph Pub. Co., 1978).

29. Fela quoted in Moore, *Fela*, 149. Emphasis in original.

30. For a useful introduction, see Esedebe P. Olisanwuche, *Pan-Africanism: The Idea and Movement, 1776–1991* (Washington, D.C.: Howard University Press, 1994); and Ronald W. Walters, *Pan Africanism in the African Diaspora: An Analysis of Modern Afrocentric Political Movements* (Detroit: Wayne State University Press, 1993).

31.     Fela quoted in Idowu, *Fela*, 150–151.

32.     Molefi Asante, *The Afrocentric Idea* (Philadelphia: Temple University Press, 1987), 125.

33.     For detailed examinations of these movements and their intricate relationships, see Tejumola Olaniyan, "Afrocentrism," *Social Dynamics* 21, no. 2 (Summer 1995): 91–105; and "From Black Aesthetics to Afrocentrism," unpublished.

34.     Fela quoted in Idowu, *Fela*, 164.

35.     Fanon, *Wretched of the Earth*, 311–316.

36.     For a general eloquent critique of this "culturalism" in African and Africanist scholarship, see Paulin J. Hountondji, *African Philosophy: Myth and Reality*, 2nd ed. (Bloomington: Indiana University Press, 1996), 156–169.

37.     See Veal, *Fela*, 178 for an episode in which Fela narrowly missed being shot dead in an attempt to test a supposedly bulletproof vest made by Hindu.

38.     For a profile of Okosun and an assessment more generous than mine, see Stewart, *Breakout*, 124–130.

39.     See Moore, *Fela*, 135. See also Idowu, *Fela*, 85–86.

40.     Fela quoted in Moore, *Fela*, 153–155.

41.     See Moore, *Fela*, 49–50.

42.     Fela quoted in Idowu, *Fela*, 149.

43.     Gramsci, *Selections from the Prison Notebooks*, 419.

44.     See Veal, *Fela*, 249.

45.     On the influential activities of Nigerian students in the country's political process, see the collection of essays *Nigerian Students and the Challenges of Leadership*, ed. Jiti Ogunye, Segun Jegede, Bash Olasupo, Lucky Akaruese, and Dipo Fashina (Lagos: Committee for the Defence of Human Rights, 1998). See also Osaghae, *Crippled Giant*, 94–95.

46.     See Idowu, *Fela*, 173.

47.     Here I am invoking Gramsci's useful distinction between "direct domination" and "hegemony." Gramsci, *Selections from the Prison Notebooks*, 12. See also Ranajit Guha's useful extension, "Dominance Without Hegemony and Its Historiography," *Subaltern Studies* 6 (1989): 210–309.

## 5. Fela, Lagos, and the Postcolonial State

1.     See Akin L. Mabogunje, *Urbanization in Nigeria* (New York: Africana Publishing Corporation, 1968), 238–311; Margaret Peil, *Lagos: The City Is the People* (Boston, Mass.: G. K. Hall & Co., 1991); Sandra T. Barnes, *Patrons and Power: Creating a Political Community in Metropolitan Lagos* (Manchester: Manchester University Press, 1986); A. G. Aderibigbe, ed., *Lagos: The Development of an African City* (London: Longman Nigeria, 1975); Abiola Dosunmu Elegbede-Fernandez, *Lagos: A Legacy of Honour* (Ibadan: Spectrum Books, 1992); and Michael J. C. Echeruo, *Victorian Lagos: Aspects of Nineteenth Century Lagos Life* (London: Macmillan, 1977).

2.   Nnamdi Inyama et al., "This Is Still Lagos: The Land of Lawlessness, Armed Robbery, Gridlock, Overpopulation and Stench," *The Guardian* (Lagos), June 23, 2003.

3.   Soyinka, "I Love My Country," *Unlimited Liability Company.*

4.   Fela quoted in Victor Dorgu, "Are the Youngsters Taking Over?" *Daily Times* (Lagos), July 28, 1968, 10.

5.   For a useful introduction to pidgin, see Mark Sebba, *Contact Languages: Pidgins and Creoles* (New York: St. Martin's Press, 1997); and Loreto Todd, *Modern Englishes: Pidgins and Creoles* (London: Blackwell, 1984).

6.   "[T]he citiness of a city lies in the absorption of its many parts into a common whirlpool. Its core experience intimates a civis: a place of civilization where people who may not have the same occupation, or accept the same ancestors, and people who may not bow to the same deity, can live within a common frame of politics, thus entrenching the possibility of shared decision-making as a permanent way of life. The city is, in this sense, an ever-ready challenge because it is continually suggesting the necessity to find a common morality that can hold people together. The city, as such, has proved to be humankind's most permanent experiment in living together beyond the ethic of hunter-gatherers." Odia Ofeimun, "Imagination and the City," *Glendora: African Quarterly on the Arts* 3, no. 2 (2001): 12.

7.   Peter Hall, *Cities in Civilization* (New York: Pantheon Books, 1998), 3.

8.   Baker quoted in Jay Babcock, "Ginger Baker," *Mean*, no. 6 (December 1999–January 2000), available online at http://www.jaybabcock.com/ginger.html.

9.   The nationalists never decolonized the—characteristically repressive—colonial state and its apparatuses but actually actively consolidated them and turned the state into the main tool of sectarian struggles for power and its perquisites. See Patrick Chabal, *Power in Africa: An Essay in Political Interpretation* (New York: St. Martin's Press, 1994). See also Irele, "The Crisis of Legitimacy in Africa: A Time of Change and Despair," *Dissent* 39, no. 3 (1992): 296–302.

10.  See Claude Ake, *Social Science as Imperialism: The Theory of Political Development*, 2nd ed. (Ibadan: Ibadan University Press, 1982). On the state, see Robert H. Jackson and Carl G. Rosberg, *Personal Rule: Prince, Autocrat, Prophet, Tyrant* (Berkeley: University of California Press, 1982); Jean-François Bayart, *The State in Africa: The Politics of the Belly*, translated by M. Harper et al. (London: Longman, 1993); Richard A. Joseph, *Democracy and Prebendal Politics in Nigeria: The Rise and Fall of the Second Republic* (New York: Cambridge University Press, 1987); Robert Fatton, *Predatory Rule: State and Civil Society in Africa* (Boulder: Lynne Rienner, 1992); Crawford Young, *The African Colonial State in Comparative Perspective* (New Haven, Conn.: Yale University Press, 1994); Basil Davidson, *The Black Man's Burden: Africa and the Curse of the Nation State* (New York: Random House, 1992); and Mahmood Mamdani, *Citizen and Subject: Contemporary Africa and the Legacy of Late Colonialism* (Princeton, N.J.: Princeton University Press, 1996).

11.  See Toyin Falola and Julius Ihonvbere, *The Rise and Fall of Nigeria's Second Republic, 1979–1984* (London: Zed, 1985).

12.  On the drama and passion of Ogun, the Yoruba deity of metallurgy and

metalwork, see Soyinka, *Myth, Literature and the African World* (Cambridge: Cambridge University Press, 1976) 140–160. On the diasporic dispersion of the deity, see Sandra T. Barnes, ed., *Africa's Ogun: Old World and New* (Bloomington: Indiana University Press, 1989).

13. Lagos pidgin is not gendered in its pronouns, but since there is no standard orthography, the accepted damaging compromise is to resort to English pronouns to aid understanding. The pidgin "e," which sounds like "he," is used for all genders, and some spell it as "i" ("I" being "Ah"). "Himself" and "herself" ideally should be "inself." Although Fela is referring to men in the song (though a "perambulator" could be male or female), my more substantive defense for using the male gendered pronoun is the gendered character of the Nigerian state.

14. See E. Bolaji Idowu, *Olodumare: God in Yoruba Belief* (London: Longman, 1962), 18–29.

15. Confounded by its deconstructive, aporetic features that were no doubt interpreted stereotypically by Christian colonial racism as "further evidence of the illogic of the natives," the missionaries successfully equated Esu with the Christian Satan. They translated Satan in the Yoruba Bible as Esu, an incomparable epistemological killing if ever there was one, as many generations of Yoruba grew up knowing Esu only as Satan. The literature on Esu, both in Africa and in the New World, is vast. See, for a few examples, Ayodele Ogundipe, "Esu Elegbara, the Yoruba God of Chance and Uncertainty: A Study in Yoruba Mythology," 2 vols. (Ph.D. diss., Indiana University, 1978); Juana Elbein dos Santos and Deoscoredes M. do Santos, *Esu Bara Laroye: A Comparative Study* (Ibadan: Institute of African Studies, 1971); Hans Witte, *Ifa and Esu: Iconography of Order and Disorder* (Soest, Holland: Kunstandel Luttik, 1984); and Robert D. Pelton, *The Trickster in West Africa: A Study of Mythic Irony and Sacred Delight* (Berkeley: University of California Press, 1980). For a recent deployment of Esu as a literary-critical interpretive tool, see Henry Louis Gates, Jr., *The Signifying Monkey: A Theory of Afro-American Literary Criticism* (New York: Oxford University Press, 1988). Esu, as Papa Labas, is also the star of the classic novel *Mumbo Jumbo* by the distinguished African-American writer Ishmael Reed.

16. "Most Africans do not really know about life. They think everything from overseas is greater, but they do not know also that everything from overseas could have gone from here to overseas and come back to us." Fela in Idowu, *Fela*, 37.

17. For a thoughtful treatment of African dependence and indigenous knowledges, see Paulin Hountondji, "Scientific Dependency in Africa Today," *Research in African Literatures* 21, no. 3 (1990): 5–15; and Hountondji's edited book *Endogenous Knowledge: Research Trails* (Dakar: CODESRIA, 1997).

18. Olikoye Ransome-Kuti quoted in "Part 2: A Tale of Two Brothers" in the series "AIDS: The Agony of Africa," by Mark Schoofs, *Village Voice*, November 10–16, 1999, available online at http://www.villagevoice.com/issues/9945/schoofs.php.

19. Microsoft® Encarta® Reference Library 2003. © 1993–2002 Microsoft Corporation.

20. See Amilcar Cabral, *Return to the Source: Selected Speeches* (New York: Monthly Review Press, 1973).

21. For a larger context in which I used these concepts to assess theories and theorists of the African state, see Tejumola Olaniyan, "Modernity and Its Mirages: Wole Soyinka and the African State," *Modern Drama* 45, no. 3 (2002): 349–357.


## 6. On the Shop Floor

1. See Raymond Williams, *Problems in Materialism and Culture* (London: Verso, 1980), 47–48, for his formulation of "the true crisis in cultural theory" as the conflict "between [the] view of the work of art as object and the alternative view of art as a practice."

2. "Culinary" is Bertolt Brecht's term. See *Brecht on Theatre*, 33–42.

3. See Veal, *Fela*, 261–262.

4. Fela quoted in Stewart, *Breakout*, 117.

5. This is Frank Thurmond Fairfax's phrase in his useful study of musical recruitment, training, apprenticeship, and retention among Nigerian popular music bands. "Fela, the Afro-Beat King: Popular Music and Cultural Revitalization in West Africa" (Ph.D. diss., University of Michigan, 1993), 87.

6. Fela quoted in Moore, *Fela*, 142. Fela's emphasis.

7. Fela quoted in Moore, *Fela*, 137.

8. See Fela's account in Moore, *Fela*, 152.

9. Benjamin, *Illuminations*, 256.

10. Fairfax, *Fela*, 358.

11. Tony Allen quoted in Veal, *Fela*, 165.

12. Veal, *Fela*, 165.

13. Fela continued: "You cannot class my music like American music, because, I said, my music is in different movements. You have to class it by movements, so you cannot say Fela is writing one song. No! Fela is writing a song with five movements. . . . It's like a symphony but in the African sense." Quoted in Stewart, *Breakout*, 117.

14. Fela quoted in Veal, *Fela*, 220. Street-corner accounts of this episode are infinitely more colorful. Here is one version: Having seated the well-suited Motown executives, Fela took his place on the bowl in the adjoining open toilet and began doing a big one. Because, he said, that is when ancient African kings decide important matters. He then started to reflect aloud on the name, "Motown," differently accenting the syllables each time, and much else. "Motown." "Mo taun." "Mo ta ohun." "Motaun." "Motown." "May the gods forbid. I cannot sell my voice," he said decisively and ended the meeting there and then. Tonally manipulated in certain ways, Motown could be made to mean "I sold my voice" in Yoruba.

15. Veal, *Fela*, 244.

16. Sweetman, reggae musician, quoted in Veal, *Fela*, 244.

17. "Strange! But something just kept attracting me to her. I didn't know why she was kicking my ass. I don't think anybody kicked my ass as much as my mother. But I dug her. I liked to hear her talk, discuss. Something always made me sit with her, to listen"; Moore, *Fela*, 41.

18. For Fela's account, see Moore, *Fela*, 62–64.

19. Cheryl Johnson-Odim and Nina Emma Mba write in their study of Fela's mother: "Funmilayo Ransome-Kuti was fiercely protective of Fela, who had often been abused by the authorities in a series of raids on his nightclub, the Shrine, and on his home. She was a frequent visitor to the Kalakuta Republic, and she and Fela were extremely close. One Nigerian observed, 'Fela became the darling of his mother towards the last stage of her life because she found in him a man who has a message for our oppressed people' (*Guardian*, Feb. 18, 1985). Though she never changed her name legally, in the early 1970s she had dropped Ransome-Kuti and substituted Anikulapo, a Yoruba word meaning 'warrior who carries strong protection' or alternatively 'hunter who carries death in a pouch.' She had done this at least partially at the suggestion of Fela, who had previously changed his own name to symbolize his disparagement of neocolonial mentality he attached to the adoption of European names. As early as the 1920s she had dropped her European given names, Frances Abigail, and used only Funmilayo and, as shown earlier, also insisted that pupils at her schools use their African rather than European names." *For Women and the Nation: Funmilayo Ransome-Kuti of Nigeria* (Urbana: University of Illinois Press, 1997), 168.

20. They were married in London in 1961, when Fela was still a student. Remi is British, of a Nigerian father and a mother who is African American, Native American, and British. See Moore's useful profiles in *Fela* 67–70 and 169–174.

21. Moore, *Fela*, 169.

22. Remi quoted in Moore, *Fela*, 169–170.

23. Remi quoted in Moore, *Fela*, 170.

24. Remi quoted in Moore, *Fela*, 170.

25. Remi quoted in Moore, *Fela*, 171.

26. Remi quoted in Moore, *Fela*, 172–173.

27. Remi quoted in Moore, *Fela*, 173.

28. Fela quoted in Moore, *Fela*, 88.

29. Fela quoted in Moore, *Fela*, 88.

30. Sandra recounts an episode in which she slapped Fela publicly for his infidelity in Moore, *Fela*, 98–99.

31. Sandra quoted in Moore, *Fela*, 102–103.

32. Sandra quoted in Moore, *Fela*, 102.

33. For more on afrobeat dance, see Sola Olorunyomi's useful discussion, *Afrobeat! Fela and the Imagined Continent* (Trenton, N.J.: Africa World Press, 2003), 157–169. For dance in Yoruba context, see Omofolabo Soyinka-Ajayi, *Yoruba Dance: The Semiotics of Movement and Body Attitude in a Nigerian Culture* (Trenton, N.J.: Africa World Press, 1998).

34. Moore, *Fela*, 177–233.

35. Moore, *Fela*, 163.

36. Alake, quoted in Moore, *Fela*, 198.

37. Moore, *Fela*, 166.

38. See Moore, *Fela*, 164–166.

39. Fela quoted in Moore, *Fela*, 234.

40. Remi quoted in Moore, *Fela*, 173.

41. See Moore, *Fela*, 35–47.

42. Fela quoted in Moore, *Fela*, 39.

43. Fela quoted in Moore, *Fela*, 234.

44. Fela quoted in Moore, *Fela*, 234.

45. Fela quoted in Moore, *Fela*, 235. Fela's idea here roughly parallels that of the former speaker of the U.S. House of Representatives, Newt Gingrich, who created an uproar in 1993 when he said that women, unlike men, lack "upper body strength": "Upper body strength matters—men, women. Because men are biologically stronger, and they don't get pregnant. And pregnancy is the period of male domination in traditional societies. On the other hand if what matters is the speed with which you can move the laptop, women are at least as fast and in some ways better. So you have a radical revolution based on technological change. And you've got to think that through. You talk about being in combat, what does combat mean? If combat means living in a ditch, females have biological problems staying in a ditch for thirty days, because they get infections. And they don't have upper body strength. I mean, some do, but they're relatively rare. On the other hand men are basically little piglets, and you drop them in a ditch and they just roll around in it and it doesn't matter. I mean these things are very real. On the other hand, if combat means being on an Aegis class cruiser managing the computer controls for twelve ships and their rockets, a female may be again dramatically better than a male who gets very, very frustrated sitting in a chair all the time, because males are biologically driven to go out and hunt giraffes." From "Transforming American Civilization," a college course taught by Newt Gingrich in 1993. Available online at http://www.voiceoftheturtle.org/dictionary/dict_u1.php#upper.

46. Fela quoted in Moore, *Fela*, 236.

47. Fela quoted in Moore, *Fela*, 236. For an extended consideration of some of the arguments vulgarized here by Fela, see Matt Ridley's insightful book *The Red Queen: Sex and the Evolution of Human Nature* (New York: Penguin, 1993), especially Chapter 6, "Polygamy and the Nature of Men," 171–207, and Chapter 7, "Monogamy and the Nature of Women," 209–44.

48. Fela quoted in Moore, *Fela*, 162.

49. 'Molara Ogundipe-Leslie, "Women in Nigeria," in *Women in Nigeria Today*, edited by WIN (London: Zed Press, 1985), 127.

50. Fela quoted in Moore, *Fela*, 156–157.

51. Moore, *Fela*, 165.

52. The primary conceptual framework through which many Nigerian scholars

assess polygamy is that of political economy. The argument is that the precapitalist, mainly agrarian mode of production dictated a large pool of labor in the family, which could only be provided by many wives bearing many children. The practice gradually acquired a cultural—that is, symbolic—value independent of the material foundation that gave it palpable logic. But such cultural forms change far more slowly that their material support, hence the continued practice of polygyny even when a large proportion of the men involved do no farming or any other business that demands a pool of labor. The practice has mutated in various interesting ways. Unlike the classical practice of all the women living in the same household, it is now common for rich men to establish different wives in different parts of town or indeed in different towns, complete with houses and automobiles. Polygyny today serves more as a symbol of status among those who still practice it than anything else, though there are the instances in which men marry second wives because of childlessness of the first wife or the quest for a child of the desired sex. For an analysis of contemporary experiences of Nigerian women, including women in different marital situations, see WIN, ed., *Women in Nigeria Today* (London: Zed Press, 1985), Part IV.

53.    Fela quoted in Moore, *Fela*, 161; Fela's emphasis. Needless, to say, someone this invested in heterosexuality can hardly be expected to be tolerant of homosexuality. For Fela, the latter is—yes, you guessed it—un-African, and unnatural: "The only kind of sexuality that is against nature is homosexuality. 'Cause it don't create life." Quoted in Moore, *Fela*, 237.

54.    Fela quoted in Abdul Oroh, "I Am Still Scratching the Surface," *African Guardian* (Lagos), October 17, 1988, 23.

55.    Fela quoted in Veal, *Fela*, 207.

56.    The album designer is not named in the MCA *Fela Originals* compact disc reproduction released in 2000. Names of designers and artists will be given except when they are not identified.

57.    Cover design by Mamuli Okotie-Eboh, artwork by Kayode Ademola, and photography by Afro Click.

58.    The reader who perceives a Derridean ring to my discussion here is not mistaken. Indeed, for Derrida in his reading of the opposition of nature and culture in Rousseau, the supplement is that which "adds itself, it is a surplus." But this is only one aspect of a supplement in Derrida's formulation of the concept. For him, a supplement is also a substitute; "it adds only to replace. It intervenes or insinuates itself *in-the-place-of;* if it fills, it is as if one fills a void"; *Of Grammatology,* translated by G. C. Spivak (Baltimore: Johns Hopkins University Press, 1976), 144–145. My different argument here is not that the supplement substitutes, but that it profoundly transforms that to which it is added. The Derridean logic would work here only if we were to consider the new transformed entity—now a complex, a composite of the supplement and that to which it is added—as a substitute for what was there before, insofar as that previous entity no longer exists.

59.    See Brecht, *Brecht on Theatre*, 33–42.

60.    Lemi Ghariokwu, interview with Tejumola Olaniyan, July 25, 2002.

61. Lemi Ghariokwu, interview with P. Letellier published on the back of the poster "Lagos Art: A Retrospective Exhibition by Ghariokwu Lemi," Lagos, Lithotec, 2001. The exhibition ran from Tuesday, November 13, to Sunday, December 9, 2001.

62. Ghariokwu has also narrated snatches of his early beginnings with Fela in many published interviews. See interview with P. Letellier; and also Tajudeen Sowole, "Fela Predicted the Way He Ended—Ghariokwu," *Sunday Concord* (Lagos), August 20, 2000, 13.

63. Lemi Ghariokwu, "Producing Fela's Album Jacket," *Glendora: African Quarterly on the Arts* 2, no. 2 (1997): 54.

64. See Tejumola Olaniyan, "The Traditions of Political Cartooning in Nigeria," *Glendora: African Quarterly on the Arts* 2, no. 2 (1997): 92–104. See also www.ijele.com/ijele/vol1.1/olaniyan.html.

65. Ghariokwu, "Producing Fela's Album Jacket," 54–55.

66. Ghariokwu, "Producing Fela's Album Jacket," 55.

67. Quoted in Helen Lee, "Lemi, Faithful Reflection of Fela," n.p.

68. Sowole, "Fela Predicted the Way He Ended—Ghariokwu," 3.

69. See interview with P. Letellier. On Roger Dean, see the BBC's interview with him, available online at http://www.bbc.co.uk/music/classicpop/interviews/int_dean.shtml.

70. For samples of the cover art of some of the bands, see http://www.art-for-a-change.com/Punk/punka.htm.

71. See, for instance, Chris Morrow, *Stir It Up: Reggae Album Cover Art* (San Francisco: Chronicle Books, 1999).

72. Interview with Tejumola Olaniyan, July 25, 2002.

73. Here is Ghariokwu, in his own words: "I became a regular companion sharing the great ideology of Pan-Africanism and having my mind's eye opened to the great thoughts of no less personages than 'The Redeemer' Kwame Nkrumah, Malcolm X, Marcus Garvey etc. I became a travelling companion on some of the trips across the West African coast. I contributed my quota to this great struggle for the emancipation from mental slavery. I found myself in the vantage position of having a pre-knowledge of the logic behind the conception of some of his magnum opuses. With a lot of hard work and dedication, the illustration and design of the covers thereby became such an easy task." Ghariokwu, "Producing Fela's Album Jacket," 55.

74. For the Nkrumah quote, see his *Axioms* (London: Thomas Nelson, 1967), 76.

75. All quotations in this paragraph from Femi Akintunde-Johnson, "I Cried When I Broke Up with Fela—Lemi Ghariokwu," *The Punch* (Lagos), July 20, 1989, 11. See also Sowole, "Fela Predicted the Way He Ended—Ghariokwu"; and interview with Tejumola Olaniyan.

76. Ghariokwu, from Akintunde-Johnson, "I Cried When I Broke Up with Fela," 11.

77. Akintunde-Johnson, "I Cried When I Broke Up with Fela," 11.

78. Akintunde-Johnson's words, summarizing Ghariokwu's, in "I Cried When I Broke Up with Fela," 11.

79. Ghariokwu, quoted in Sowole, "Fela Predicted the Way He Ended—Ghariokwu," 13.

80. All the quotations in this paragraph are from a profile of Femi Osunla in the exhibition brochure of *Scenes from the Underground*, 5. For reviews of the exhibition, see Nseobong Okon-Ekong, "The Many Faces of the Weird One," *Thisdayonline*, January 8, 2003, available online at www.thisdayonline.com/archive/2002/02/25/20020225art01.html; and Mcphilips Nwachukwu and Prince Osuagwu, "The Camera Stories of *Abami Eda*," *Vanguard*, February 28, 2002, available online at http://www.vanguardngr.com/news/articles/2002/February/28022002/ar328202.htm.

81. See *Scenes from the Underground*, 5.

82. *Scenes from the Underground*, 5.

83. Dapo Olorunyomi, "Osunla and the Challenge of Nigerian Visual Historiography," in *Scenes from the Underground*, 2.

84. Olorunyomi, "Osunla and the Challenge of Nigerian Visual Historiography," 2.

85. Femi Osunla, interview with Tejumola Olaniyan, Lagos, July 2002.

86. See *Scenes from the Underground*, 5.

87. See Saul Rubin, *Offbeat Marijuana: The Life and Times of the World's Grooviest Plant* (Santa Monica, Calif.: Santa Monica Press, 1999), 159–197.

88. Fela, in Moore, *Fela*, 73.

89. Fela, in Moore, *Fela*, 73.

90. See Lynn Zimmer and John P. Morgan, *Marijuana Myths, Marijuana Facts: A Review of the Scientific Evidence* (New York: Lindesmith Center, 1997), 92–96.

91. Fela, in Moore, *Fela*, 73.

92. Fela, in Veal, *Fela*, 54–55.

93. Rubin, *Offbeat Marijuana*, 169.

94. Quoted in Rubin, *Offbeat Marijuana*, 169.

95. Rubin, *Offbeat Marijuana*, 172.

96. Ghariokwu, "Producing Fela's Album Jacket," 55.

97. Idowu, *Fela*, 98–99.

98. For more detailed account, see Fairfax, *Fela*, 383–385.

99. Richard Rudgley, *Essential Substances: A Cultural History of Intoxicants in Society* (New York: Kodansha International, 1993), 3–4.

100. Rudgley, *Essential Substances*, 172–175.

101. Rudgley, *Essential Substances*, 175.

### 7. Pedagogue, Pedagogy, and the Pedagogic Form

1. Here is the process: beneath the common toilet in a house is a metal container that collects the waste. At regular daily or weekly intervals, a waste collector in a mask—*agbe poo*, literally chamber-pot carrier, but idiomatically, shit

carrier—accesses the container from its hatch that opens out behind the house and empties the contents into a bigger barrel. He does that for a few houses in the neighborhood until his barrel is full. He then carries the barrel to a waste disposal pit some distance away, followed inevitably by a trail of thick stench. All of this happens in the few daylight hours before nightfall, so the carriers are seen though they cannot be recognized as perhaps your next-door neighbor. Although it is their shit being carried, pedestrians, of course, instinctively slink to the other side of the street at the sight of an approaching *agbe poo*.

2. Fanon, *The Wretched of the Earth*. All quotations from 149, 153.

3. Mabinuori Idowu writes that Fela delivered over sixty lectures in 1980/1981 at institutions of higher learning in Nigeria. Here is his account of an interesting episode at the University of Ife (now Obafemi Awolowo University): "When other members of the discussion panel were being introduced as professor or doctor so and so, students who had had occasions to listen to Fela's marathon lectures, insisted that he too must be addressed as professor. The chairman of the occasion . . . refused to address Fela as a professor. However, seeing that the large audience stood its ground, the chairman asked Fela: 'Are you a professor?' Fela sharply retorted, 'It is the people's wish.' At this juncture, he was introduced as Professor Fela Anikulapo-Kuti and thereafter the symposium commenced in full force." *Fela*, 173–174.

4. W. J. T. Mitchell, ed., *On Narrative* (Chicago: University of Chicago Press, 1981); Philip Brophy, "Film Narrative, Narrative Film, Film Music, Music Narrative, Narrative Music," *Cinema Papers* 71 (1989), available online at http://media-arts.rmit.edu.au/Phil_Brophy/FilmNarrativeMusic.html; Mieke Bal, *Narratology: Introduction to the Theory of Narrative* (Toronto: University of Toronto Press, 1998).

5. See Theo Van Leeuwen, *Speech, Music, Sound* (London: Macmillan, 1999), 14–25.

6. Van Leeuwen, *Speech, Music, Sound*, 14.

7. Thanks to Professor dele jegede of Indiana University for pointing out this connection to me at the 2000 African Studies Association Conference in Knoxville, Tennessee, United States.

8. Fela quoted in Veal, *Fela*, 260.


## 8. The Cosmopolitan Nativist

1. See, for instance, Fela Stanovsky, "Fela and His Wives: The Import of a Postcolonial Masculinity," *Jouvert: A Journal of Postcolonial Studies* 2, no. 1 (1998), available online at http://social.chass.ncsu.edu/jouvert/v2i1/stan.htm.

2. John Howe, "Fela Anikulapo-Kuti: An Honest Man," *New Left Review* 225 (September 1997): 130.

3. John McCole, *Walter Benjamin and the Antinomies of Tradition* (Ithaca, N.Y.: Cornell University Press, 1993), 295.

4. If it is not difficult to imagine that different historical periods in all societies will create discourses of self-differentiation and gleeful self-promotion and

legitimation from preceding eras, then ideas of the "modern" as such cannot be alien to any society. By "modern" and "modernity" in this chapter, I am referring to capitalist modernity, that phenomenon of European aggressive self-propagation worldwide described so well by Karl Marx in *The Communist Manifesto*. Relevant to my consideration is Aime Cesaire's characterization of the specific form that modernity's encounter with Africa took as, on the whole, a "historical tragedy": "[T]he great historical tragedy of Africa has been not so much that it was too late in making contact with the rest of the world, as the manner in which that contact was brought about; that Europe began to 'propagate' at a time when it had fallen into the hands of the most unscrupulous financiers and captains of industry; that it was our misfortune to encounter that particular Europe on our path, and that Europe is responsible before the human community for the highest heap of corpses in human history." *Discourse on Colonialism* (New York: Monthly Review Press, 1972), 23. See also Henri Lefebvre's useful study, *Introduction to Modernity: Twelve Preludes, September 1959–May 1961* (London: Verso, 1995), 168–238.

5.   As in many other areas of contemporary African intellectual production in which it appears, "nativism," supposedly the clamorous "return-to-roots" reaffirmation of native, indigenous traditions against a stifling encroachment by the foreign, has a very elastic character. Nativism here has strangely refused to be bound by its conceptual "tribal" or ethnic delimitation and has been unapologetically transnational, continental. In other words, nativism in African discourses rarely speaks in the name of this or that ethnic culture as of African cultures generally. Ordinarily, such transnationalism can hardly be described as "nativist"; that it generally is now is a testament to the power and ability of European racialism to cheapen and simplify complexity in its own interest. This is what Frantz Fanon means when he writes that "[c]olonialism did not dream of wasting its time in denying the existence of one national culture after another. Therefore the reply of the colonized peoples will be straight away continental in breadth" (*The Wretched of the Earth*, 212). See also Adeleke Adeeko's useful book on nativism in African literary discourse, *Proverbs, Textuality, and Nativism in African Literature* (Gainesville: University Press of Florida, 1998); and Kwame A. Appiah, *In My Father's House: Africa in the Philosophy of Culture* (New York: Oxford University Press, 1992), 47–72.

6.   Basil Davidson, the distinguished historian, laments: "[T]he historian, emerging from the study of past centuries when African generally knew no such misery and crisis but, generally, a slow expansion of wealth and self-development, meets questions not to be avoided. What explains this degradation . . . ? How has this come about?" *The Black Man's Burden*, 9.

7.   See Olaniyan, "Afrocentrism."

8.   See Fairfax, *Fela*, 294–295.

9.   Immediately before the excerpt, he appeals to one of the core groups already won over by Fela, the students: "Student come and dance our music / Apala is very easy f'enikeni" (Students come and dance our music / Apala is very easy for anyone). And later on in the track, he claims for *apala* two points that

might also be perceived as afrobeat's advantages: that it is a music for the "educated," meaning western educated, and that it is cosmopolitan. *Apala* too, argues Ishola, is for the educated and is cosmopolitan:

| | |
|---|---|
| Educated fellow to ba ti sensible | Sagacious educated fellows |
| to mo nipa music kakiri | well versed in music worldwide |
| Educated guy to ba ti sensible | Astute educated guys |
| to mo nipa music kakiri | deeply knowledgeable in music |
| l'on bawajo. | dance to our music. |
| Titi lo'de Cologne, lo de Cotonou | From Cologne to Cotonou |
| Titi lo'de London, d'America | And London to America |
| Na ma wa ninu a'lare | We are known as leading entertainers. |

"Oroki Social Club," *Oroki Social Club* (Decca [West Africa] 1971).

10. *Agbada* is the classic Yoruba men's dress; it is the largest of the three pieces consisting of itself, *sokoto,* and *buba.* The three pieces, minus the cap, are made of no less than ten yards of clothing. *Gele* is the classic women's headgear, the third in the three-piece outfit of *iro* and *buba.*

11. "Apparently," because Fela argues vehemently that his orchestra only appears to be western but it is really not: "In fact all the musical instruments the whiteman is using today were invented here in Africa. Violin was stolen from Sankore University in Timbuktu, and taken to Italy during the Roman-Portuguese trade." Quoted in Idowu, *Fela,* 158.

12. See, for instance, Iyorchia D. Ayu, "Creativity and Protest in Political Culture: The Political Protest in Popular Music of Fela Anikulapo-Kuti," in *Essays in Popular Struggle* (Oguta, Nigeria: Zim Pan African Publishers, 1986), 1–55.

13. Zygmunt Bauman, "Modernity and Ambivalence," in *Globalization and Modernity,* ed. Mike Featherstone (London: Sage Publications, 1990), 144.

14. Bauman, "Modernity and Ambivalence" 144.

15. Tejumola Olaniyan, *Enchanting Modernity: A Cultural Biography of the Post-colonial African State.* Book in progress.

16. Bauman, "Modernity and Ambivalence," 144.

17. Take, for instance, the famous case of Chinua Achebe on the question of the place of English language in African literature. In the early 1960s, he wrote with optimism of his taming capacity: "I feel that the English language will be able to carry the weight of my African experience. But it will have to be a new English, still in full communion with its ancestral home but altered to suit its new African surroundings" ("The African Writer and the English Language," in *Morning Yet on Creation Day: Essays* [London: Heinemann, 1975], 62). In spite of all the accolades he received for his mastery and distinctive use of English (the "stranger"), Achebe issued, a decade later, a lament that describes the self-suspicion I am talking about: "[T]he fatalistic logic of the unassailable position of English in our literature leaves me more cold now than it did when I first spoke about it. . . . And yet I am unable to see a significantly different or a more emotionally comfortable resolution of that problem" ("Preface," in *Morning Yet on Creation Day: Essays* [London: Heine-

mann, 1975], xiv). We may have no such exemplary statements from Wole Soyinka, but his aggressive, take-no-prisoners ransacking of the properties and inner recesses of English in order to speak his world indicates no less an anxiety. And since the one and only egalitarian relationship between two living languages is translation, the most promising project of taming so far—in spite of such remaining untamable factors as the European alphabet and some categories of narrative-making—has been Ngugi wa Thiong'O's resort to writing in Gikuyu and then having his work translated into English.

18. See, for instance, Howe's useful analysis: "When Fela spoke—as he often did—in the name of 'Africa', he may have been projecting some of the attitudes of a famous, eccentric, successful, Westernized, upper-class Yoruba anarchist and bohemian on a largely uncomprehending continent; but people understood that the Africa he referred to was a colonized Africa whose private history had been disrupted by outside forces and needed to be relaunched. This *knack of being wrong, but right,* endeared Fela to his constituents." "Fela Anikulapo-Kuti: An Honest Man," 130, emphasis added.

19. Timothy Brennan, *At Home in the World: Cosmopolitanism Now* (Cambridge, Mass.: Harvard University Press, 1997), 2.

20. This is what Karl Marx means in one of his eloquent characterizations of capitalist modernity in *The Communist Manifesto:* "It compels all nations, on the pain of extinction, to adopt the bourgeois mode of production; it compels them to introduce what it calls civilization into their midst, i.e., to become bourgeois themselves. In one word, it creates a world after its own image"; translated by A. J. P. Taylor (1848; reprint, London: Penguin, 1967), 84.

### 9. The Political, the Libidinal

1. The libidinal is that realm of emotional and psychic energy in the psychological composition of a person that is connected to the basic human instincts. See Sigmund Freud, *Standard Edition of the Complete Psychological Works of Sigmund Freud,* 24 vols., translated under the general editorship of James Strachey, in collaboration with Anna Freud, assisted by Alix Strachey and Alan Tyson (New York: W. W. Norton, 1953–1974), 18:90. For a detailed accessible definition, see Laplanche and Pontalis, *The Language of Psycho-Analysis,* translated by Donald Nicholson-Smith (New York: W. W. Norton, 1973), 236–240. However, I am more indebted to Jacques Lacan in my use of the concept here; see *The Seminar,* Book II: *The Ego in Freud's Theory and in the Technique of Psychoanalysis, 1954–55,* translated by Sylvana Tomaselli (New York: W. W. Norton, 1988).

2. In *The Seminar,* Lacan situates libido in the imaginary psychic order: "Libido and the ego are on the same side. Narcissism is libidinal" (326).

3. This is why I think we can better conceive the "political" in the comprehensive sense as encompassing both the realms of the artificially demarcated sphere of politics where issues of immediate governance are discussed *and* all the other areas that are cordoned off and assumed to be "not political" but are in fact constituted by the struggle of active competing interests over

symbolic production and hence over all resources and opportunities; the immediately palpable context of the "political" is that quintessential compromise arrangement we call "society." I have benefited from Ernesto Laclau and Chantal Mouffe, *Hegemony and Socialist Strategy: Toward a Radical Democratic Politics* (London: Verso, 1985). See also Mouffe, *The Return of the Political,* where she writes, "The political cannot be restricted to a certain type of institution, or envisaged as constituting a specific sphere or level of society. It must be conceived as a dimension that is inherent to every human society and that determines our very ontological condition"; (London: Verso, 1993), 3.

4.    See also Jean-François Lyotard, *Libidinal Economy,* translated by I. H. Grant (Bloomington: Indiana University Press, 1993).

5.    This is no doubt part of the reason John Howe describes Fela as an "anarchist." See his "Fela Anikulapo-Kuti: An Honest Man," 130.

6.    "Politics is identical to political reality and political reality, as all reality, is first, constituted at the symbolic level." Yannis Stavrakakis, *Lacan and the Political* (London: Routledge, 1999), 71.

7.    Dylan Evans, *An Introductory Dictionary of Lacanian Psychoanalysis* (New York: Routledge, 1996), 161.

8.    Evans, *An Introductory Dictionary of Lacanian Psychoanalysis,* 82.

9.    See Evans, *An Introductory Dictionary of Lacanian Psychoanalysis,* 114–116; and Laplanche and Pontalis, *The Language of Psycho-Analysis,* 250–252.

10.   Lacan, "Some Reflections on the Ego," *International Journal of Psycho-Analysis* 34 (1953): 14. See also Evans, *An Introductory Dictionary of Lacanian Psychoanalysis,* 114–116.

11.   This is a foundational point, a description, and not just a criticism. "There is no society and social reality without exclusion; without it, the world collapses into a psychotic universe." Stavrakakis, *Lacan and the Political,* 34.

12.   "The imaginary is . . . rooted in the subject's relationship to his own body (or rather to the image of his body). . . . [T]he imaginary is manifested above all on the sexual plane, in such forms as sexual display and courtship rituals"; Evans, *An Introductory Dictionary of Lacanian Psychoanalysis,* 83.

13.   The reality would of course repeatedly dawn on Fela that the signifier has no originary signified. He was booed by the Berlin Jazz Festival audience in 1978 for not playing "African music" but instead playing mere disco. Fela responded: "I want you to scream and shout more, because the more you shout, the more you convince me, that you all wish Afro-Beat were a German music. But one unfortunate thing for you is that the music is an authentic African music a product from the authentic African music archives." Idowu, *Fela,* 71. Fela justifiably played the "race" card here, but what would be his response to Africans who might make a similar charge as the one the Germans made? No doubt that they are suffering from "colomentality"—another suture for the dispersed nature of what "Africa" is to even Africans. It is not that what is "Africa" cannot be programmatically articulated; it is just that that articulation would have to be acknowledged as partisan and only one in many possible articulations. The problem was that Fela assumed that his own articulation is

or ought to be universally shared or is so unimpeachable that everyone ought to see and agree to it without debate.

14. Homi Bhabha, *The Location of Culture* (New York: Routledge, 1994), 189.

15. "If the social does not manage to fix itself in the intelligible and instituted forms of a society, the social only exists, however, as an effort to construct that impossible object. Any discourse is constituted as an attempt to dominate the field of discursivity, to arrest the flow of difference, to construct a centre. We will call the privileged discursive points of this partial fixation, nodal points. (Lacan has insisted on these partial fixations through his concept of *points de capiton,* that is, of privileged signifiers that fix meaning of a signifying chain)." Laclau and Mouffe, *Hegemony and Socialist Strategy,* 112.

16. Fela quoted in Veal, *Fela,* 253.

17. Fela quoted in Veal, *Fela,* 236.

18. Stavrakakis, *Lacan and the Political,* 81.


## 10. Conclusion

1. I am indebted to Wole Soyinka's account in *Myth, Literature and the African World,* 27–28.

2. Lemi Ghariokwu recalls, "I remembered vividly that sometimes in 1976, I suggested to Fela that he should start producing young people. And as is characteristic of Fela, he just cut me and said . . . 'Am I a producer? Lemi, don't start again.' What brought about my suggestion then was the way I saw the reggae music growing. You have hundreds if not thousands of reggae musicians and I thought Afrobeat too should develop along that line. Now I'm happy that many people are playing Afrobeat. We need more musicians to join the train." Interview with Sowole, "Fela Predicted the Way He Ended— Ghariokwu," 13.

3. For a more detailed profile of Allen, see Benson Idonije, "Drum Rains Descend . . . with Tony Allen," *The Guardian* (Lagos), April 19, 2002.

4. See Veal's detailed discussion in *Fela,* 257–260.

5. In liner notes to his LP *Hope* (1993).

6. See Veal, *Fela,* 256–259.

7. See liner notes for *Red Hot + Riot.*

8. Tony Allen quoted in liner notes by Carter Van Pelt to *Afrobeat . . . No Go Die.*

9. Antibalas, "Antibalas . . . Musical Insurrection." This is from the band's "Biography," available at http://www.antibalas.com/pages/index2.html, accessed February 6, 2003 (click on "Biographies"). By December 2003, the title of the biography had changed to a much-less-political and more entertainment-oriented "Antibalas Will Help You Find Your 'Inner Freak'!" The band had reworded its self-description less polemically as well: it is "carrying on the Afrobeat tradition begun by Fela Anikulapo-Kuti. Based in New York, the band combines highlife, jazz, funk, and traditional African rhythms and informs all of it with unabashed political conviction. The band's sound is

rooted in monstrous horns and bass, polyrhythmic beats and funky breaks, and furious lyrics in English, Yoruba and Spanish."

10. Matt Cibula, "'Lip Service Too Much': Antibalas Grows Up," available online at http://www.antibalas.com/pages/index2.html.

11. "Antibalas: Proudly Providing 'America's Only Live Afrobeat Party,'" *Weekend All Things Considered,* August 21, 2001, available online at http://www.npr.org/programs/watc/features/2001/antibalas/010825.antibalas.html.

12. Tosin Ajirire, "From Kora to Grammy: Femi Kuti Reaps Dad's Reward," *Tempo,* February 6, 2003, Available online at http://allafrica.com/stories/200302060780.html.

13. "Truly, Femi's shows in those days had attracted little or no crowd. Most people, including Fela, did not see the wisdom in his decision to quit the Egypt 80 band to form his own band. But Femi's day of glory came in 1991. It was at the Shrine. He performed so well that Fela could not conceal his excitement as he got up to dance. Afterward, Fela got the microphone and announced that Femi was the only musician who could play Afrobeat like him." Ajirire, "From Kora to Grammy."

14. Femi quoted in Veal, *Fela,* 256.

15. Femi told a journalist in 1988: "Most of us who love him are no longer around him as we should be because we cannot stand some of the things which happen around him. . . . If I go to him now and tell him I want to stop people selling drugs around the Shrine, I will make a lot of enemies and he too will not listen to me." Quoted in Veal, *Fela,* 206.

16. Femi quoted in Veal, *Fela,* 257.

17. Femi quoted in Jay Babcock, "Femi Kuti: The Son Also Grooves," *Mean,* no. 6 (December 1999–January 2000), available online at http://www.jaybabcock.com/femi.html.

18. UNICEF, "Femi Kuti is UNICEF's Newest Special Representative," press release, June 12, 2002, available online at http://www.unicef.org/newsline/02pr34femi.htm.

19. Femi Anikulapo-Kuti, "Commentary: Speaking Out against AIDS," 2000, available online at http://www.unicef.org/pon00/mysong.htm.

20. Olakunle Tejuoso and Dapo Adeniyi, "Interview with Lagbaja (Bisade Ologunde)," *Glendora International* (Lagos), February 24, 1995, available online at http://allafrica.com/stories/200105210262.html.

21. Lagbaja quoted in Tejuoso and Adeniyi, "Interview with Lagbaja."

22. "I chose to use the mask as a symbol that represents the facelessness, the voicelessness, the seemingly lack of identity of the common man. And I thought since I felt they were faceless the best thing to communicate that would be to use a mask. I wanted a name that would communicate the same message. The Yoruba word Lágbájá means nobody in particular, and depending on the context of its use, it could mean anybody, somebody." Lagbaja, in Adam Wasserman, "Lagbaja, 'The Masked Man,'" 2001, available online at http://www.afropop.org/multi/interview/ID/9.

23.   Lagbaja quoted in Tejuoso and Adeniyi, "Interview with Lagbaja."

24.   Banning Eyre, "Lagbaja," available online at
      http://www.afropop.org/explore/artist_info/ID/192/Lágbájá.

25.   Lagbaja explains in an interview, "Through the use of technology, I strung
      parts of his voice, sentences, phrases, syllables together, to make the message
      that I wanted to communicate." See Wasserman, "Lagbaja, 'The Masked
      Man.'"

26.   Fela quoted in Moore, *Fela*, 257 (Fela's emphasis).

# Bibliography

Achebe, Chinua. "The African Writer and the English Language." In *Morning Yet on Creation Day: Essays,* 55–62. London: Heinemann, 1975.

———. "Preface." In *Morning Yet on Creation Day: Essays,* xiii–xiv. London: Heinemann, 1975.

———. *The Trouble with Nigeria.* Oxford: Heinemann, 1983.

Adeeko, Adeleke. *Proverbs, Textuality, and Nativism in African Literature.* Gainesville: University Press of Florida, 1998.

Aderibigbe, A. B., ed. *Lagos: The Development of an African City.* London: Longman Nigeria, 1975.

Adorno, Theodor W. "On Popular Music." *Studies in Philosophy and Social Sciences* 9 (1941): 17–48.

———. "Perennial Fashion: Jazz" (1955). In *Prisms,* 119–132. Cambridge, Mass.: MIT Press, 1981.

———. *Essays on Music.* Berkeley: University of California Press, 2002.

Agawu, Kofi. *Representing African Music: Postcolonial Notes, Queries, Positions.* New York: Routledge, 2003.

Ajaegbu, Hyacinth I. *Urban and Rural Development in Nigeria.* London: Heinemann, 1976.

Ajirire, Tosin. "From Kora to Grammy: Femi Kuti Reaps Dad's Reward." *Tempo,* February 6, 2003. Available online at http://allafrica.com/stories/200302060780.html.

Ake, Claude. *Revolutionary Pressures in Africa.* London: Zed Press, 1978.

———. *Social Science as Imperialism: The Theory of Political Development.* 2nd ed. Ibadan: Ibadan University Press, 1982.

Akintunde-Johnson, Femi. "I Cried When I Broke Up with Fela—Lemi Ghariokwu." *The Punch* (Lagos), July 20, 1989, 11.

Akpabot, Samuel Ekpe. *Foundation of Nigerian Traditional Music.* Ibadan: Spectrum Books, 1986.

Alli, M. Chris. *The Federal Republic of Nigerian Army: The Siege of a Nation.* Lagos: Malthouse, 2002.

*The Amazing and Perilous Odyssey of Fela Anikulapo-Kuti.* San Francisco: Revolution Books, 1985. First issued in *Revolutionary Worker,* no. 305 (May 13, 1985).

Ani, Marimba. *Yurugu: An African-Centered Critique of European Cultural Thought and Behavior.* Trenton, N.J.: Africa World Press, 1994.

Anikulapo-Kuti, Fela. "Chief Priest Say: If Expenses of 80,000 Pilgrims . . . " *Daily Times* (Lagos), January 1, 1976, 24.

———. "Afrika Shrine." *The Punch* (Lagos), August 25, 1979, 12.

———. "Chief Priest Say: For Pope Country . . . " *The Punch* (Lagos), February 26, 1982, 19.

Anikulapo-Kuti, Femi. "Commentary: Speaking Out against AIDS." 2000. Accessed May 6, 2003. Available online at http://www.unicef.org/pon00/mysong.htm.

Antibalas. "Antibalas . . . Musical Insurrection." n.d. Accessed February 6, 2003. Available online at http://www.antibalas.com/pages/index2.html.

"Antibalas: Proudly Providing 'America's Only Live Afrobeat Party.'" *Weekend All Things Considered*, August 21, 2001. Available online at http://www.npr.org/programs/watc/features/2001/antibalas/010825.antibalas.html.

Appiah, Kwame A. *In My Father's House: Africa in the Philosophy of Culture*. New York: Oxford University Press, 1992.

Asante, Molefi. *The Afrocentric Idea*. Philadelphia: Temple University Press, 1987.

———. *Kemet, Afrocentricity and Knowledge*. Trenton, N.J.: Africa World Press, 1990.

Attali, Jacques. *Noise: The Political Economy of Music*. Translated by Brian Massumi. Minneapolis: University of Minnesota Press, 1985.

Ayu, Iyorchia D. "Creativity and Protest in Political Culture: The Political Protest in Popular Music of Fela Anikulapo-Kuti." In *Essays in Popular Struggle*, 1–55. Oguta, Nigeria: Zim Pan African Publishers, 1986.

Babcock, Jay. "Femi Kuti: The Son Also Grooves." *Mean*, no. 6 (December 1999–January 2000). Accessed January 15, 2004. Available online at http://www.jaybabcock.com/femi.html.

———. "Ginger Baker." *Mean*, no. 6 (December 1999–January 2000). Accessed January 15, 2004. Available online at http://www.jaybabcock.com/ginger.html.

Badie, Betrand, and Pierre Birnbaum. *The Sociology of the State*. Translated by A. Goldhammer. Chicago: University of Chicago Press, 1983.

Bal, Mieke. *Narratology: Introduction to the Theory of Narrative*. Toronto: University of Toronto Press, 1998.

Barber, Karin. "Popular Reactions to the Petro-Naira." *The Journal of Modern African Studies* 20, no. 3 (1982): 431–450.

Barnes, Sandra T. *Patrons and Power: Creating a Political Community in Metropolitan Lagos*. Manchester: Manchester University Press, 1986.

———, ed. *Africa's Ogun: Old World and New*. Bloomington: Indiana University Press, 1989.

Barthes, Roland. "Whose Theater? Whose Avant-Garde?" In *Critical Essays*, 67–70. Translated by R. Howard. Evanston, Ill.: Northwestern University Press, 1972.

Bauman, Zygmunt. "Modernity and Ambivalence." In *Globalization and Modernity*, ed. Mike Featherstone, 143–170. London: Sage Publications, 1990.

Bayart, Jean-François. *The State in Africa: The Politics of the Belly*. Translated by M. Harper et al. London: Longman, 1993.

Benjamin, Walter. *Illuminations: Essays and Reflections*. Translated by Harry Zohn. New York: Schocken Books, 1969.

Ben-Jochannan, Y. *The Black Man of the Nile and His Family*. New York: Alkebu-lan Books, 1972.

Bernal, Martin. *Black Athena: The Afroasiatic Roots of Classical Civilization*. Vol. 1. New Brunswick, N.J.: Rutgers University Press, 1987.

Bhabha, Homi. *The Location of Culture*. New York: Routledge, 1994.

Blyden, Edward Wilmot. *Christianity, Islam and the Negro Race*. London: W. B. Whittingham, 1887.

Brecht, Bertolt. *Brecht on Theatre: The Development of an Aesthetic*. Translated by John Willett. New York: Hill and Wang, 1964.

———. *The Caucasian Chalk Circle*. Translated by James and Tania Stern. 1948. Reprint, London: Methuen, 2000.

Brennan, Timothy. *At Home in the World: Cosmopolitanism Now.* Cambridge, Mass.: Harvard University Press, 1997.

Brophy, Philip. "Film Narrative, Narrative Film, Film Music, Music Narrative, Narrative Music." *Cinema Papers* 71 (1989). Accessed January 15, 2004. Available online at http://media-arts.rmit.edu.au/Phil_Brophy/FilmNarrativeMusic.html.

Brown, James, and Bruce Tucker. *James Brown: The Godfather of Soul.* New York: Macmillan, 1986.

Cabral, Amilcar. *Return to the Source: Selected Speeches.* New York: Monthly Review Press, 1973.

Cesaire, Aime. *Discourse on Colonialism.* New York: Monthly Review Press, 1972.

Chabal, Patrick. *Power in Africa: An Essay in Political Interpretation.* New York: St. Martin's Press, 1994.

Chabal, Patrick, and Jean-Pascal Daloz. *Africa Works: Disorder as Political Instrument.* Oxford: James Currey, 1999.

Cibula, Matt. "Lip Service Too Much: Antibalas Grows up." Accessed May 5, 2003. Available online at http://www.antibalas.com/pages/index2.html.

Collins, John. *West African Pop Roots.* Philadelphia: Temple University Press, 1992.

Crawford, Young. *The African Colonial State in Comparative Perspective.* New Haven, Conn.: Yale University Press, 1994.

Davidson, Basil. *The Black Man's Burden: Africa and the Curse of the Nation State.* New York: Random House, 1992.

Davis, Ossie. "On Malcolm X." In *The Autobiography of Malcolm X,* 464–466. New York: Ballantine Books, 1965.

Delano, Isaac O. *The Singing Minister of Nigeria: The Life of the Rev. Canon J. J. Ransome-Kuti.* London: United Society for Christian Literature, 1942.

———. *Josaiah Ransome-Kuti: The Drummer Boy Who Became a Canon.* Ibadan: Oxford University Press, 1968.

Derrida, Jacques. *Of Grammatology.* Translated by G. C. Spivak. Baltimore: Johns Hopkins University Press, 1976.

Diop, Cheikh Anta. *The African Origins of Civilization: Myth or Reality.* Westport, Conn.: Lawrence Hill, 1974.

———. *Civilization or Barbarism: An Authentic Anthropology.* Westport, Conn.: Lawrence Hill, 1991.

Dorgu, Victor. "Are the Youngsters Taking Over?" *Daily Times* (Lagos), July 28, 1968, 10.

dos Santos, Juana Elbein, and Deoscoredes M. dos Santos. *Esu Bara Laroye: A Comparative Study.* Ibadan: Institute of African Studies, 1971.

Drake, St. Clair. *Black Folk Here and There: An Essay in History and Anthropology.* 2 vols. Los Angeles: Center for Afro-American Studies, University of California, 1987–1990.

DuBois, W. E. B. *The Souls of Black Folk.* 1903. Reprint, New York: Vintage, 1990.

Echeruo, Michael J. C. *Victorian Lagos: Aspects of Nineteenth Century Lagos Life.* London: Macmillan, 1977.

Elegbede-Fernandez, Abiola Dosunmu. *Lagos: A Legacy of Honour.* Ibadan: Spectrum Books, 1992.

Essien-Udom, Essien Udosen. *Black Nationalism: A Search for an Identity in America.* New York: Dell, 1964.

Euba, Akin. *Essays on Music in Africa.* Vol. 1. Bayreuth: Bayreuth African Studies, 1988.

———. *Yoruba Drumming: The Dundun Tradition.* Bayreuth: E. Breitinger, Bayreuth University, 1990.

Evans, Dylan. *An Introductory Dictionary of Lacanian Psychoanalysis*. New York: Routledge, 1996.

Eyre, Banning. "Lagbaja." Accessed April 17, 2003. Available online at http://www.afropop.org/explore/artist_info/ID/192/Lágbájá.

Fairfax, Frank Thurmond. "Fela, the Afro-Beat King: Popular Music and Cultural Revitalization in West Africa." Ph.D. diss., University of Michigan, 1993.

Falola, Toyin, and Julius Ihonvbere. *The Rise and Fall of Nigeria's Second Republic, 1979–1984*. London: Zed, 1985.

Fanon, Frantz. *The Wretched of the Earth*. Translated by Constance Farrington. 1961. Reprint, New York: Grove Press, 1963.

———. *Black Skin, White Masks*. Translated by C. L. Markmann. New York: Grove Press, 1967.

———. *Toward the African Revolution*. Translated by Haakon Chevalier. New York: Grove Press, 1969.

Fatton, Robert. *Predatory Rule: State and Civil Society in Africa*. Boulder: Lynne Rienner, 1992.

Freire, Paulo. *Pedagogy of the Oppressed*. Translated by Myra Bergman Ramos. New York: Continuum, 1970.

Freud, Sigmund. *Standard Edition of the Complete Psychological Works of Sigmund Freud*. 24 vols. Translated under the general editorship of James Strachey, in collaboration with Anna Freud, assisted by Alix Strachey and Alan Tyson. New York: W. W. Norton, 1953–1974.

Frith, Simon. *Performing Rites: On the Value of Popular Music*. Cambridge, Mass.: Harvard University Press, 1996.

Gates, Henry Louis, Jr. *The Signifying Monkey: A Theory of Afro-American Literary Criticism*. New York: Oxford University Press, 1988.

Ghariokwu, Lemi. "Producing Fela's Album Jacket." *Glendora: African Quarterly on the Arts* 2, no. 2 (1997): 54–56.

Gordimer, Nadine. "Living in the Interregnum." In *The Essential Gesture: Writing, Politics and Places*, edited by S. Clingman, 261–284. London: Penguin, 1989.

Graham, Ronnie. *The Da Capo Guide to Contemporary African Music*. New York: Da Capo Press, 1988.

Gramsci, Antonio. *Selections from the Prison Notebooks*. Edited and translated by Q. Hoare and G. N. Smith. New York: International Publishers, 1987.

Grass, Randall F. "Fela Anikulapo-Kuti: The Art of an Afrobeat Rebel." *The Drama Review* 30, no. 1 (1986): 131–148.

Gridley, Mark C. *Jazz Styles: History and Analysis*. Englewood Cliffs, N.J.: Prentice Hall, 1994.

Guha, Ranajit. "Dominance without Hegemony and Its Historiography." *Subaltern Studies* 6 (1989): 210–309.

Hall, Peter. *Cities in Civilization*. New York: Pantheon Books, 1998.

Heywood, Andrew. *Political Ideologies: An Introduction*. London: Macmillan, 1992.

"Highlife on the 'Net." Accessed October 20, 2002. Available online at http://www.antibalas.com/pages/index2.html. (Recently retitled "Antabalas will Help You Find Your 'Inner Freak'!")

Hountondji, Paulin J. "Scientific Dependency in Africa Today." *Research in African Literatures* 21, no. 3 (1990): 5–15.

———. *African Philosophy: Myth and Reality*. 2nd ed. Bloomington: Indiana University Press, 1996.

———, ed. *Endogenous Knowledge: Research Trails*. Dakar: CODESRIA, 1997.

Howe, John. "Fela Anikulapo-Kuti: An Honest Man." *New Left Review* 225 (September 1997): 127–133.

Idonije, Benson. "Koola Lobitos . . . The Beauty of Melody." *The Guardian* (Lagos), October 13, 1999, 52.

———. "Old or New, Palmwine Is Truly Enchanting." *Glendora: African Quarterly on the Arts* 3, no. 2 (2001): 17–22.

———. "The Legendary Highlifer." In *Scenes from the Underground: Exhibition of Fela Anikulapo-Kuti's Photographs*, 6–9. Brochure. Lagos: The News and Femi Osunla, 2001.

———. "Drum Rains Descend . . . with Tony Allen." *The Guardian* (Lagos), April 19, 2002.

Idowu, E. Bolaji. *Olodumare: God in Yoruba Belief*. London: Longman, 1962.

Idowu, Mabinuori Kayode. *Fela: Why Blackman Carry Shit*. Ikeja, Nigeria: Opinion Media Limited, 1986.

Inyama, Nnamdi, et al. "This Is Still Lagos: The Land of Lawlessness, Armed Robbery, Gridlock, Overpopulation and Stench." *The Guardian* (Lagos), June 23, 2003.

Irele, Abiola. "The Crisis of Legitimacy in Africa: A Time of Change and Despair." *Dissent* 39, no. 3 (1992): 296–302.

Jackson, Robert H., and Carl G. Rosberg. *Personal Rule in Black Africa: Prince, Autocrat, Prophet, Tyrant*. Berkeley: University of California Press, 1982.

James, George G. M. *Stolen Legacy: The Greeks Were Not the Authors of Greek Philosophy, but the People of North Africa, Commonly Called the Egyptians*. 1954. Reprint, San Francisco: Julian Richardson Associates, 1976.

Johnson-Odim, Cheryl, and Nina Emma Mba. *For Women and the Nation: Funmilayo Ransome-Kuti of Nigeria*. Urbana: University of Illinois Press, 1997.

Jones, Charles E., ed. *The Black Panther Party Reconsidered*. Baltimore: Black Classic Press, 1998.

Joseph, Richard A. *Democracy and Prebendal Politics in Nigeria: The Rise and Fall of the Second Republic*. New York: Cambridge University Press, 1987.

Kofsky, Frank. *John Coltrane and the Jazz Revolution of the 1960s*. Rev. and expanded ed. New York: Pathfinder, 1998.

Lacan, Jacques. "Some Reflections on the Ego." *International Journal of Psycho-Analysis* 34 (1953): 11–17.

———. *The Seminar*. Book II: *The Ego in Freud's Theory and in the Technique of Psychoanalysis, 1954–55*. Translated by Sylvana Tomaselli. New York: W. W. Norton, 1988.

Laclau, Ernesto, and Chantal Mouffe. *Hegemony and Socialist Strategy: Toward a Radical Democratic Politics*. London: Verso, 1985.

Laplanche, J., and J.-B. Pontalis. *The Language of Psycho-Analysis*. Translated by Donald Nicholson-Smith. New York: W. W. Norton, 1973.

Lawson, William. *The Western Scar: The Theme of the Been- to in West African Fiction*. Athens, Ohio: Ohio University Press, 1982.

Lazarus, Neil. *Nationalism and Cultural Practice in the Postcolonial World*. Cambridge: Cambridge University Press, 1999.

Lee, Helene. "Lemi, Faithful Reflection of Fela." Originally published in *Liberation*, March 28, 2001. Translated by Adolf Onwuka. Reproduced on the back of the poster "Lagos Art: A Retrospective Exhibition by Ghariokwu Lemi," Lagos, Lithotec, 2001.

Lefebvre, Henri. *Introduction to Modernity: Twelve Preludes, September 1959–May 1961.* London: Verso, 1995.

Legum, Colin. *Africa since Independence.* Bloomington: Indiana University Press, 1999.

Letellier, P. "Ghariokwu Lemi, 'Lagos Art': Interview with Lemi Ghariokwu." Exhibition poster. Lagos: Lithotec, 2001.

Lyotard, Jean-François. *Libidinal Economy.* Translated by I. H. Grant. Bloomington: Indiana University Press, 1993.

Mabogunje, Akin L. *Urbanization in Nigeria.* New York: Africana Publishing Corporation, 1968.

Mamdani, Mahmood. *Citizen and Subject: Contemporary Africa and the Legacy of Late Colonialism.* Princeton, N.J.: Princeton University Press, 1996.

Marx, Karl, and Friedrich Engels. *The Communist Manifesto.* Translated by A. J. P. Taylor. 1848. Reprint, London: Penguin, 1967.

Mbembe, Achille. "The Banality of Power and the Aesthetics of Vulgarity in the Postcolony." *Public Culture* 4, no. 2 (1992): 1–30.

———. *On the Postcolony.* Berkeley: University of California Press, 2001.

Mbembe, Achille, and Janet Roitman. "Figures of the Subject in Times of Crisis." *Public Culture* 7, no. 2 (1995): 323–352.

McCartney, John T. *Black Power Ideologies: An Essay in African American Political Thought.* Philadelphia: Temple University Press, 1992.

McCole, John. *Walter Benjamin and the Antinomies of Tradition.* Ithaca, N.Y.: Cornell University Press, 1993.

Middleton, Richard. *Studying Popular Music.* Milton Keynes: Open University Press, 1990.

———, ed. *Reading Pop: Approaches to Textual Analysis in Popular Music.* Oxford: Oxford University Press, 2000.

Mitchell, W. J. T., ed. *On Narrative.* Chicago: University of Chicago Press, 1981.

Mohammed, Bala. *Africa and Nonalignment: A Study in the Foreign Relations of New Nations.* Kano: Triumph Pub. Co., 1978.

Moore, Carlos. *Fela, Fela: This Bitch of a Life.* London: Alison & Busby, 1982.

Morrow, Chris. *Stir It Up: Reggae Album Cover Art.* San Francisco: Chronicle Books, 1999.

Mouffe, Chantal. *The Return of the Political.* London: Verso, 1993.

Nketia, J. H. Kwabena. *The Music of Africa.* New York: W. W. Norton, 1974.

Nkrumah, Kwame. *Africa Must Unite.* London: Heinemann, 1963.

———. *Consciencism: Philosophy and Ideology for Decolonization and Development with Particular Reference to the African Revolution.* London: Heinemann, 1964.

———. *Neo-Colonialism: The Last Stage of Imperialism.* New York: International Publishers, 1966.

———. *Axioms.* London: Thomas Nelson, 1967.

Nwabueze, B. O. *Military Rule and Social Justice in Nigeria.* Ibadan: Spectrum Books, 1993.

Nwachukwu, Mcphilips, and Prince Osuagwu. "The Camera Stories of Abami Eda." *Vanguard,* February 28, 2002. Available online at http://www.vanguardngr.com/news/articles/2002/February/28022002/ar328202.htm.

Nzimiro, I. *The Nigerian Civil War: A Study in Class Conflict.* Enugu: Fourth Dimension, 1979.

Obasanjo, Olusegun. *My Command: An Account of the Nigerian Civil War, 1967–1970.* London: Heinemann, 1981.

Ofeimun, Odia. "Imagination and the City." *Glendora: African Quarterly on the Arts* 3, no. 2 (2001): 11–15, 137–141.

Ogundipe-Leslie, 'Molara. "Women in Nigeria." In *Women in Nigeria Today*, edited by WIN, 119–131. London: Zed Press, 1985.

Ogundipe, Ayodele. "Esu Elegbara, the Yoruba God of Chance and Uncertainty: A Study in Yoruba Mythology." 2 vols. Ph.D. dissertation, Indiana University, 1978.

Ogunmola, Kola. *Palmwine Drinkard: Opera after the Novel by Amos Tutuola*. Translated by R. G. Armstrong. Ibadan: Institute of African Studies, University of Ibadan, 1968.

Ogunye, Jiti, Segun Jegede, Bash Olasupo, Lucky Akaruese, and Dipo Fashina, ed. *Nigerian Students and the Challenges of Leadership*. Lagos: Committee for the Defence of Human Rights, 1998.

Okon-Ekong, Nseobong. "The Many Portraits of the Weird One." *Thisdayonline*, January 8, 2003. Accessed May 9, 2003. Available online at www.thisdayonline.com/archive/2002/02/25/20020225art01.html.

Olaniyan, Tejumola. *Scars of Conquest, Masks of Resistance: The Invention of Cultural Identities in African, African American and Caribbean Drama*. New York: Oxford University Press, 1995.

———. "Afrocentrism." *Social Dynamics* 21, no. 2 (Summer 1995): 91–105.

———. "The Traditions of Political Cartooning in Nigeria." *Glendora: African Quarterly on the Arts* 2, no. 2 (1997): 92–104.

———. "Africa: Varied Colonial Legacies." In *A Companion to Postcolonial Studies*, edited by Sangeeta Ray and Henry Schwarz, 269–281. Oxford: Blackwell, 2000.

———. "Modernity and Its Mirages: Wole Soyinka and the African State." *Modern Drama* 45, no. 3 (2002): 349–357.

———. "From Black Aesthetics to Afrocentrism." Unpublished, 2002.

———. "Interview with Femi Osunla." Unpublished, 2002.

———. "Interview with Lemi Ghariokwu." Unpublished, 2002.

———. "Economies of the Interstice." In *Problematizing Blackness: Self Ethnographies by Black Immigrants to the United States*, edited by Percy C. Hintzen and Jean Muteba Rahier, 53–64. New York: Routledge, 2003.

Olisanwuche, Esedebe P. *Pan-Africanism: The Idea and Movement, 1776–1991*. Washington, D.C.: Howard University Press, 1994.

Olorunyomi, Dapo. "Osunla and the Challenge of Nigerian Visual Historiography." In *Scenes from the Underground: Exhibition of Fela Anikulapo-Kuti's Photographs*, 2. Exhibition brochure. February 17–23, 2002. Lagos: The News, 2002.

Olorunyomi, Sola. "Another Township Tonight." *Glendora: African Quarterly on the Arts* 3, no. 2 (2001): 24–35.

———. *Afrobeat! Fela and the Imagined Continent*. Trenton, N.J.: Africa World Press, 2003.

Olson, Gary A., and Irene Gale, eds. *(Inter)Views: Cross-Disciplinary Perspectives on Rhetoric and Literacy*. Carbondale: Southern Illinois University Press, 1991.

Omojola, Bode. *Nigerian Art Music, with an Introductory Study of Ghanaian Art Music*. Ibadan: Institut Français de Recherche en Afrique (IFRA), 1995.

Oroh, Abdul. " 'I'm Still Scratching the Surface.' " *African Guardian* (Lagos), October 17, 1988, 20–23.

Osaghae, Eghosa E. *Crippled Giant: Nigeria since Independence*. Bloomington: Indiana University Press, 1998.

Padmore, George. *Pan-Africanism or Communism.* 1956. Reprint, Garden City, N.Y.: Anchor Books, 1972.

Peil, Margaret. *Lagos: The City Is the People.* Boston, Mass.: G. K. Hall & Co., 1991.

Pelton, Robert D. *The Trickster in West Africa: A Study of Mythic Irony and Sacred Delight.* Berkeley: University of California Press, 1980.

Peters, Jimi. *The Nigerian Military and the State.* London: Tauris Academic Studies, 1997.

Plato. *The Republic.* Translated by B. Jowett. New York: Vintage Books, 1972.

———. *The Essential Plato.* Translated by B. Jowett. New York: QPB Club, 1999.

Reed, Ishmael. *Mumbo Jumbo: A Novel.* 1972. New York: Simon and Schuster, 1996.

Ridley, Matt. *The Red Queen: Sex and the Evolution of Human Nature.* New York: Penguin, 1993.

Rodney, Walter. *How Europe Underdeveloped Africa.* Washington, D.C.: Howard University Press, 1972.

Rubin, Saul. *Offbeat Marijuana: The Life and Times of the World's Grooviest Plant.* Santa Monica, Calif.: Santa Monica Press, 1999.

Rudgley, Richard. *Essential Substances: A Cultural History of Intoxicants in Society.* New York: Kodansha International, 1993.

Sada, P. O., and J. S. Oguntoyinbo, eds. *Urbanization Processes and Problems in Nigeria.* Ibadan: Ibadan University Press, 1978.

Sandoval, Chela. *Methodology of the Oppressed.* Minneapolis: University of Minnesota Press, 2000.

Sankara, Thomas. *Thomas Sankara Speaks: The Burkina Faso Revolution 1983–87.* Translated by Samantha Anderson. New York: Pathfinder, 1988.

Schoofs, Mark. "Part 2: A Tale of Two Brothers." *Village Voice,* November 10–16, 1999. Accessed May 24, 2003. Available online at http://www.villagevoice.com/issues/ 9945/schoofs.php.

Schoonmaker, Trevor, ed. *Fela: From West Africa to West Broadway.* New York: Palgrave Macmillan, 2003.

Sebba, Mark. *Contact Languages: Pidgins and Creoles.* New York: St. Martin's Press, 1997.

Silverman, Kaja. *The Subject of Semiotics.* New York: Oxford University Press, 1983.

Simmel, George. "The Metropolis and Mental Life." In *On Individuality and Social Forms,* edited by Donald N. Levine, 324–339. 1903. Reprint, Chicago: University of Chicago Press, 1971.

Sowole, Tajudeen. "Fela Predicted the Way He Ended—Ghariokwu." Interview. *Sunday Concord* (Lagos), August 20, 2000, 13.

Soyinka, Wole. *Myth, Literature and the African World.* Cambridge: Cambridge University Press, 1976.

———. *Art, Dialogue and Outrage: Essays on Literature and Culture.* Ibadan: New Horn Press, 1988.

Soyinka-Ajayi, Omofolabo. *Yoruba Dance: The Semiotics of Movement and Body Attitude in a Nigerian Culture.* Trenton, N.J.: Africa World Press, 1998.

Stanovsky, Derek. "Fela and His Wives: The Import of a Postcolonial Masculinity." *Jouvert: A Journal of Postcolonial Studies* 2, no. 1 (1998). Accessed January 15, 2004. Available online at http://social.chass.ncsu.edu/jouvert/v2i1/stan.htm.

Stavrakakis, Yannis. *Lacan and the Political.* London: Routledge, 1999.

Stewart, Gary. *Breakout: Profiles in African Rhythm.* Chicago: University of Chicago Press, 1992.

Taiwo, Olufemi. "On the Misadventures of National Consciousness: A Retrospect on

Frantz Fanon's Gift of Prophecy." In *Frantz Fanon: A Critical Reader,* edited by Lewis Gordon, Tracy Sharpley-Whiting, and Renee T. White, 255–270. Oxford: Blackwell, 1996.

Tamuno, T. N., and S. C. Ukpabi, eds. *Nigeria since Independence: The First 25 Years.* Vol. 6: *The Civil War Years.* Ibadan: Heinemann Educational Books, 1989.

Tejuoso, Olakunle, and Dapo Adeniyi. "Interview with Lagbaja (Bisade Ologunde)." *Glendora International* (Lagos), February 24, 1995. Accessed May 8, 2003. Available online at http://allafrica.com/stories/200105210262.html.

Tenaille, Frank. *Music Is the Weapon of the Future: Fifty Years of African Popular Music.* Chicago: Lawrence Hill, 2002.

Thomas, T. Ajayi. *History of Juju Music: A History of African Popular Music from Nigeria.* Jamaica, N.Y.: Thomas Organization, 1992.

Todd, Loreto. *Modern Englishes: Pidgins and Creoles.* London: Blackwell, 1984.

Tucker, Robert C., ed. *The Marx-Engels Reader.* New York: W. W. Norton, 1972.

Tutuola, Amos. *The Palm-Wine Drinkard and His Dead Palm-Wine Tapster in the Dead's Town.* New York: Grove Press, 1953.

UNICEF. "Femi Kuti Is UNICEF's Newest Special Representative." Press Release, June 12, 2002. Accessed May 12, 2003. Available online at http://www.unicef.org/newsline/02pr34femi.htm.

van der Merwe, Peter. *Origins of the Popular Style: Antecedents of Twentieth-Century Popular Music.* New York: Oxford University Press, 1989.

Van Leeuwen, Theo. *Speech, Music, Sound.* London: Macmillan, 1999.

Van Sertima, Ivan. *They Came before Columbus.* New York: Random House, 1976.

Vaughan, Olufemi. *Nigerian Chiefs: Traditional Power in Modern Politics, 1890s–1990s.* Rochester: University of Rochester Press, 2000.

Veal, Michael E. "Jazz Music Influences on the Work of Fela." *Glendora Review: African Quarterly on the Arts* 1, no. 1 (1995): 8–13.

———. *Fela: The Life and Times of an African Musical Icon.* Philadelphia: Temple University Press, 2000.

Walters, Ronald W. *Pan Africanism in the African Diaspora: An Analysis of Modern Afro-centric Political Movements.* Detroit: Wayne State University Press, 1993.

Ward, Brian. *Just My Soul Responding: Rhythm and Blues, Black Consciousness, and Race Relations.* Berkeley: University of California Press, 1998.

Wasserman, Adam. "Lagbaja, 'the Masked Man.'" 2001. Accessed May 12, 2003. Available online at http://www.afropop.org/multi/interview/ID/9.

Waterman, Christopher Alan. *Juju: A Social History and Ethnography of an African Popular Music.* Chicago: University of Chicago Press, 1990.

Willetts, Peter. *The Non-Aligned Movement: The Origins of a Third World Alliance.* New York: Nichols Pub. Co., 1978.

Williams, Chancellor. *The Destruction of Black Civilization.* Chicago: Third World Press, 1987.

Williams, Raymond. *Problems in Materialism and Culture.* London: Verso, 1980.

WIN. *Women in Nigeria Today.* London: Zed Press, 1985.

Witte, Hans. *Ifa and Esu: Iconography of Order and Disorder.* Soest, Holland: Kunstandel Luttik, 1984.

Woodson, Carter G. *The Miseducation of the Negro.* 1933. Reprint, Trenton, N.J.: Africa World Press, 1990.

X, Malcolm. *The Autobiography of Malcolm X.* New York: Ballantine Books, 1965.

Yinger, J. Milton. *Countercultures: The Promise and Peril of a World Turned Upside Down.* New York: The Free Press, 1982.

Young, Crawford. *The African Colonial State in Comparative Perspective.* New Haven, Conn.: Yale University Press, 1994.

Zimmer, Lynn, and John P. Morgan. *Marijuana Myths, Marijuana Facts: A Review of the Scientific Evidence.* New York: Lindesmith Center, 1997.

# Discography

**Fela Anikulapo-Kuti (formerly Fela Ransome-Kuti)**

MCA Records began in 2000 to re-release Fela's songs—many of which were already out of print or available only in scattered compilations—in their original form onto compact discs. It was a boon to my search, given my incomplete and scratched LP collection, cartons of cassettes collected over the years but without proper song list or other discographic details, compact disc compilations without original release dates, and yes, many, many libraries pleading lost Fela LPs. The discography below is based largely but not exclusively on the now easily available compact discs. The advantages of doing this are many. The compact disc would be the format in which the songs would exist for the foreseeable future; it is therefore redundant to reproduce discographic details of formats that no longer exist. Also, scholars and enthusiasts searching for particular songs would find it easier to locate the compact disc volume below in which it is published. What is needed most to retrieve from original publication details are the dates, and I have supplied them in parentheses below. In tracking dates of original release, I have benefited from Toshiya Endo's Web discography (http://biochem.chem.nagoya-u.ac.jp/~endo/EAFela.html) as well as the discography in Michael E. Veal's biography, *Fela*. The arrangement below follows the original dates of release of the songs, in rough chronological order, and not the publication date of the compact disc volume.

*With Koola Lobitos*

*Koola Lobitos 64–68/The '69 Los Angeles Sessions.* MCA, 2001. "Highlife Time," "Omuti Tide," "Ololufe Mi," "Wadele Wa Rohin," "Laise Lairo," "Wayo" (1st Version), "My Lady Frustration," "Viva Nigeria," "Obe," "Ako," "Witchcraft," "Wayo" (2nd Version), "Lover," "Funky Horn," "Eko," "This Is Sad."

*With Africa 70*

*Fela with Ginger Baker Live!* MCA, 2001. "Let's Start" (1971), "Black Man's Cry" (1971), "Ye Ye De Smell" (1971), "Egbe Mi O (Carry Me I Want to Die)" (1971), "Ginger Baker & Tony Allen Drum Solo" (1978).
*Why Black Man Dey Suffer.* African Songs Limited AS 0001, 1971. "Why Black Man Dey Suffer," "Ikoyi Mentality versus Mushin Mentality."
*Shakara/London Scene.* MCA, 2000. "Lady" (1972), "Shakara (Oloje)" (1972), "J'Ehin J'Ehin (Chop-Teeth Chop-Teeth)" (1970), "Egbe Mi O" (1970), "Who're You" (1970), "Buy Africa" (1970), "Fight to Finish" (1970).
*Roforofo Fight/The Fela Singles.* MCA, 2001. "Roforofo Fight" (1972), "Go Slow" (1972), "Question Jam Answer" (1972), "Trouble Sleep Yanga Wake Am" (1972), "Shenshema" (1970), "Ariya" (1970).
*Open & Close/Afrodisiac.* MCA, 2001. "Open & Close" (1972), "Swegbe and Pako" (1972),

"Gbagada Gbagada Gbogodo Gbogodo" (1972), "Alu Jon Jonki Jon" (1973), "Jeun Ko Ku (Chop and Quench)" (1973), "Eko Ile" (1973), "Je'Nwi Temi (Don't Gag Me)" (1973).

*Confusion/Gentleman.* MCA, 2000. "Confusion" (1975), "Gentleman" (1973), "Fefe naa Efe" (1973), "Igbe" (1973).

*Everything Scatter/Noise for Vendor Mouth.* MCA, 2001. "Everything Scatter" (1975), "Who No Know Go Know" (1975), "Noise for Vendor Mouth" (1975), "Mattress" (1975).

*Expensive Shit/He Miss Road.* MCA, 2000. "Expensive Shit" (1975), "Water No Get Enemy" (1975), "He Miss Road" (1975), "Monday Morning In Lagos" (1975), "It's No Possible" (1975).

*Alagbon Close/Kalakuta Show.* Victor, 1994. "Alagbon Close" (1974), "I No Get Eye for Back" (1974), "Kalakuta Show" (1976), "Don't Make Ganran Ganran" (1976).

*Ikoyi Blindness/Kalakuta Show.* MCA, 2001. "Ikoyi Blindness" (1976), "Gba Mi Leti ki N'Dolowo (Slap Me Make I Get Money)" (1976), "Kalakuta Show" (1976), "Don't Make Garan Garan" (1976).

*J.J.D./Unnecessary Begging.* MCA, 2001. "J.J.D. (Johnny Just Drop)" (1977), "Unnecessary Begging" (1976), "No Buredi (No Bread)" (1976).

*Monkey Banana/Excuse O.* MCA, 2001. "Monkey Banana" (1976), "Sense Wiseness" (1976), "Excuse O" (1976), "Mr. Grammartologylisation Is the Boss" (1976).

*Yellow Fever/Na Poi.* MCA, 2000. "Yellow Fever" (1976), "Na Poi" 1975 Version (1976), "Na Poi" (Part 1 & 2) (1972), "You No Go Die . . . Unless" (1972).

*Zombie.* MCA, 2001. "Zombie" (1976), "Mister Follow Follow" (1976), "Observation Is No Crime" (1977), "Mistake" (Live at the Berlin Jazz Festival—1978).

*Upside Down/Music Of Many Colours.* MCA, 2001. "Upside Down" (1976), "Go Slow" (1976), "2000 Blacks Got to Be Free" (1980), "Africa Centre of the World" (1980).

*Stalemate/Fear Not for Man.* MCA, 2000. "Stalemate" (1977), "Don't Worry about My Mouth O (African Message)" (1977), "Fear Not for Man" (1977), "Palm Wine Sound" (1977).

*Opposite People/Sorrow Tears and Blood.* MCA, 2000. "Opposite People" (1977), "Equalisation of Trouser and Pant" (1977), "Sorrow Tears and Blood" (1977), "Colonial Mentality" (1977).

*Shuffering and Shmiling/No Agreement.* MCA, 2000. "Shuffering and Shmiling" (1978), "No Agreement" (1977), "Dog Eat Dog" (1977).

*V.I.P./Authority Stealing.* MCA, 2000. "V.I.P. (Vagabonds in Power)" (1979), "Authority Stealing" (1980).

*Coffin For Head of State/ Unknown Soldier.* MCA, 2000. "Coffin for Head of State" (1981), "Unknown Soldier (1979).


*With Egypt 80*

*Original Sufferhead/I.T.T.* MCA, 2000. "Original Sufferhead" (1982), "Power Show" (1982), "I.T.T." (1979; with Africa 70).

*Perambulator/Original Sufferhead.* Victor, 1999. "Perambulator" (1983), "Frustration" (1983), "Original Sufferhead" (1982), "Power Show" (1982).

*Live In Amsterdam.* MCA, 2001. "M.O.P. (Movement of the People) Political Statement Number 1" (1984), "You Gimme Shit I Give You Shit" (1984), "Custom Check Point" (1984).

*Army Arrangement.* MCA, 2001. "Army Arrangement" (1985), "Government Chicken Boy" (1985).

*Teacher Don't Teach Me Nonsense.* MCA, 2001. "Teacher Don't Teach Me Nonsense" (1986), "Look and Laugh" (1986), "Just Like That" (1990).

*Beasts of No Nation/O.D.O.O.* MCA, 2001. "Beasts of No Nation" (1989), "O.D.O.O. (Overtake Don Overtake Overtake)" (1989).

*Overtake Don Overtake Overtake.* Shanachie, 1990. "Confusion Break Bones" (1990), "Overtake Don Overtake Overtake" (1989).

*Underground System.* Stern's Records, 1992. "Underground System" (1992), "Pansa Pansa" (1992).


*Unreleased*

"Chop and Clean Mouth: New Name for Stealing" (1990s)
"B.B.C.: Big Blind Country" (1990s)
"Stranger: Allahaji, Allahaji" (1990s)
"Music against Second Slavery" (1990s)
"Bamaiyi" (1990s)
"Clear Road for Jagba Jagba" (1990s)
"Cock Dance" (1990s)
"Condom, Scallywag, & Scatter" (1990s)
"Akunakuna: Sen. Bro. of Perambulator" (1980s)
"Country of Pain" (1980s)
"O.A.U." (1980s)
"Government of Crooks" (1980s)
"Football Government" (1970s)
"Male" (1970s)
"Nigerian Natural Grass" (1970s)


**Other Artists**

Allen, Tony. *No Accommodation for Lagos* (with Afrika 70) and *No Discrimination* (Tony Allen and the Afro Messengers). Evolver, 2002.
———. *Jealousy/Progress* (with Afrika 70). Evolver, 2002.
———. *N.E.P.A. (Never Expect Power Always).* Celluloid/Moving Target, 1985.
Anikulapo-Kuti, Femi, and the Positive Force Band. *No Cause for Alarm.* Polygram, 1989.
———. *M.Y.O.B. (Mind Your Own Business).* Kalakuta, 1991.
———. *Femi Kuti.* Tabu, 1995.
———. *Shoki Shoki.* Barclay, 2000
———. *Fight to Win.* Barclay, 2001.
Antibalas' Afrobeat Orchestra. *Liberation Afro Beat Vol. 1.* Ninja Tune, 2001.
Antibalas. *Talkatif.* Ninja Tune, 2002.
Hendrix, Jimi. *Electric Ladyland.* Track Reco, 1968.
Ishola, Haruna, and His Apala Group. *Oroki Social Club.* Decca (West Africa), 1971.
Lagbaja. *We Before Me.* Indigedisc, 2001.
———. *Me.* Motherlan' Music, 2000.
———. *We.* Motherlan' Music, 2000.
———. *Abami.* Motherlan' Music, 2000.
———. *C'est Un African Thing.* Motherlan' Music, 1996.

———. *The Colours of Rhythm.* Motherlan' Music, 1993.

Lawson, Cardinal Rex, and His Mayor's Band of Nigeria. *Rex Lawson's Greatest Hits.* Timbuktu Records, 1997.

Marley, Bob. *Songs of Freedom* (4 CD set). Tuff Gong, 1999.

Masekela, Hugh. *Hope.* Worldly/Triloka, 1993.

Obey, Ebenezer, and His Inter-Reformers Band. *Operation Feed the Nation.* Decca, 1976.

Obey, Ebenezer, and His International Brothers. *E Sa Ma Miliki.* Decca, 1970.

Okosun, Sonny. *The Ultimate Collection.* AVC Music, 2001.

———. *Liberation.* Shanachie, 1982.

Rudder, David. *International Chantuelle.* Lypsoland, 1999.

Soyinka, Wole. *Unlimited Liability Company.* Featuring Tunji Oyelana and His Benders. Ewuro Productions, 1983.

Tosh, Peter. *Legalize It.* Columbia, 1976.

Ukwu, Celestine. *Greatest Hits.* Timbuktu Records, 1997.

Various artists. *Afrobeat . . . No Go Die! Trans-Global African Funk Grooves.* Shanachie, 2000.

Various artists. *Red Hot + Riot.* MCA, 2002.

# General Index

*Page numbers in italics refer to illustrations.*

# Song Index

TEJUMOLA OLANIYAN is Professor of English and African Languages and Literatures at the University of Wisconsin, Madison. He is author of *Scars of Conquest/Masks of Resistance: The Invention of Cultural Identities in African, African-American, and Caribbean Drama.* He is co-editor (with John Conteh-Morgan) of *African Drama and Performance* (Indiana University Press).